LIVING WITH JUNG

Volume 1

LIVING WITH JUNG

"Enterviews" with Jungian Analysts

VOLUME 1

Robert and Janis Henderson

Spring Journal Books
New Orleans, Louisiana

Published by
Spring Journal, Inc.;
627 Ursulines Street #7
New Orleans, Louisiana 70116
Tel.: (504) 524-5117
Fax: (504) 558-0088
Website: www.springjournalandbooks.com

Cover design by:
Michael Mendis
24 Blackfriars Street
London, Ont. N6H 1K6
Canada

Printed in Canada
Text printed on acid-free paper

Library of Congress Cataloging in Publication Data Pending

DEDICATION

This volume is dedicated
to our creative sons, whom we will love forever:

REV. RYAN W. HENDERSON
and
CHAD R. HENDERSON

About the Front Cover

The photograph on the front cover of this volume was taken by Robert Henderson in 1973. It shows the front door of C. G. Jung's house in Kusnacht, Switzerland. Above the door is an inscription in Latin: "VOCATUS ATQUE NON VOCATUS DEUS ADERIT." Translated into English, the inscription reads: "Called or not called, God will be there." In a conversation with Murray Stein, Robert Henderson asked about the significance of the inscription. Stein replied:

> I believe this is a quote from Erasmus, a fellow resident of Basel. Jung had it carved in stone and placed above the entrance to his house on Lake Zürich in Kusnacht. The house was built not too long after his marriage to Emma Rauschenbach in 1903, and Jung had an important hand in the design. So this was a very self-conscious statement of his spiritual attitude as a thirty-something-year-old doctor. Since Jung set up his private practice in his home, his patients confronted this statement at the beginning of every therapeutic session. It cannot have been lost on them that Jung was a spiritual man. The motto made his home into a kind of sacred space, a *temenos*, where the care of souls took place. I think the message was this: No matter what your attitude may be, whether you believe in a Deity or not, the presence of God will be a part of the work undertaken here. He was inviting them into that experience. I think it must have had quite a profound effect on his patients.

As Stein implies, the front door of a house is an invitation to enter private space, and the image of Jung's front door here echoes the kind of entering that was involved in the interviews in this volume, a idea that is also conveyed by the word "*enter*views" in the book's subtitle.

Contents

Acknowledgments

Janis and I are thankful to each of the individuals who consented to being interviewed by us for this volume: Adolf Guggenbühl-Craig, Jane and Jo Wheelwright, C. Toni Frey-Wehrlin, James A. Hall, John Beebe, Joseph L. Henderson, Russell Arthur Lockhart, Patricia Berry, Murray Stein, Thomas Kirsch, Fred Gustafson, and Gilda G. Frantz. They are all exceptional people and it was pure joy to spend the moments we did with them. I would also like to thank each of them for graciously providing the photographs that accompany the interviews herein.

I am grateful to the following publishers for granting us permission to reproduce previously published material in this volume: The C. G. Jung Institute of Los Angeles for the following interviews, first published in *Psychological Perspectives*: "Eyes in the Night Country" (Vol. 30, 1994), "A Lifetime of Marriage" (Vol. 32, 1995), "Deepening The Soul" (Vol. 46, 2004), "At Home with Himself" (Vol. 47, 2004), and "Softening the Heart" (Vol. 49, 2006); Karnac Books for the following interview, first published in *Harvest: Journal for Jungian Studies*: "Groomed to be a Jungian" (Vol. 51, No. 1, 2005); and Spring Journal, Inc. for the following interviews, first published in *Spring: A Journal of Archetype and Culture*: "Let It Be" (Vol. 64, 1998) and "We Will Know Where We Are When We Get There" (Vol. 67, 2000). These interviews have been re-edited for this volume.

Much appreciation and gratitude goes to special close friends who gave encouragement and support: Richard Allen, William and Pat Baugh, David Boulton, Catherine Chissell, Steve and Colleen Davis, Priscilla and Paul DerAnanian, Tyler Dudley, James and Liza Ervin, Kathleen Foley, Susan Erwin, Diane and Gary Gagnon, Linda Garrido, Norma Gomez, Fred and Karen Gustafson, James Hall, Debbie and Don Hamer, Colette Hanlon, Margaret and Robert Henderson, Ryan and Kristina Henderson, and Chad, Jennifer, and Stella Grace Henderson, David and Marilyn Henderson, Richard and Ann Henderson, Doris Jones, Joyce Laughlin,

ACKNOWLEDGMENTS

Malcolm Marler, Mark and Valerie McKinney, Lee and Tom Nielson, Sharon Oliver, Judy and Lew Parker, Michael and Gina Pines, Richard and Genevieve Risinger, Carl and Della Schultz, Edgar and Jean Sprenger, Earl and Sylvia Thompson, Ernie and Johanna Treichler, Charles and Mae Willliams, Barbara and Jim Willis, Leslie and John Wertam, Patricia and Raymond Wright, the staff, Board of Directors, Tuesday Group, and Dream Seminar at the Pastoral Counseling Center, Inc.

Finally, we wish to acknowledge our indebtedness to our publisher, Nancy Cater, and our editor, Michael Mendis, for their efforts in bringing this volume to publication.

Robert Henderson

Preface

Being interviewed by Robert Henderson is like spending an hour in analysis: you are confronted with questions and issues that stimulate reflections, which circle around themselves until you realize that making the circle is itself the point of the work. In the end, you find that you have managed to circumambulate yourself. This is a most revealing process. I've been afraid to peek at what my colleagues have said about themselves—my own revelations were so personal! There is in all of us engaged in the private work of listening to other people's lives a certain reticence about inserting too much of ourselves into our interaction with them. Like the priest who remains unseen while the confession is taking place, we shy away from bringing the vision of own lives into the center of the confessional space.

Yet, as Jeffrey Kirpal has recently observed, all disciplines that deal with sacred matters must hold the tension between the secrets that must be kept and the revelations that must be shared. It is important to the patient in analysis that the analyst should also be the person he or she is—not just one who is likely to have struggled with the same issues, but one who has actually struggled with them in particular ways. Sooner or later, every analyst has to give his or her own account, in the patient's presence, of this. Sometimes, an unexpected sigh is enough for the patient to know the analyst "has been there too" in some unique way. Not infrequently, a somewhat more detailed explanation of the analyst's experience is necessary, and if well timed and sensitively delivered, the honest account is welcome and remembered later by the patient as part of the healing. Other revelations seem tactless and intrusive. No one has yet figured out how much of the analyst is too much, how much is too little, and how much is enough.

I would imagine that some readers who pick up this book have been in analysis with, or have thought of going into analysis with, some of the people whose interviews are included here. They will have to decide, as I have had to do, whether to read these particular interviews. To such readers, I would offer this advice: if you think the relative anonymity you may need your analyst to have is going to be violated, stay out of those pages. If you're not sure, try to imagine how you might feel if you were exposed to something that you would rather not know about someone whom you may need to remain unseen—for the present, at least—on the other side of the confessional. On the other hand, I would also ask such readers not to condemn the analyst who has made her or his own confession in these pages. Jung himself said that his psychology was his "personal confession." It serves the integrity of the field to have the personal experiences of those who are taken as authorities on depth psychological matters available to public inspection.

Robert Henderson stands out among interviewers of analysts as one who enables the people he interviews to define their own agenda. How differently each of us has chosen to develop the legacy of Jung and to grow, through Jungian training, into the analysts we have become! Reading each new interview, one is tempted to ask, "How in the world could an analyst have chosen to emphasize *that*?" Perhaps the better question would be, "How is it that an analyst with that particular history can have something to offer to people whose lives are so different?" For that is the true mystery disclosed by this book, one that Robert Henderson approaches with the lightest of touches, but does not neglect, I believe, to address in every interview. If you look between the lines of his questions, you will notice that he is always gently but firmly asking us—engaged as we are in this difficult, all-consuming work—to identify the source of the energy we bring to the business of hearing people out so that they can declare themselves more authentically. Perusing these valuable interviews, one finds that even though he is not a Jungian analyst, one wants to ask Robert Henderson that very same question.

John Beebe

I cannot understand the mystery; but I am always conscious of
myself as two (as my soul and I).
—Walt Whitman

The *interview* is a curious literary form. The intention would seem to be the harvesting of *facts,* related to a person's life and work, often with a determined sense of seeking something that will help us *understand* and *explain* that life, that work. Decidedly, this setup is voyeuristic, and certainly the interviewer's effort is to satisfy the audience's desire for a *peep* into a life otherwise hidden from view. As audience we are like the legendary Peeping Tom, the only one who saw Godgifu ("Lady Godiva") riding naked through the town while all others dutifully drew their blinds against her nakedness in compliance with the religious orthodoxy of *not* seeing. While it is said that Tom was struck blind—or worse (thus raising the question of what cost there is to seeing), it is not difficult to imagine that there were many who peeked through their blinds and glimpsed the truth.

We *do* want to see! This desire is insatiable. The largest-selling newspapers are those market tabloids shrieking out, in gaudy headlines and pictures, the proffered "truth." The veracity of this truth matters less than the *desire* to see, a desire requiring ever more extremes to be even momentarily satisfied. Hence, *privacy* becomes a lost value. Indeed, the eye of the collective to which we all belong is a *hungry* eye, a devouring eye. Nothing embodies this cyclopean hunger as much as the camera, its subsequent development as film, then as television, and now *all* of these combined in the Internet's "browsing" instantaneity—the act of *feeding* by continual nibbling. In the case of a figure such as Jung, we all know how eagerly the eye seeks photographs of him and his haunts and his circle, and this eventually gets satisfied, as in *Word & Image* [an illustrated biography of Jung edited by Aniela Jaffé]; then we want to see those pictures *move,* and this too gets satisfied, as in *Face to Face* [John Freeman's BBC interview with Jung, first aired in 1959]; then we want to see him *live* on TV—alas, too late. All of these are manifestations of the impulse to see *into,* to catch a glimpse of the actual life of the man—not just his work, not just those books on the shelf. And when we have run out of firsthand accounts, then we want to hear from and see those who knew him, worked with him, were affected by him. This too gets satisfied, as in *Matter of Heart* [a 1985 documentary film on the life and work of Jung, containing interviews with those who knew him personally]. This volume, this *book*—interviews with those who in one way or another were impacted fatefully by Jung—is yet another attempt to satisfy that thirst to *see.* Yet, there is *no* film here, *no* TV, *no* website address— interviews in *words* only. Is this a *difference* worth noting, worth commenting on? I think so.

As I was reading over these interviews, a dream, in voice only, said to me, "Not *inter*views—*enter*views!" As a word addict, I sensed right away what was being urged on me. I knew that "inter" emphasized the idea of *between, among, reciprocity*—the *collective* eye—that urge to *see into* that we share among us, between us—our mutual hunger for "viewing." But what of "enter," the idea of going *into*, going *within*? Do words provide ways of entry that the "literal" images of photography, film, and TV do not? I believe so, and I believe this entry has something to do with *imagination*.

What is this about? We get close to an answer, I think, if we reflect on Roland Barthes's insight into the essence of the photograph: "Whether or not the subject is already dead, every photograph is this catastrophe." Let us extend this and say that every interview is this catastrophe as well. Death looms large here: *quick*, get some "last words" before these elders *die*. *Preserve* something of their spirit before they are gone—and luckily this preservative impulse was followed, since some of those interviewed here *are* now indeed gone. If we are aware that the root of the word "preserve," *ser-*, is also the root of our word *hero*, we can sense that what we are doing in this preserving is trying to save the spirit of those who are in one way or another our heroes. Heroes are those who labor to preserve what is discovered, what is valued, what is cherished, and it is heroic as well to preserve something of the deeds and the spirit and the soul of our heroes— Hera's efforts on behalf of her Heracles.

Barthes contributes another important idea when he differentiates between *studium* and *punctum*. In relation to these interviews, the *studium* qualities would be all those conscious intentionalities of the interviewer and his subjects. On the other hand, the *punctum* refers to those strange, odd, even offhand details—different for each of us—that stand out in such a way as to make the interview come *alive*, to become an *enter*-view, an entry way, a way into an *imaginal* encounter with these figures. Conceived of in this way, these interviews will not become mere relics, to be examined and mined for the facts they contain and then forgotten, but will forever be a *source* for an imaginal *life* that succeeding generations can enter into. It is for the preservation of *that* possibility that Rob and Janis Henderson and Spring Journal Books are to be commended.

So, if the interviewers did not ask the questions you hoped they would, do not despair. Imagine yourself as the interviewer, and imagine through to the response; and if it helps to have some images to start with, imagine riding with Pat Berry on the back of her motorcycle as she whizzes across the wide open spaces; or linger at the side of stroke-bound James Hall as he types his next book heroically one slow key at a time; or, listen in on the intimate spats of Joe and Jane Wheelwright—you get the point: imagine on, imagine on, imagine on. These volumes provide endless fodder for that. Plenty of *puncta* in these pages! Jung did not want to be a "Jungian" in the sense that he did not seek his identity in the collective. In these pages you will find that view in good company; you will encounter first-person accounts of long lives spent in the pursuit of being one's individual and unique self.

Remember that Godgifu ("God's Gift") never actually rode through the market place for all to see (as an early version has it), or through town for no one to see (as a later version tells it); and there is no evidence whatever for a Peeping Tom either (as even later versions added). So, even when the *facts* are known well enough to dispel misconceptions about the literal truth, the psychic propensity for *deeper* truth will preserve what imagination gives birth to. Don't insist on facts here, don't psychoanalyze the analysts. Instead, enter into Keats' view of *negative capability* and inhabit the space where one becomes "capable of being in uncertainties, mysteries, doubts, without any irritable reaching after fact and reason." Jung would have liked that. You will too.

Russell Arthur Lockhart

Several years ago, a northwest-coast Indian woman remarked to me that her people value stories, and that the elders regularly share them with the people. She went on to say that if ever there were no more stories to tell, they would cease to be a people. Bob and Jan Henderson's book is about stories. Here is an intensive undertaking involving several interviews with elders first of all, elders in the deepest sense of that word, who actually worked with or knew C. G. Jung personally. Blended in with the insights of this distinguished group are interviews with younger analysts, who are nevertheless old enough to have had the opportunity of working, during their training, with many of the individuals who personally knew and worked with Jung.

Anyone interested in the history of analytical psychology will be interested in this book for its historical references, the deeply personal experiences by noted analysts, its readability and the variety and depth of stories shared. It can be read from cover to cover or randomly with any chapter. But its uniqueness is in the idea of story. We live in an age that is in serious danger of losing its stories. Our linear idea of time tends to sever us from our past, making it something that happened long ago, now over, a tale to be told rather than a story that is vital and still shaping our lives. Does the past ever really go away? Or does it continue to live in the micro-cells of our psyche and accumulate in what we call our ancestral inheritance? We do not need big stories only, like the ones we learned in school as children growing up. Perhaps, more than these, we need little stories of the specific kind that make up the marrow and tissue of our lives and that help direct, define, and sustain us as individuals in our darker and lighter moments. I remember, as a child, listening to the stories told by my grandparents, who were born at the end of the 19th century. I have no doubt that these stories still live within me and influence my life, even if in unconscious ways.

Years ago, the Hendersons shared with me their idea of conducting interviews with noted analysts who had personally known and worked with C. G. Jung. It began as one interview, which was published in a Jungian journal. And then there was another and yet another. What was meant to be only individual interviews for separate publication in journals took on a life of its own. The process of gathering the interviews became a story in itself. And the stories collectively have become one common story that reflects the experience of any individual trying to live life as fully and as passionately as it was meant to be lived. Never mind the mistakes and successes, the degrees and credentials. This is every person's story in that it brings us to reflect on the story we are living personally or, more accurately, is living us. In a wonderfully honest and respectful manner, Bob and Jan have gathered an archival treasure for those interested in the life and work of C. G. Jung. In so doing, they have not only been gatherers and custodians of the stories of others, but creators of a story of their own, which has helped us all better remember who we are as a people of this inheritance.

Fred Gustafson

LIVING WITH JUNG

"Enterviews" with Jungian Analysts

JANIS AND ROBERT HENDERSON

Introduction

ORIGINAL VISION

In 1991 a vision came to me. I saw that the line of people who had worked with C. G. Jung and were still alive was growing shorter. By then I had been well entrenched in analytical psychology for over 30 years through personal analysis, countless educational opportunities throughout the United States and Switzerland, and continual reading. I thought of the elderly Jungians still alive and wondered if they would share with me how Jung had touched their lives. When I enrolled in the 1992 summer course at the Jung Institute in Zürich, it seemed like the perfect opportunity for me to follow my vision, so I wrote a letter to Adolf Guggenbühl-Craig. His gracious willingness to meet with me was the beginning of this incredible adventure.

I had long felt something special in the writings of the people who knew Jung. For them Jung was not only a profound teacher of important transforming concepts, but also a healer in their lives, as they were drawn to him because of personal suffering. As an extravert, I love asking questions, and I discovered that most of the people I interviewed enjoyed having questions asked of them, and they answered these questions in an open and direct manner. There are many ways to learn about the psychology of Jung, and I believe these interviews offer yet another way. They show how devoted students of Jung used creative means to understand and integrate his psychology into their personal and professional lives.

Each interview has its own fascinating story associated with it. For example, after the interview with Dr. Guggenbühl-Craig was first published, I wrote a letter to Jane and Jo Wheelwright in care of the San Francisco Jung Institute, as I had no other way of contacting them. The Institute forwarded the letter, and it eventually reached the Wheelwrights on their ranch on the coast of central California, where they were living out their retirement in seclusion. As they read my letter, they felt deeply touched and invited Janis and me to their ranch for a weekend, which turned out to be one of the highlights of our lives. Jo said that the interview would be "one last shot out to the world" for them. And he was right: they both died a few years after the visit.

I did not have the privilege of knowing Jung personally, but I had the opportunity to visit his spacious home in Kusnacht, Switzerland on three occasions. On the first visit, in 1973, I was able to take a photograph of the front door of the house (it makes a fitting front cover for this volume). In 1992 and 1995, I had the privilege of meeting with Jung's son, Franz, for several hours. On one occasion, Franz left me alone with one of his father's dream journals, and I discovered that Dr. Jung recorded his dreams in small black notebooks. My visits to Jung's home left me feeling that he was, in many ways, a very ordinary man, who lived his life to the best of his ability. He had as much difficulty dealing with his shadow as he did with his genius. It is from him that I derived the inspiration to live poetically and soulfully. His rich insights have helped me find meaning and depth in the healing work of my calling, pastoral psychotherapy.

Rumi expressed the power that friends add to meaningful adventures when he wrote:

OF BEING WOVEN

The way is full of genuine sacrifice.
The thickets blocking your path are anything
that keeps you from that, any fear that you may be broken
into bits like a glass bottle.

This road demands courage and stamina, yet it's full of footprints!
Who are these companions?
They are rungs in your ladder. Use them!
With company you quicken your ascent.
You may be happy enough going along, but with others
you'll get farther, and faster.

Someone who goes cheerfully by himself to the customs
house to pay his traveler's tax will go even more
lightheartedly when friends are with him.

INTRODUCTION

Every prophet sought out companions.
A wall standing alone is useless, but put three or four walls
together, and they'll support a roof and keep grain dry and safe.

When ink joins with a pen, then the blank paper can say something.
Rushes and reeds must be woven to be useful as a mat. If
they weren't interlaced; the wind would blow them away.

Like that, God paired up creatures, and gave them friendship.

May the beauty of the single rose be forever in our hearts and may
we all be blessed by the keeper of the stars.

Robert Henderson
Glastonbury, CT
May 2006

ADOLF GUGGENBÜHL-CRAIG, M.D.

Adolf Guggenbühl-Craig, M.D., is a Jungian analyst and psychiatrist, the former Chair of the C. G. Jung Institute in Zürich, and former President of the International Association for Analytical Psychology. He maintains a private practice in Zürich and is the author of a number of books on contemporary issues, including *Power in the Helping Professions* (Spring Publications, 1971), *Eros on Crutches* (Spring Publications, 1980), *The Old Fool and the Corruption Myth* (Spring Publications, 1992), and *Marriage Dead or Alive* (Continuum, 2001). We met in Dr. Guggenbühl's office in Zürich in the summer of 1992. He impressed us as a very warm, thoughtful, and generous man whose passion for living was strong.

EYES IN THE NIGHT COUNTRY

ADOLF GUGGENBÜHL-CRAIG AT 70

The shadow is so strong that we always live it anyway. What we can do is to become more conscious of how the shadow insinuates into our lives and therefore not fall into its hands without realizing it.

—Adolf Guggenbühl-Craig

PERSONAL MATTERS

ROB HENDERSON (RH): You have had a long and distinguished career and life. I consider you to be one of the most readable and helpful of all Jungian writers. Can you tell us a little about your family and personal interests?

ADOLF GUGGENBÜHL-CRAIG (AG): I am married and have five children and eight grandchildren. All my children and grandchildren live around Zürich, so I can stay in close contact with them. For my wife and me, the family is very important. We try to keep the members together. Of course, they are all very different—and this is a challenge in every family. You don't get to choose your family members—so you are always in contact with people within the family who are very different from yourself.

Personally, I am very interested in local politics, but now, being 70 years old, I no longer participate actively. I have a very deep interest in history, especially the history of Switzerland and that of small countries and nations. It would be wrong to say that for me religion is only a personal interest. Religion is not an interest, it is an ongoing experience or state of mind. I am very much influenced by the reformed kind of Protestantism established by Zwingli and Calvin.

THE SHADOW, EROS, AND AGGRESSION

RH: You have written a lot about the shadow. How would you describe its influence on us?

AG: The shadow is the great destroyer within us; the suicidal maniac and the murderer in each of us. The shadow is not some casual psychological force that we don't want to see or that we repress. We repress many quite harmless things because of cultural constraints. The shadow is a genuine psychological force in itself. It is the destructive side in all of us, perhaps corresponding to what Freud understood as the death instinct.

RH: How do you cope with the shadow? How do you stay connected to the shadow?

AG: Even if you don't want it to, the shadow always tries to influence, connect with, and stimulate you. It's nearly impossible to know if your motives and desires are connected to the shadow or not. It's often extremely difficult for us to see our own destructiveness. Even when I do recognize the effects of the shadow, it still might be difficult for me to resist those effects. For instance, I might be very nice to my wife, but in reality my niceness is an attempt to dominate and manipulate her. I might consciously try to help a patient get out of his painful confusion until I suddenly discover that I might do him more harm than good. My wish to confront the patient with his pathology in order to help him might actually stem from an unconscious desire to cause him pain and confusion. I don't have the impression that I am a particularly good, gentle, and kind man. Whenever I have thought that I am not so bad after all, when I am actually quite pleased with myself, I often discover that I become destructive. The shadow is really a very twisted force. It makes me doubt my *eros*, which at times might be the genuine *eros*. One thing is certain: if you consider yourself a saintly person, you probably are under the domination of the shadow.

RH: What would you suggest to those saintly people who want to connect with the shadow?

AG: We don't really *want* to connect with the shadow. The shadow connects with *us* and our job is to notice and be aware of it. In our dreams, fantasies, and feelings, the shadow is always there. Some people are extremely naïve concerning their own shadow. The just don't see it. And yet, even

8

though they don't see it, they continually build new defenses against it. We all dislike—and even hate—some people. We think we have a right to those feelings—that these people "deserve" our hatred.

RH: What are some of the negative feelings common to "honest" people?

AG: Most honest people hate with surprising intensity. They are completely convinced that the other person, group, or country is simply wrong and is acting very strangely. Some people deserve to be hated, but often the hate is more about ourselves than about the people we hate. For example, with good reasons, most decent people hated the Nazis during World War II. This kind of hatred is not necessarily an expression of the shadow. But often there is something very satisfying in that hate, and so the question must be asked: Do we not hate because we also *enjoy hating* and relish the thought of destruction? During the War, when we heard on the news that a particular German city was destroyed by bombs, we would often feel a deep sense of satisfaction. We enjoyed knowing the forces of evil were suffering. And yet, in this joy at the defeat of the forces of evil, one might have detected a pure joy in destruction *per se*. The shadow is in touch with us all the time. The question is: *How do we live with it?*

RH: What does it mean "to live with the shadow"?

AG: It does *not* mean to be nasty and disagreeable, to steal, cheat, lie, betray your friends, or murder. Sometimes an analyst will tell his or her client to become more aggressive, to be more openly nasty, to be less timid and decent, in order for the client to become more whole by developing this "other" side. But that advice springs from a complete misunderstanding of the nature of the shadow. The shadow is so strong that we *always* live it anyway. What we *can* do is become more conscious of how the shadow insinuates itself into our lives, and thus avoid falling inadvertently into its "hands."

SEX, SPIRIT, PORNOGRAPHY, AND ABUSE

RH: You have written a great deal about sexuality. Jung once said that spiritual problems are also sexual problems and vice versa. What do you think he meant?

AG: I don't know if Jung used those very words, but we have an important issue here. Freud tried to reduce all psychic phenomena to sexuality, and by sexuality he meant a basic biological instinct connected to the survival of the species. To Jung, sexuality was more than a biological drive and an instinct to propagate the species. For instance, sexual fantasies are not just an expression of our desire to procreate, but can also be understood as symbols of individuation. All the sexual fantasies we have are, in some way, connected to the symbol of the union of opposites (or the *coniunctio oppositorum*). Is the "Song of Songs" in the Old Testament just a beautiful, sexually explicit, pornographic song? Or is it a spiritual song? It is probably both. It is certainly not just a pornographic song—otherwise it would hardly have been accepted into the Old Testament. For the writer of the "Song of Songs," longing for a woman is a symbol of the longing of Israel for God (or the longing of everyone for God). All sexual feelings have a spiritual dimension and perhaps all religious feelings have a sexual dimension. Freud would say that the "Song of Songs" is a sexual song, slightly mistaken as a religious song, while Jung might say that the "Song of Songs" is a mystical, spiritual song, slightly mistaken as a sexual song!

RH: That's a wonderful way to say it. Are you familiar with that line in one of Fellini's films, "When I see a beautiful, sexy woman, I feel more religious?"

AG: When you see a beautiful, sexy woman, the biologist would say that your glands start working because the human race has to propagate in order to survive. But that's not all. When you see a beautiful, sexy woman, you become enthusiastic, both physically and spiritually, because in the beauty of the woman you find the symbol of the other—or the anima—which, ultimately, is the symbol of God. So experiencing the beauty of another human being, or being sexually attracted to another human being, is something that touches us in many ways, from our biology to our longing for God.

RH: Are men who are always seeking beautiful women revealing a spiritual quest?

AG: Well, maybe—and maybe not. But it's more likely that beneath promiscuous behavior in many men and women lies a desperate need for a spiritual connection.

RH: I find that sexuality continues to be repressed in our culture. You once wrote that "we talk now more about our sexual lives, but that has only produced more liars." Given the repression of sexuality, how do you account for the popularity of pornography? I read a quote recently stating that nearly 70 percent of the movies made these days are pornographic.

AG: The accuracy of that statement depends very much on how you define pornography. First, is sexuality really repressed, as you say? I think some parts of sexuality are always repressed and other parts are not. The need to express sexuality cannot be completely eliminated. And this need is perhaps partially met by pornography. It does not actually astonish me that there is so much pornography. It astonishes me that there is not more. Young people nowadays certainly live their sexuality much more openly than young people did when I was young. On the other hand, the slightest erotic feeling of parents toward children or adults toward children is immediately decried as perverted, incestuous, and forever damaging. In this sense, the Victorians were much less repressed sexually. Pornography doesn't worry me too much. I have made a very strange observation. While I was a psychiatric adviser at a home for delinquent girls and boys between the ages of 10 and 20, I discovered that those who had an interest in pornography generally had a better prognosis socially. They later led more useful and fruitful lives than those who were not interested in pornography at all.

RH: How do you make sense of that?

AG: Those for whom sex was just a quick, mechanical type of affair did not have the ability to fantasize. The spiritual life relies on the ability to fantasize and symbolize. Those fascinated with pornography already had developed the symbolic ability and were one step closer to a spiritual life. Spiritual life requires imagination, and pornography develops the imagination.

RH: And yet we have so many people who are vehemently opposed to pornography.

AG: I am not saying that we should promote pornography. Pornography is too complicated an issue for one to be simply *for* or *against* it. I think people who are fascinated by pornography are not really lost souls. In fact, they might be on their way to a spiritual life.

RH: Very little has ever been written about masturbation. Historically, it has been viewed as the cause of one illness after another. How do you view masturbation?

AG: First of all, a lot has been written about masturbation in the past. More important than the actual act of masturbation are the fantasies that accompany it. Masturbation is a curse when it becomes compulsive and purely mechanical. But as long as it is associated with fantasies, it could be the beginning of a deeply psychological life.

RH: How do you understand sexual addiction in relation to spiritual life?

AG: In all addictions, human beings try to find something spiritual. They try to find it, but they do not find it. That's why they are unable to stop and they become addicted. Sexual addiction is, in some ways, a failed attempt to come to a deeper understanding of life. Because one always fails, one has to keep trying again and again.

RH: Why do you think there is so much attention paid today to sexual abuse and sexual harassment?

AG: Sexuality has a demonic side. It has a tremendous power because it's not only physical, but also spiritual. Everything can be expressed through sexuality. For instance, the shadow or destructive force in us can be experienced through sexuality. The demonic side of sexuality can do a great deal of damage. Since sexuality is more recognized now, its demonic side has to be looked for in the sideshows of sexuality. The demonic side is now lived out and experienced in sexual abuse and harassment. But there is more connected with this interest in sexual abuse and harassment. The myth of the victim is very important today. Everyone is a victim and nobody seems to be an actor. Or, to put it differently, all decent people are victims and all "others" are aggressors. Or, all women are victims and all men are rapists. Or, all children are victims and adults are sexual predators. This general glorification of victimhood leads to the increased interest in sexual abuse and harassment. In my supervision of therapists, I have listened to many a therapist describe a patient who, for example, had a dream of being touched by her father (or something similar). The therapist then tries to convince the patient that she was sexually abused by her father. Then, often out of weakness or a desire to please, the patient tells the therapist that, indeed, she *was* abused by her father.

RH: A desire to please?

AG: Yes, to please the therapist. The actual phenomenon of sexual abuse and harassment certainly exists, but not to the extent that it is claimed to exist today, and it is certainly not as harmful as it is made out to be. Children do arouse physical, semi-erotic feelings in their parents. It is pleasurable to have a child sit on your lap and to cuddle her or him. This is a wonderful experience for the parents and very important for the child. The child feels a special affirmation from the physical joy the parents have in holding her or him. Often, even these harmless feelings of physical pleasure are labeled "sexual abuse." Another reason why sexual abuse and harassment have gained such widespread "popularity" is that we are always looking for a root cause to explain what happens to us psychologically. Today it is fashionable to say that sexual abuse is the cause of every psychopathology.

RH: There is also a lot of concern today about sexuality within the professional therapeutic relationship. What is your understanding of this issue?

AG: There is plenty of sexual abuse happening within therapy. In the transference and countertransference, sexuality is a very important part of the therapeutic process. And there is, of course, a temptation to act this out concretely. But the danger or incidence of sexual abuse in therapy is highly overestimated. Abuse in psychotherapy happens much more in other areas. For example, patients are often abused financially. We have come to realize that psychotherapy can have a number of disastrous effects. Sexual abuse just happens to be very easy to pin down; both the man and woman know if they have slept together. I have seen many patients abused by their therapists, but in my experience, sexual abuse is rare compared to these other types of abuse, such as the abuse of power and influence over the patient. Some therapists play with their patients as if they were puppets. They try to change their patients' lives or, out of jealousy, destroy their patients' marriages.

RH: Is there a "Jungian view" of homosexuality and heterosexuality, and if so, what is it?

AG: Jung himself seemed to have been very critical of homosexuality, as were most of his contemporaries. But we certainly understand now that sexuality cannot be explained solely in terms of the biological drive to propagate our species. Sexuality takes many forms, and one of them is homosexuality. Thus, just as heterosexuality can be part of our spiritual quest, so too can homosexuality.

By the way, I don't like the phrase "*spiritual quest*" so much. It sounds too spiritual! Maybe it would be better to talk about our *passion for understanding life* or for *coming closer to God*.

GOD, DREAMS, AND ORGANIZED RELIGION

RH: Jung said he did not "believe" in God but rather that he "knew" God. Do you believe in God or do you know God?

AG: I don't quite know what Jung meant by *know*. For myself, I believe in God; I don't know God.

RH: That quote by Jung is very important to a lot of people.

AG: So it seems—and it is a very striking answer that Jung gave. When I was younger, I thought it was a classic *senex* answer—Jung, the wise old man, had to know everything, even God. Later, I thought it was a trickster answer. Jung said many things instinctively knowing that people would wonder about them later.

Jung certainly had a very special connection to God, so he couldn't just say, like everybody else, "I believe in God." He had to say something special to express his special relationship. But I still think it is a bit arrogant to say, "*I know God*."

RH: Do you feel, as one book says, that dreams are "God's forgotten language"?

AG: I don't think that dreams are a forgotten language at all. Many people talk about their dreams. Children talk about their dreams very often. Dreams may be obscure or perverse, but not forgotten. People all over the world talk about their dreams—so in that sense, dreams are not a forgotten

14

language. Of the more than four billion people in the world, I think most of them take dreams very seriously. They say they were scared by them or mention them in one way or another. "God's forgotten language" is a good journalistic title, but are dreams more God's language than the language you and I talk? Everything is God's language. God talks through everything and in everything—not only in dreams, but in poetry, in songs, in pictures, in buildings, in houses, etc. People hear God in different places. Fellini talks to God when he sees a beautiful, sexy woman. If I have a particular dream, God might be talking to me. Or if I am ill, he might be talking to me through my illness too.

RH: Are interpretations of the unconscious to be taken as the discernment of God's will? I hear people say that their dreams told them to do something and this is how they follow God.

AG: "God moves in a mysterious way his wonders to perform." We don't know the plans of God and we can't understand them. Dreams are dreams and are first and foremost an expression of our unconscious—and the unconscious is not God. Or we could say: The unconscious is an expression of God, like everything else is. The unconscious is not a special field for God, where we see God more clearly. In this sense, dreams are not a message from God. People who think they can discern God's voice in their dreams very often cannot stand the uncertainties of life, the inherent inability to know what God really wants. So they comfort themselves with the illusion that they can understand or read God's will in their dreams.

RH: Then what do you say to people who claim they came to Zürich to study to become a Jungian analyst because the unconscious led them here and therefore it is God's will?

AG: I probably would say that they should go back to where they came from, or that they are definitely inflated. How do they know that God is talking through that particular dream? They could say that a deep voice within told them to come to Zürich. So they come to Zürich, knowing that this might be the right thing or the wrong thing to do.

RH: How do you work with your own dreams?

AG: When I wake up during the night or in the morning, I try to remember my dreams. I fantasize around them. I talk about them with my wife. I try to understand them. But very often I don't. I just let their images influence me one way or another.

RH: It appears that organized religion is in decline around the world. Why do you think this is so?

AG: Apparently people nowadays are less constrained to live and express their religious needs in a particular organization. Modern people have religious experiences walking down the street, seeing movies, etc. Churches have lost their monopoly on religious experience and this makes it very difficult for any given organized denomination. But that does not mean that the church is not important, just because it attracts far fewer people. The fact remains … where else can you pray and perform religious rituals along with other like-minded people other than in a church? And to pray to God, to try to get into communion with God, you need other people around you. I don't know why this is so, but it seems to me it is certainly so.

RH: You have known many ministers and priests in your work. What have you found to be some of the common shadow issues of the clergy?

AG: It seems to me that, very often, the clergy are inclined to ignore the demonic side of life and of our psyches. They want to see a harmony everywhere. They want to see God's wonderful world in everything and they miss the devilish side of our existence. I think their shadow issues often involve a lack of belief in God. In some way, they seem inflated and think they know everything; they seem to think the world is simple and they can understand it. And sometimes they even think they understand God.

RH: Meaning that they don't need God because they have the power to do anything?

AG: Officially, they are ministers of God, and yet behind that role is the inflated idea that they can do without God.

RH: How would you describe a healthy minister or priest?

AG: I don't know if anybody needs to be healthy! Why should a minister or priest have to be healthy? I think the very claim of healthiness is a perversion. I think a good minister or priest, like anybody else, is one who struggles with doubt. Ministers and priest—like you and me—are seekers, not achievers. Like everyone else, they are on their way, but have not yet arrived.

RH: In your book *Power in the Helping Professions*, you write about the need for friendships. Do you have such friendships in your life?

AG: It seems so. First, there is my wife, my children, and the rest of my family, and then I have friends I need quite often for different reasons. I don't know what I would do without these people. I have never worked alone. I have always had a partner with whom to exchange ideas and concerns. I meet some friends every Saturday morning for breakfast. I especially cultivate relationships with other men. Friends are people you can rely on and talk to about intimate things. Friends are people you can love, hate, and long for. Friendship is an intense connection, not just a casual thing. I think we all need friends, not just acquaintances or comrades.

Marriage, Power, and Death

RH: I really enjoyed your book, *Marriage Dead or Alive*, especially your views on what causes marriage to fail. Could you summarize those here?

AG: Everybody is on a journey, looking for the meaning of life. Everybody is looking for God in one way or another. So, two married people are always two people seeking the secret of life. This keeps the couple together and, at the same time, leads to a great deal of friction, because each one is striving for the ultimate goal in life, but in a different way. Marriage doesn't work when one partner has no interest in the way the other is seeking God and the meaning of life. But even if both are seekers, there are still innumerable battles and fights.

RH: What are your views on divorce?

AG: I think nowadays people get divorced too easily. You marry, and then you run into the first difficulties, and so you get divorced. But, if a couple definitely sees that they are not meant for each other, they should get divorced as soon as possible. In that sense, it is quite healthy that many people do divorce and don't go on torturing each other for life. I guess I would say: One should not give up on the marriage too easily, but one should also have the freedom to end the marriage when one sees that the different ways of individuation are too divergent.

RH: You have some interesting ideas about the power complex. People are often seduced by power. Have you found a good way to relate to power?

AG: A good way to relate to power is to try to get some and then use it ethically. Often we are envious of people who have power, but that envy is an indirect means of damaging the self. So I suggest that we all try to relate to power by not shying away from it.

RH: In your fascinating book *The Old Fool and the Corruption of Myth,* you wrote, "Let us bury the wise old man and instead be inspired and guided by the old fool." Can you give an example of the old fools you have known who inspired and guided you?

AG: It would take too long to give examples! I have known many men and women who behaved strangely, oddly, and foolishly, and yet seem to have had some kind of special wisdom. And I have also seen many old people who felt under a certain obligation to appear wise, and therefore became insincere and hypocritical.

RH: What is your view of death? How do you see your own death at this point in your life?

AG: That is a difficult question. There is nothing we know about death, or life after death, or non-existence after death. Therefore, we can project anything we want into the existence or non-existence after our death. Death scares me. What scares me the most is that I will be separated after death from all the people I like—but will I really be separated? I don't know. I don't trust people who say they are not afraid of death. On the other hand, I feel very strongly that there is a longing for death, because dying means that perhaps we will finally get the answers to all the endless questions we have lived with in this life.

If you want to go your individual way, it is the way you make for yourself, which is never prescribed, which you do not know in advance, and which simply comes into being of itself when you put one foot in front of the other. If you always do the next thing that needs to be done, you will go most safely and sure footedly along the path prescribed by your unconscious. Then it is naturally no help at all to speculate about how you ought to live. And then you know, too, that you cannot know it, but quietly do the next and most necessary thing. So long as you think you don't know what this is, you still have too much money to spend in useless speculation. But if you do with conviction the next and most necessary thing, you are always doing something meaningful and intended by fate. [Letter to Frau V., December 15, 1933, *C. G. Jung Letters, Vol. 1: 1906-1950*, Princeton University Press, 1973.]

—C. G. Jung

JANE AND JO WHEELWRIGHT, M.D.

True elders in the Jungian community, Jane and Jo Wheelwright were analyzed and trained by C. G. Jung and Toni Wolff in the 1930s, and were instrumental in founding the C. G. Jung Institute of San Francisco in the early 1940s. We interviewed them in the spring of 1994, when they were both eighty-nine years old and shortly after they had celebrated their sixty-fifth wedding anniversary. Our weekend interview took place at their home in a secluded area of the Hollister Ranch near Point Conception in Central California in front of a huge picture window overlooking an ancient Chumash burial ground and the Pacific Ocean. Very few visitors came to the house then, and neither Jane nor Jo often left it. There were pictures on the wall of Jo and his close pals, Erik Erikson, Gregory Bateson, Michael Fordham, and Joe Henderson. On another wall was a letter from C. G. Jung, dated July 3, 1939, certifying Jo as a Jungian analyst. Jo knew of no one else who ever received such a letter of certification from Jung. Both Jo and Jane were very lively. Jo's humor and wonderful personal stories and Jane's deep thoughtfulness and earthiness were touching. Our weekend with them was full of shared experiences, belly laughter, and the reflections of two people who have spent a lifetime together and are able to describe their journey with its full impact. Jo died in 1999. Jane died in 2004.

• 2 •

A LIFETIME OF MARRIAGE
Jane and Jo Wheelwright at 89

The older you get, the more you become different.

—Jane Wheelwright

Before I understood something about typology, I used to think Jane was imitating a Mack truck.

—Jo Wheelwright

Encountering Jung

Rob Henderson (RH): Jung was very important to your marriage, wasn't he?

Jo Wheelwright (Jo): If it hadn't been for Jung and his concept of psychological types, I think we would have broken up. We had not been married very long and were traveling in Europe, living very intimately because we were traveling third and fourth-class. Fighting is normal in a marriage, but our fights were beyond fighting. I told Carey Baynes that I thought Jane and I might break up. She gave me a copy of Jung's newly published *Psychological Types*. Reading that book was a very powerful experience for me. It changed my life. I talked again to Carey, and she said, "You'd better go see Jung." I said, "You mean the guy who wrote the book?" She said, "Yes, he lives here in Zürich."

Jane Wheelwright (Jane): At first Jung wouldn't see us because he didn't want to work with people our age. We were in our twenties. But Carey talked him into it!

Jan Henderson (JH): So the problems in your marriage got you into Jungian psychology?

J<small>ANE</small>: We each thought the other one was being mean or perverse or unpleasant. We didn't realize that we were made so differently.

J<small>O</small>: We were in tough shape by the time we landed in Jung's office. Usually Jung saw people once a week. I saw him every day for three or four weeks.

J<small>ANE</small>: Jung said: "I can't promise you that this is going to work out. You will just have to find your own way." I felt trapped, but I knew the marriage had to be worked out. I didn't have enough intuition to follow Jung. I didn't know what he was talking about.

RH: What was it like to be a patient of Jung's?

J<small>O</small>: You would have thought that since he was such a big noise in the world, there wouldn't be room for anyone else but him in his consulting office. His personality *did* fill the room but not at his patients' expense. I was in a pretty vulnerable state when I met Jung. I described my ego as a dandelion. But with him I never felt threatened, bossed around, or overwhelmed. I felt relaxed and I could be open. I trusted him.

J<small>ANE</small>: I knew from the beginning that our marriage would be difficult. We are so opposite. I am the thinking type and Jo is the feeling type. I am the introvert and Jo is the extravert. We come from very opposite places. I was oriented toward the negative and Jo toward the positive. The more positive he got, the more negative I got!

J H: You went to see Jung as a result of a real need in your life, not out of intellectual curiosity.

J<small>O</small>: We were hurting. I couldn't face living the rest of my life without Jane. I don't want to say that my basic reason for living is cowardliness. But I couldn't imagine life without Jane.

J<small>ANE</small>: I couldn't imagine life without Jo, either. Jung's theories are very helpful for people who are trying to understand their own experiences, for his ideas provide a wider context. With Jung's ideas you are part of a larger group—the collective—but the journey is your own, individual journey.

RH: Knowing Jung as you did, how do you think he would feel about today's Jungian psychology?

Jo: During my forty-odd years of teaching in the psychiatric department of the University of California Medical School in San Francisco, I have seen a gravitation toward Jung and a lessening of the Freudian monopoly. My guess is that this shift is because of Jung's discovery and championing of the archetypes. This means a focus on nature as opposed to personal history.

JANE: After all, archetypes and instincts are the same phenomenon.

JH: As a result of knowing and working with Jung personally, do you feel something about analytical psychology that future generations can never feel?

JANE: Possibly. As a sensation type, I function best when I am in a reality situation. Hence, contact with Jung gave me a more all-round sense of the man who discovered the reality of the psyche and consequently—possibly—a more real sense of the psyche itself. It is possible that first-generation Jungians are the most convinced of the importance of the psyche.

Jo: Certainly. Those who worked with Jung are uniquely affected by that fact.

MARRIAGE AND TYPOLOGY

RH: Is it more natural for Jo to do all the talking and Jane to do all the listening?

JANE: If I want to talk, I just make a loud noise and he shuts up. That's understood. [*Laughter*]

Jo: That used to be a bad problem for us. Before I understood something about typology, I used to think Jane was imitating a Mack truck.

JANE: I was! It took a Mack truck to stop Jo! We ran smack into this problem early in our marriage. I got lazy because of Jo's extraversion. I have had to learn to be more extraverted because we live in an extraverted society. I am a minority person in our society. I have had to do something about it. If I could make the effort, then I would do better, I felt. Jo gets such a kick out of talking, and I'm glad he does. He doesn't get all that many kicks any more, so it's all right with me. Have you noticed that Jo's hair is pretty short? Well, a few days ago we went to Santa Barbara where we have this cute little hairdresser. I looked over as Jo was getting his hair cut and the two of them were talking away, and I think that's why his hair got cut so short!

JH: So, Jane, in being married to Joe, you have had to learn about the value of talking?

JANE: I have had to learn it. I have also learned about the outer world. I was oblivious to it, especially having grown up on this vast ranch. I think the extravert has to help the introvert find out about the outer world. Jo is able to set an extraverted tone in conversations. He puts the focus on a "people level." But as an introverted thinker, I have to change to another level before I can respond.

Jo: And Jane has been my guide into the inner world. Our marriage has brought up our inferior functions, and we have been able to help each other with them. It is part of the individuation process.

JANE: We do need help on our inferior side. And I think that is one of the important things about marriage. Usually one spouse can do this and the other spouse can do that, and they both help each other find out about things they wouldn't otherwise know by themselves. I've become much more extraverted since I have been around Jo. Even in spite of his taking over as much as he does, I have seen the sense of extraversion, where it fits, and how much people get out of it.

RH: Typology has been extremely important to your marriage, hasn't it?

JANE: It was the only connection we had, except for sex, companionship, and our attachment to nature as the governing principle.

JH: When you learned about the typological differences, did you find that the anger and frustration in your marriage began to fade?

JANE: Yes. It didn't mean we didn't fight any more. But we got along better. And I found it exciting to be with someone who was different from me, because of all the things I could learn about my inferior functions.

RH: Jane, did you "learn" an extraversion that was similar to Jo's, or do you feel you have learned it your own way?

JANE: I do have a different extraversion from Jo's. Mine is more in the impersonal world and Jo's is much more of a personal expression.

Jo: She is an intellectual and I am a mushy, old feeling type.

JANE: I had to learn about feeling. I had to learn that it was a good thing. I have learned that from Jo.

Jo: When I was sixty-five, I did some work with Joe Henderson. He told me that Jo Wheelwright, the extravert, was finished. I was still lecturing all over the place and seeing more patients than I could count. He helped me realize that I had played the game in the outer world and that I was through—not that it was time to die, but that I needed to find the other world. That's what living on this ranch has done for me. I knew Jane needed to return here before she died. But living here has helped me to be reborn into the inner world. Jane is like an inner-world guide for me. I am still growing and very much alive. But now, a good week for me is one in which I see no one else except Jane. For the first seventy years of my life, the most important element for me was relationship. Since the age of eighty, the focus has shifted to my own psychological development—to become what is in me to become.

J H: Since the age of eighty, what has become of your extraverted side?

Jo: I lived it out! [*Laughter*]

RH: Jane, you are known as an introverted thinker. How would you describe that part of yourself?

JANE: My thinking imposes itself on me. For most of my life I have kept journals to accommodate its insistence. I call my thinking "little brain waves." They seem to have a life of their own, and they have no respect for outside circumstances. Because my thinking is aligned with my introversion, it is difficult for me to relate to people in extraverted situations, but not when the milieu is introverted. Introverted thinking in a woman takes her out of the stereotypic classifications that most people depend on. In special situations, with chosen people, that combination is a big asset.

RH: Has it helped your writing career?

JANE: Yes, my writing is geared to the impersonal subjective bias.

MARRIAGE AND CONFLICT

JO: One of the key things I have found in sixty-five years of marriage is that you have to fight. If your relationship is not strong enough to stand the fights that occur, forget it. You are going to get divorced as sure as God made little green apples.

JANE: The negative is just as important as the positive for the Jungian world.

JO: The bottom line is nobody's the boss.

JH: Sometimes you hear it said that parents should not fight in front of their children.

JANE: I think it is a big revelation for children to see that you fight and yet stick together. There are many times when the shadow has to get into the picture. Otherwise, there is no depth. We fought in front of our daughter and son because at the time, we were not that smart—we did it because we could not help it.

RH: What do you think it means when a couple fights?

JO: I think it is a process of withdrawing projections. If your wife doesn't do what you expect her to do, then Bingo! Jane was very allergic to intuition. Fighting is caused by getting hit on a blind spot.

JANE: When couples are exaggeratedly different, as we are, there are more than the average number of blind spots. I kept saying, prove it. Jo would grasp at something out of the blue, and I'd say prove it. Where are the facts?

JO: I would say *facts*—who the hell cares about facts! *I'm* telling you it is true—and off we would go.

JANE: He would say it was true, but what he meant was that it was true *for him*. This no longer happens.

JH: Do you feel your marriage keeps your own individuation process alive?

Jo: Yes. It brings us to our inferior functions, although you don't ever make it all the way to becoming what it is in you to become. Jane and I still step on each other's toes. I don't think our marriage has gotten either easier or harder. But our relationship would not have a chance if we didn't pay allegiance to ourselves and become as individually whole as we can become.

JANE: We couldn't get along if we didn't keep working on our unconscious areas.

Jo: There are still unconscious areas, but when you think about it, Jane and I are together now twenty-four hours a day—or maybe thirty-six hours some days!

JANE: There is a tension in our relationship that nudges us both toward consciousness.

RH: Do you think that you have lived longer because of your marriage and the tension that pushes you toward consciousness?

JANE: I think so.

Jo: But we also have long-life genes in both family trees.

MARRIAGE, AGING, AND SUFFERING

RH: How has Jo's blindness and Jane's deafness affected your relationship with each other?

Jo: It certainly leads to a lot of petty quarrels and irritations with each other. I'll say something to Jane and she doesn't hear me. How do you say nice things and at the same time have to shout as loud as you can? Her deafness makes communication more difficult.

JANE: Jo's blindness does the same for me.

JH: How has losing your sight affected you, Jo?

Jo: I have been a visual person aesthetically. There are so many beautiful things here on the ranch and by the ocean. Gradually they are going out of my world. Those islands off the coast—I used to love to watch them. They are gone now. The beautiful fields ... and now they are starting to turn gold. I feel it as a real loss. And I can't see Jane any more. I always used to like to watch Jane, and I can't do that now. She is just a blur to me. Her white hair is one thing I cling to because it shows when other things don't. I want to go back. I have the feeling that I owe God something. I believe I was put on this earth for a purpose. Some of us never find out why we're here. Probably the majority don't find out. With Jane's help, I did. It started with a repetitive dream I had in which I nursed Jane back to life instead of her nursing me.

RH: What is your purpose?

Jo: It is to become what is in me to become. And that is thanks to Albert. I call God *Albert*. And all the beauty here is thanks to Albert. He can be pretty mean, too. We had a gale here not long ago—winds up to ninety-five miles per hour. I sat here watching the big window move in and out and thought it wasn't very good. I have to accept what Albert sends to me as part of the price of admission. We have to pay a price to be alive.

RH: Aren't blindness and deafness pretty heavy prices to have to pay? Some might consider it a punishment or something that shouldn't happen to good people.

Jo: Some people never accept the price they are asked to pay. Albert says there are no freebies. This is the price of such a long life.

JANE: I know what Jo means. I see it more in terms of fate or the inevitability of what happens. I see my hearing loss as part of a pattern that I am being drawn along, and I don't see who is pulling me. I see myself going in a certain way that is all right. Many things come to me. It has a lot to do with nature. The animals have an instinct that works for them, as when a day-old quail knows its mother. Jung tells us that archetypes are instincts, and vice versa.

JH: Would you call yourselves "soulmates"?

Jo: I think so.

JANE: "Soulmates" is a tricky word. It means companionable and communicative. It means real connections. It also suggests the challenge that is required in a relationship to bring out consciousness. The individuation process goes on for your whole life. The older you get, the more different you become. When you are very old, you have become more different than you have ever been before.

Jo: You also become more alike because of the development of the inferior function. At any rate, our communication is greatly improved, despite deafness and blindness.

JH: Does marriage get harder as you get older?

JANE: There are still difficulties in being married in old age.

Jo: We still fight.

JANE: You have to get to the point where you can say to each other, "I'm different from you and I see it this way. I'm sorry. I can't do anything else." If you can get to where you can say that to each other, it gets much easier.

Jo: I have never been particularly vain. I wore the three-piece suits and neckties. But as I have become older, I've gotten to a stage where I don't really care, even a little bit, what I look like. I don't want to upset people, so I don't go around in my underdrawers, but I wouldn't mind. Women in their forties and fifties stop having periods, and I have stopped shaving. Until I was eighty, I would lie about my age. In our type of business, being too young is a drawback. If you are too young, people won't come to you because they figure you don't know anything about life. So I would always say I was a bit older than I really was.

JANE: As I have gotten older, my intuition has increased. I am speculating more and Jo is speculating less.

MARRIAGE AND LOVE

Jo: There is a difference between being *in love* and *loving*. It seems to me that the good Lord has seen fit to make opposites attract each other. The man seems to plaster his anima on the woman, and the woman seems to plaster her animus onto the man. That's what I call being in love; it is aesthetic and lovely, but it is a little bit narcissistic, because what you are really in love with is your own anima or animus. *Being in love becomes an exercise in narcissism.* But then, pretty soon, you start to become irritated because what your partner should be doing is not being done. And vice versa. Then the fighting begins. If there is some kind of basic connection between the two, the marriage will hold together for the resolution to occur, so that you can withdraw the projections. As they are withdrawn, you can actually perceive who the woman or man you are living with is as a person. Before that, *you have been passionately in love with yourself.*

JH: How have you each come to understand what love is?

JANE: The hard way! [*Laughter*]

RH: There is a lot of controversy these days over the issue of what is masculine and what is feminine. Jung has been criticized for this, especially by feminists and the men's movement.

JANE: There are masculine characteristics in women and feminine characteristics in men long before they discover what they are and how they appear and what effect they have on others. I think too many feminists identify with the animus, but are not conscious of it and cannot "see" it in action.

JO: The animus is an important and positive component of a woman's psychology. For a feeling-type man like myself, the anima tends to be negative. Because of my feeling function, I could never identify with men.

"BASING YOUR WHOLE LIFE ON ONE DREAM"

RH: What do you do with your dreams?

JANE: I write mine down and keep them. I have a whole suitcase of them. I don't know what to do with them. I have never thrown them out. I will probably give them to my daughter. We are close.

JO: I hardly ever have dreams! I was a washout as a patient. I did have a few that were very important, but I was never very good at analyzing dreams. I was always afraid that Jane would be a better analyst than I would. But then I discovered something very important. The people I could not help at all Jane was good with, and the people whom she wasn't able to help worked well with me. I realized then that we didn't have to compete. I once said to Mike Fordham, "You folks are always rattling around with dreams and the collective unconscious, but what I am interested in is the interaction between myself and the person I am working with." It is through that relationship that I was able to gain access to the unconscious.

JANE: Jo, you almost always told me your dreams. I don't know whether you knew it, but I wrote all of them down for you. Jo's dreams are very simple, direct, and to the point.

Jo: Like the dreams of an eleven-year-old! I used to drive Toni Wolff crazy. She would plead with me, "Please, Jo, have a dream."

JH: What did you talk about, if you didn't have dreams? That could drive some Jungians crazy. [*Laughter*]

Jo: Well, it was sixty-five years ago, and I'm not sure I can remember exactly. I think we spent our time working our way out of the transference and countertransference. I did have one dream I remember. I had had a series of repetitive dreams in which I would be in an auto accident and badly hurt, and Jane would nurse me back to health. That night I dreamt that the accident happened, but this time Jane was hurt and I nursed her back to health. This may sound crazy, but to me the dream meant that I was to be an analyst. I told Jung the dream and that I felt I had finally found out what I was here for. He laughed and said he thought there was more to it than that, but that I was on the right track. Can you imagine basing your whole life on one dream?

JANE: Sally, the woman I wrote about in *Death of a Woman,* was able to keep herself alive because she became interested in dreams. Whenever I would go to see her, she looked like a skeleton. But she was excited and would say to me, "I just had an interesting dream," and we would talk about it. And the color would come back into her face.

"In Life There Are No Freebies"

RH: What do you think Jung meant when he said he knew God?

Jo: I understand just what he meant since I have come to know nature by living on this ranch.

Jane: In Jung's letters, he always explained that his experience of God was real but that he did not know what the image of God was made of. In the movie of Jung [*Face to Face*] he said he did not *believe* in God, he *knew*. In a letter he said that knowing makes belief unnecessary. I couldn't say that. I have seen such extraordinary things in nature that no one except a god or devil could figure out. I believe that there is a power beyond me, which I find more impressive than what the Bible or religious leaders talk about.

Jo: I have always believed there is a higher power. I am not a churchgoer. As I said, I call God *Albert.* I don't know why. Before I was blind, I used to drive over to get the groceries once a week, and I hallucinated all the way. I used to talk to Albert. When my sight began to go, I fretted a lot. I kept saying, "Albert, why me?" I would be talking out loud, and I would see the startled faces of people looking at me. One night I realized—not in a dream, just at night—that here I am in my eighties, and I am going blind because in life there are no freebies. There is a price for living. This is the price I am paying for being in relatively good shape at the age of eighty-nine. I have to pay my dues, so I am going blind. Following the hallucination, I swear to you, I heard low laughter. I don't think of God as a dear old man, like Leonardo da Vinci with a white beard. God is Albert. I have hallucinatory conversations with Albert, and my image of "him" is as a man and a woman. "He" is both.

Marriage and Death

Jo: Several years ago, we wondered how our children felt about us living so long. Did they think we would live forever—especially when it came to thinking about what we would pass along in terms of the furniture, rugs, and artwork? So we decided to have a mock death. They would take turns going through all the valuable stuff we had collected over the years. They were each free to take whatever they wanted. I recently worked out that our son John is now five times richer than I am. He doesn't have to wake up in the middle of the night and say, "Isn't that old bastard ever going to pop off?"

JANE: I found it a great relief to just get rid of everything.

JO: I never think about what death will be like. I think if Jane died first, I would proceed to die very quickly. I used to feel secure because I had a tube with ten morphine-sulfate tablets in it—enough to kill a fair-sized giraffe. I felt safe. When we moved out here to the ranch, I don't know where the tube went. Now that I am retired, I will have to get one of my M.D. friends to prescribe the tablets. Without Jane, there wouldn't be enough left for me to continue. I had thoughts from time to time about taking an overdose, but I wouldn't as long as Jane is alive. I don't want to leave her alone.

JANE: I think the unconscious functions are more available as we grow older. The more balanced the two sides are, maybe, the easier the death. I see patterns as I think of death, something that could be a mandala pattern, like a square or circle. It lasts for just a short time. Perhaps a mandala symbol would appear if death is imminent. I think there is an archetype you identify with, and then you ease into death. As you get nearer to death, you get into deeper levels of the unconscious. Is death going to be a bad experience or a good one? We heard that Jung died in his sleep. That is a good way to go. But we don't know about ourselves.

JH: What would you like to be remembered for?

JO: For starting—with Jane—the first Jungian analyst training program [in San Francisco] in the world.

JANE: Donald Sandner once told me that he thought my book, *Ranch Papers* [Lapis, 1988], was one of the best Jungian books ever written. I like it the best of everything I have done. Maybe I could be remembered for that.

RH: Jung encouraged people to formulate their own views of life after death. What do you feel will happen when you die?

JANE: I know Jung suggested that, but I think it may be more appropriate for intuitives. It is not appropriate for me. I have had a few dreams, perhaps about life after death. One, in particular! I am trying to go through a huge, dense forest to some circular objective but do not know my way. The trees are taller than any I have ever seen.

RH: As they approach death, some couples find comfort in believing that they will be reunited in the afterlife, or in heaven.

JANE: I feel that death will end our relationship, but it will not end the changes and development that came out of so many years together— if there is an afterlife. So far, I have not feared that death will change the meaning of our relationship.

Jo: I do not believe in survival after death. I think that relationship stops at death and therefore there is no choice in the matter. I can only join in the cyclical creativity of nature. I have asked that my ashes be used as fertilizer.

To this day, God is the name by which I designate all things which cross my willful path violently and recklessly, all things which upset my subjective views, plans, and intentions and change the course of my life for better or worse. [Interview with Frederick Sands, June 2, 1961 (4 days before he died), *Good Housekeeping,* December 1961.]

— C. G. Jung

It is tremendously important that people should be able to accept themselves. Otherwise the will of God cannot be lived …. [*The Vision Seminars*, Vol. 1, 1976, p. 134.]

— C. G. Jung

C. TONI FREY-WEHRLIN, PH.D.

After receiving his Ph.D. in Philosophy at the University of Zürich, Toni Frey-Wehrlin enrolled at the Jung Institute in Zürich and underwent analysis with C. A. Meier, later training under Michael Fordham in London. In 1964, along with C. A. Meier, Carl Briner, and Heinrich Fierz, he established the world's first and only inpatient Jungian psychiatric clinic, the Zürichberg Clinic in Switzerland. For decades, he maintained a private practice in Zürich, which he started in 1958, and taught at the Jung Institute, where he was an analyst and training supervisor. He also actively supported Susan Bach in her work with severely ill children. His writings include: "The Treatment of Chronic Psychoses," "Oedipus in Gethsemane: Archetypal Aspects of Homosexuality," "C. G. Jung—Light and Shadow," "Reflections on C. G. Jung's Concept of Synchronicity," "Problems of Dream Interpretation" and "Defiance and Compliance—What is a Jungian?" We interviewed Toni in the spring of 1996, when he was 70 years old. We met him on the banks of the Hudson River near Rheinbeck, New York at the Valeur Mansion, where he was leading a week-long workshop for mental health professionals. Though his body was somewhat frail, his mind was quick and his heart was warm and open. Toni died in 2002. He and his wife, Rita, were married for over 40 years with three daughters and four grandchildren.

• 3 •

LET IT BE
C. Toni Frey-Wehrlin at 70

The shadow confronts us with everything that is foreign to us,
everything we don't want or that we hate. But out of the shadow
also comes much that makes us and our lives valuable. Without
shadow there is no creativity.

—C. Toni Frey-Wehrlin

Encountering Jung

ROB HENDERSON (RH): You have described yourself as part of the
almost extinct species of those who actually met Jung in person. What
impact has meeting Jung had on you?

TONI FREY-WEHRLIN (TF): It was quite impressive to me that he was
such a huge man. He was a tower, an athlete, and a giant physically. That
was quite impressive, not only the weight of his personality, but his whole
physical appearance. That is something I will never forget. Whether that
made a difference in my views on Jungian psychology or not is another
question. But the man—he was colossal. You could imagine him as a
dairyman in the Alps, carrying huge cheeses around on his back. There
are pictures of him taking off his jacket, screaming and yelling, jumping
around. He was an enormously vital personality—full of vitality and
energy.

RH: Was his physical appearance overwhelming to others as well?

TF: I remember a passage from Jones's biography of Freud in which
Freud and Jung were talking about alcoholism, and Freud fainted. Jung
just picked him up and carried him to the sofa.

RH: So, he was a strong man?

TF: He was. I remember the passage in *Memories, Dreams, Reflections* in which Jung, after his break with Freud, said that getting through his night sea journey was a matter of "sheer force." When Jung was in Africa, some natives started a ritual and became more and more excited. They started waving their spears and dancing around the fire, and when they became really aggressive and dangerous, Jung felt threatened and suddenly started shouting at them in Swiss German as if to say "how dare you," and soon the whole thing calmed down. And if you had met Jung, you would believe it.

RH: How old were you when you met Jung?

TF: Thirty. He was 80.

RH: Did you have much contact with him?

TF: He was quite withdrawn at that time. He seldom came to the Institute. I don't know if he ever lectured at the Institute. He once gave a student an exam in the fundamentals of analytical psychology. He asked the student: "If I were a street cleaner and you had to explain analytical psychology to me, how would you proceed?" After half an hour of listening to the man, he flunked him.

RH: Where did you hear that story?

TF: It's one of the many stories that circulated at the Institute. There are lots of stories like that about Jung, but most of them are apocryphal. There's no way of knowing what really went on, since only Jung and the other person were present.

JH: Do you think he was aware of how strong his personality was?

TF: I am quite sure he was. And he used it very well. Jung invited projections more than the average person would. He also offered a big hook for these projections. Jung often reacted bizarrely to things, if judged from a scientific viewpoint.

RH: You have described Jung as a "mythical" figure. What do you mean by that?

TF: I mean that the projections he constellated were of the archetypal kind. He really was the wise old man, the giant behind the mountains or in the cave. That's how one experienced him. This is something people need. A leading figure—in the good sense, and in the bad sense—like the Führer in Germany. People need this kind of figure in times of transition, when values are collapsing or changing. They need a guiding figure to tell them what is good and what is evil. Jung constellated that in a very deep way. He invited the projection.

RH: When you say "invited," are you saying there was something intentional?

TF: No. But real. You know the famous hook for the projection. It just happened to him.

JH: Does that mean that his life was also taken over by a myth?

TF: Absolutely. The big question for him after the separation from Freud was: "Which myth am I living?" He was convinced everyone was living a myth. He was trying to determine which myth he was living. Then came the famous dream in which he shot Siegfried down from the wagon.

RH: Then that told him which myth he was living?

TF: Yes, that told him that he had been living the myth of the hero up to that point. And after the separation from Freud, that was the end of his living the hero myth. That is why he withdrew from all his official functions at the psychoanalytic society. He withdrew from Zürich University and from the Burghölzli Psychiatric Hospital. He abandoned his career. His career could have gone God knows where—but he withdrew into his own inner world. He had his practice, he traveled around the world, and he wrote his books.

RH: He started to live out of another myth then?

TF: Of course.

RH: He left the hero myth and started to get into the myth of the wise old man?

TF: Yes, I think he got into a number of myths then. The wise old man, and you mentioned yesterday his book, *Answer to Job*. I think he also identified with Job.

RH: That is a very interesting book. I don't hear too many people talking about that book.

TF: I can imagine. When it came out—I think it was 1952—I was in the midst of my analysis with Meier, and Meier said it was a mistake to publish the book then, as it was fifty years too early.

RH: Is that right? It was really interesting for me yesterday, when I told you what I thought Jung was saying in that book, to have you say that you thought the same thing, because I never thought I really understood it, even though I have read it many times.

TF: It is a very difficult book to understand, and I am far from pretending that I understand it. It is one of the books by Jung that I read every three or four years, and when I find something important, I make a mark in the margin, and I hope that if I ever reach 100, the whole book will be marked ... [*laughter*] ... because you don't see what is in the book unless you have really experienced it. The other book of this kind is *The Psychology of the Transference*.

RH: You feel the same way about that book?

TF: I have marked about half of it so far.

RH: Like we were saying yesterday, one thing Jung is saying in *Answer to Job* is that God has a dark side—we call that Satan—and that God is partly unconscious; and because he is unconscious, there are things that happen in the world that happen because of God's unconsciousness.

TF: Yes.

RH: That explains why bad things happen to good people—some of that is because God is unconscious.

TF: Yes. God is like an emotional person. When you have been gripped by an emotion, you might say afterwards: "I don't know myself any more. I did this and that, but how could I have done or said that?

I didn't know myself to be like that." Well, something else has taken over: the complex.

RH: So God gets taken over by a complex?

TF: Yes. I think that is a very difficult thing for you to understand with your theological training. Jung sees God as a person, as a human being.

RH: It makes sense to me—if we are made in God's image. I have also had the experience of sharing these ideas in churches, and I can remember in one particular church, the minister had given a sermon that morning about God being love and good, and I came out with some of these ideas in an evening group. The minister got so angry that I thought he was going to punch me. I was very embarrassed, but that is the kind of reaction that these ideas get—at least in the church.

TF: Where does evil come from then, if God is almighty and all loving? Why does evil happen? This is where the question comes up of whether Jung was a Gnostic or not.

RH: What do most people misunderstand about Jung?

TF: He is often seen as a mystic. I think this is because he wrote about things that cannot be described in the language of positive science. I do not think Jung is a mystic. He understood himself to be an empiricist and a scientist.

RH: And yet a lot of medical people—who are scientists—would discount Jung.

TF: In a paper she wrote shortly before she died, Susan Bach wrote about a case involving a man from the United States who called her for an appointment. She said she didn't have any time but that he could call back later and maybe she could find some time that evening. She hung up and then a client called to cancel his appointment—therefore making it possible for her to see the man who had called earlier. She related this synchronistic—that is, meaningful—coincidence in order to demonstrate the "charged" atmosphere of the case. As we were about to publish this paper, one of the doctors advised us to omit the reference to this incident because he considered it "unscientific." It would appear that it is "unscientific" to describe phenomena that don't fit a positivist worldview.

RH: But would Jung have seen this as a fact?

TF: Of course—and he published such facts. And because he published such facts, he is called a mystic. He was a scientist who reported what he observed.

RH: As far as the biographies of Jung go, you do not like the idealizing ones.

TF: No, not at all. I like Stern's book [Paul J. Stern, *C. G. Jung: The Haunted Prophet* (George Braziller, 1976)]. I haven't read it for some time, but I remember some passages that were the same, word for word, as things Meier had told me. It is reliable. Stern is skeptical and critical of Jung—and why not? I do not think he is hostile. He spent quite a bit of time and energy writing the book.

RH: Do you think the biographies by von Franz, van der Post, and Hannah have done a disservice to Jung?

TF: I don't know. In the long run probably not. These things correct themselves. I had to smile at certain passages. For instance, when Hannah writes about Jung's relationship with Toni Wolff, she describes the shifting of Jung's affections away from his daughters as a "sacrifice." So he sacrificed himself and projected his anima onto Toni Wolff, and the proof that this was the right thing to do was that all four daughters got married. [*Laughter*] That goes too far for my taste.

RH: Do you think enough has been said about the Jung-Wolff relationship?

TF: I believe we know what there is to know about this relationship. I can hardly imagine that yet more correspondence will come to light. The old alchemists sometimes exchanged correspondence about their work with their "*soror mystica*." Jung's work is available to us. Toni Wolff also had a few papers published. We actually know more about Jung's relationship with Sabina Spielrein, and in their correspondence one can discern the birth, so to speak, of the notion of the anima. In my opinion we know much too little about Emma Jung.

RH: You feel a biography of Emma Jung would be helpful. Why?

TF: I can't imagine Jung's life work being what it was without Emma. Let's not forget that despite being a genius—which is beyond doubt—he was also the son of a poor parson. By going on to marry this immensely rich woman, he was able to build his houses in Kusnacht and Bollingen. It was with the help of her money that he was able to work for six months a year and spend the rest of the time writing his books and traveling to Africa or India. Here's another little anecdote: after Emma died, a friend visited Jung, and Jung told him that he had just got a bill for coal and that he didn't know what to do because he'd never paid a coal bill before. She took care of all the expenses—even those involving the education of the children. She looked after the children and generally sheltered Jung from day-to-day problems. When she died, the money was, to a large extent, gone. She never said a word. She just paid the bills.

RH: So Jung was not able to provide for the family.

TF: No. I found a bill he had written for an American patient for two consultations in the 50s. The total sum was 50 Swiss francs. That would have been considered very cheap and much less than he could have asked for.

JH: Jung didn't have time to get involved.

TF: He didn't have the time, the interest, or the energy for that kind of thing.

JH: He needed someone to run his life, in a way—to make sure he had clothing and food.

TF: He had to be taken care of.

RH: Everyone we have talked to about Jung has said that Emma was a very wonderful and generous person. She raised the kids and ran the home.

TF: And that is never mentioned in his autobiography. She is mentioned twice in half a sentence. He took her for granted. That was the old system in Switzerland, and perhaps everywhere in the world 100 years ago. The wife was in the shadow of the man. I remember a book that came out in the 40s or 50s, written by the wife of a famous man— the title was *I Helped My Husband.* [*Laughter*]

RH: Is that particularly Swiss?

TF: I would say we stuck to that system much longer. Women didn't get the vote in Switzerland until 1971. Before then they couldn't vote— in the oldest democracy in the world!

JH: So the Women's Movement has not arrived in Switzerland as it has in the United States?

TF: I think it has now. There was an accelerated development. I can see that in my kids. My wife and I still follow the traditional system: I earn and she manages the house. But our children haven't adopted this approach. They can't take it any more.

RH: We hear lots of wild stories about what happened in the sessions with Jung. You have called them legends. Does that mean they may not have taken place?

TF: They contribute to our impression of Jung's personality. Perhaps these incidents didn't actually take place, but they could have. They have their value. But remember: who witnessed these events? People came out of a session with Jung and said, "Oh God!" [*Laughter*] A woman worked with him for three weeks before realizing that he didn't have a beard. [*Laughter*] In the fourth week she looked at him and said: "Professor Jung, did you shave off your beard?" [*Laughter*] She had seen the Wise Old Man for three weeks.

RH: Did you get that from the woman who said that—or is it one of the legends?

TF: That's one of the legends.

RH: That's one thing I liked about you when I was in your seminar in Zürich. You know all the legends, don't you?

TF: I have heard the gossip about Jung—and I like gossip. But I see this in my own practice. Clients have come back after a week or a year to say that they were very impressed by something I had said, and they quote me. And I think, "That's not me! It's impossible that I said that." Now my first reaction might be that the client heard something I did not say because he or she *needed* to hear it—or that syntonic countertransference made me say such a thing. I am not like a computer during the session. I am a living system that reacts to the patient. So it's possible for a reaction to come out of a corner of myself that I haven't yet seen.

RH: You have used that word "syntonic" before. What exactly does it mean?

TF: That's from Michael Fordham. In his *Notes on the Transference* he speaks of countertransference. It is an emotional reaction by the analyst. It can be based on an unconscious complex in the analyst. There is something in the analyst that has not been analyzed yet, and it comes up in the session. It's usually disastrous for the analysis when the analyst's own unconscious material comes into the treatment. But it is also possible that a complex wants to come up that is the client's business, but the client doesn't want to face it and fights it, pushing it down. It then tries to come up again—not in the client, but in the analyst. And then the analyst has an emotional reaction which actually belongs not to him or her, but to the client.

RH: So when you say something to the client, it might have originated in the client's complexes?

TF: The anger that a particular client feels towards her mother, for example, might be something she is fighting against. When she tells me a story about her mother, as she is telling it, I find myself getting angrier and angrier. I say to myself: this may be her anger that is coming up in me because I am less resistant to it. I can tell my client that I don't know what this is, but that when I hear what she says, I find myself becoming increasingly angry. I can ask her, "Don't you feel this anger?" or suggest that she may have felt the anger but did not allow herself to express it.

RH: And the more the client denies the anger, the more you feel it?

TF: Right. And that is a syntonic reaction. That is one of the new things discovered and formulated after Jung—but within the Jungian tradition—by Michael Fordham.

THE JUNGIAN CLINIC

RH: The Jung Clinic—or, as it is called in your country, "Klinik am Zürichberg"—did you begin it?

TF: I was the initiator and one of the cofounders, along with C. A. Meier, Carl Briner and H. K. Fierz. Briner was the husband of one of the first graduates of the Jung Institute in Zürich, Mary Briner. He was also the president of a large Swiss insurance company.

RH: How did the idea for the Clinic come to you?

TF: I came back from England in 1958, following my Jungian clinical training. I had a friend who ran a small psychiatric clinic near Zürich. He asked me to come and do psychotherapy there. I was looking to start my practice, so I accepted. I saw patients at the clinic, and when they were dismissed, they would come to me as private patients. Within two months I had a full caseload. I got highly interested in clinical work with schizophrenics and would go to the clinic three times a week. On one occasion, I returned to the clinic to see my patients after a day or two and found that one of them had been given a sedative by one of the doctors. The patient had apparently stopped speaking for a day or two and had become a cause for concern. This episode provoked a very infantile reaction of defiance in me. Well, in alchemy you start out with shit and you make gold out of it. [*Laughter*] I thought: if things are going to be like this, I want my own clinic. The Swiss economy was booming in the 60s, and we were able to start the venture with 10,000 Swiss francs. At that time, that was about $2,000. I also worked at the Binswanger Clinic by Lake Constance, together with Fierz and a whole team of other psychotherapists, all of whom were keen to join the new venture.

RH: Meier helped you?

TF: He was in agreement—he was a sort of figurehead—and was interested in the project.

RH: He had also been your analyst, so you had a relationship with him.

TF: I had a transference. [*Laughter*]

RH: You said you were the initiator. Does that mean Meier contributed just his name?

TF: Yes, yes. But I must admit he also went around and did some fund-raising—which was not very successful. But he did find a man—an ex-patient of his—who was quite wealthy and gave us 300,000 Swiss francs interest-free, and with that we were able to purchase the building and pay the expenses for the first few months. We had two patients when we began.

RH: You went out and purchased property in Zürich?

TF: It was an old villa on the Zürichberg, near the big Waldhaus Dolder Hotel. It had ten or twelve rooms and would have been suitable for a family with two children. Later, it came out that it had belonged to the von Franz family up until 1946. I remember finding some maps from the Austrian general staff in a cupboard. The late Baron von Franz was a colonel in the old Austrian army. I see this coincidence as a synchronism, and I'm sorry that Frau von Franz never chose to visit the building in its new function, which must have been significant for her as well. There were other buildings on the grounds, which we were able to expand into as the Clinic grew. And then we bought a third property nearby, also on the Zürichberg. By the time I was kicked out of the Clinic for poor management, the original 10,000 Swiss francs investment had been transformed into 10 million, thanks to soaring property prices. [*Laughter*]

JH: Can you go back and talk about what was going on as you began work in the Clinic? How did you start formalizing what you wanted to do with patients? How were you bringing your training into the Clinic?

TF: I had had my Jungian training, and at that time was convinced that Jungian psychology could cure almost anything, that it should be applied. And, after all, Jungian psychology came out of the psychiatric clinic. There would be no concepts of the collective unconscious or the archetype without Jung's experience with psychotics. Jung saw the parallels between what he observed in these people and what he had read in old manuscripts, the archaic fantasies in schizophrenics, for example—which Freud had never observed. Freud's practice was for neurotics.

RH: So, really, you thought you were reclaiming the territory where Jungian psychology had begun.

TF: That was one side of it. There was also what I would call, in hindsight, an overestimation—the idea that Jungian psychology could cure schizophrenia. It was a time when there was a huge wave in favor of psychotherapy for the psychoses. Everybody thought that psychotherapy was the answer to psychosis. That enthusiasm has declined a bit since then, and nowadays I have a different view, but that was the initial impetus. Over the years, I have seen more and more of what we cannot cure—and I don't think we will ever be able to. The proportions have been one-third cured, one-third improved, and one-third unchanged. These statistics were first published in the middle of the 19th century, and they remain unchanged even today, despite all the therapies. I've heard that there are over 500 different methods of psychotherapy. It was a bit of a crisis for me to witness the re-evaluation of the role of Jungian pychology: if it doesn't cure, what *does* it do? Why should we use it and run up all these expenses? Imagine what it cost to give each patient at the Clinic three hours of one-to-one psychotherapy from a Jungian specialist. That's quite an amount.

RH: After you began the Clinic, you started to get some other ideas.

TF: You interviewed John Perry. Well, we had decided to present our way of working at the Clinic at the 1977 Jungian Congress in Rome. Then I heard that Perry intended to present a paper at the same Congress in which he would claim that he was able to cure 23 out of 25 schizophrenic patients in three months using only psychotherapy. It was incredible—and it was clear we couldn't compete with that. So we decided to do the opposite, and my paper on the treatment of chronic psychosis was born. We formulated an alternative, which aimed not to cure but to "accompany." A certain percentage of chronic patients cannot be rehabilitated. If you look at our world, you soon realize it is somewhat crazy, and it is not for everyone. Quite a bit of stamina is needed to get through life, and there are some who simply don't have the stamina for it. They need a place to be. A patient remains a human being, even if he or she is a chronic patient. If the patient has the opportunity to talk for three hours a week with an intelligent partner in a stable relationship, this will change his or her quality of life. It is a question of being human— and very often, of course, the impetus for both the Clinic and the patients is a religious one. Jung makes this statement in a letter dated 28 August, 1945: "I am not interested in curing neurosis. My interest is in the numinous and I have to lead my patients to an experience of the numinous. If you can have this experience you are freed from the curse of the illness."

JH: Was that your guiding principle in starting the Clinic?

TF: No. I read this statement only much later.

RH: Then your whole notion of what Jungian psychology was about changed a lot from the time you began the Clinic.

TF: Yes, but the recognition that healing is not the main objective is only one side of that. The change in my opinions also had a lot to do with getting older. At 40 you think differently about God and the beyond than you do at 70. At 70, you are a bit closer to it, and it gets more interesting. [*Laughter*] Anyway, to get back to curing the patient, in order to get licenses and have therapy costs covered by the health insurance companies these days, we have to provide statistical evidence that proves the effectiveness of Jungian methods. But in the analytic session, Jung's concerns were very different. If the patient is cured, it's a welcome side-effect, but it is not the main objective.

RH: The Clinic was started in about 1961—is that right?

TF: No. The Foundation was established in 1963, and we opened the Clinic on April Fool's Day, 1964.

JH: On purpose? [*Laughter*]

TF: No ... [*laughter*] ... it was just a coincidence. [*More laughter*]

Jung's Funeral

RH: Jung died in 1961.

TF: I remember Jung's funeral. It was a nightmare—it was never-ending. Everybody who spoke went on for about half an hour. It was there that I had the idea that we must do something to carry on the work. "Now's the time to open the Clinic!" I thought.

RH: Where did that come from? What was the connection to Jung's death?

TF: It was my own infantile defiant reaction to want my own clinic, as I already mentioned. And then there was the funeral, and I said: "Now is the moment to do it."

RH: Let's talk about Jung's funeral, since you were actually there.

TF: I was there. It was in the church in Kusnacht, and the church was packed full of people. One speaker spoke for almost an hour. The service was even interrupted for a break so that everyone could get out and have a pipe or cigarette or what have you. [*Laughter*] Then we went back in again.

RH: Who was the speaker who went on for an hour?

TF: Hans Schaer.

RH: Was he a minister?

TF: He was. And for those people who had been working with Jung this was a tremendous experience, and they got carried away by their emotions. I am quite sure Schaer had prepared a speech to last for 15 minutes, not 50. He just got carried away by his emotions and could not stop.

RH: What was it like for you to be there?

TF: Interesting! I was not deeply touched and felt no sense of personal loss. Jung was a mythical figure for me, but his death was not a personal loss. I had not lost a father or something like that. I needed Jung as a mythical figure in the sense of having a need for a huge leading ideal.

50

Being a Jungian Analyst

JH: What drew you to the study of Jungian psychology and inspired you to make it your life work?

TF: It just fell into place with my prerequisites for a personal philosophy. Each of us has his or her own particular temperament, and that's why we are drawn to one philosophy or another. What Jung had to offer was very close to what I needed.

JH: Looking back, do you think that your myth was to be a healer and Jungian psychology offered you a way to live that myth?

TF: Maybe. I was always interested in religion. I am an only child, and as a boy I had an illustrated Bible I would read—especially the Old Testament, because the pictures were so much more interesting. [*Laughter*] I had a strong inclination towards that and towards reading and being by myself. I had very strong ambitions in many directions. I was convinced that I was much better and more gifted than my peers at school. I had a strong drive towards power. I wanted to be somebody. This is a myth of the Frey family—that they are better than others. And we need to prove it. [*Laughter*]

JH: The notion that you were better or had to be better than others attracted you to someone who presented something that was better than what others had to offer?

TF: Yes. The notion of individuation—of being unique and special—was particularly attractive. You have to get as close as possible to being yourself. That probably caught my fancy. I have always been a philosopher, basically.

JH: I get the feeling that for you there was a value system beyond that. Your interest in religion, etc. implies …

TF: A messianic element was certainly present. I was quite convinced that I had something to offer the world, something that could improve it. And I had a very strong sense of justice. As you know, my daughters were involved in the Zürich riots. I was the offspring of a family of conservative Zürich bankers, yet I was enormously proud of my daughters when they rebelled in the streets, threw stones at the police, smashed windows along Bahnhofstrasse, and showed these moneyed people what the real values of life were. It was a very easy switch from one political view to the other. It all happened within three weeks.

RH: I can identify with that. They were living your unlived life. When our kids do something like that, I feel that same pride.

TF: Since then, my relationship to most of my less immediate family has changed. I have lots of cousins around Zürich. We still see each other every year or two for a dinner, but I have lost all inner contact with them.

RH: You mean with the bankers?

TF: Yes, the Gold Coast, Zürichberg banking, Bahnhofstrasse attitude. [*Laughter*] I am really indebted to my daughters for how they helped me.

Working with C. A. Meier

RH: Toni, how did you come to hear of Jung in the first place?

TF: Well, my father died of a heart attack in 1950. At the time, I was a student in the philosophy seminar at Zürich University. The seminar consisted of about 12 students and two professors, and one of the students was Peter Walder. Walder was just completing his degree in psychology and was writing his dissertation on Jung. Well, his father died on the same day as mine, and that brought us together. We got acquainted and he introduced me to Jung. Incidentally, he became an analyst in Zürich— he died about ten years ago. Well, as we discussed Jung, I began to read his writings. The first book I read was *The Psychology of Alchemy.* Then Walder started analyzing me. [*Laughter*]

JH: Formally?

TF: Informally. He would invite me for tea and ask about my dreams. Then I met another student, John Phillips, who is now an analyst in New York. He was one of those eternal students at Zürich—he was studying philosophy, but never did complete his degree. He told me that

I was absolutely mad to be fiddling about with the unconscious with Peter Walder. He said, "You have to have a *real* analyst, and the best in Zürich is C. A. Meier." I went to see Meier—because I couldn't complete my dissertation. I was totally blocked. Without the dissertation I couldn't get my degree.

RH: That was your presenting problem to Meier?

TF: Yes.

RH: And what did Meier say to you?

TF: He never said anything. [*Laughter*] He just moaned and grumbled and picked the dead leaves out of the plants on his desk and sometimes he cleaned his nails or had tea. He never said anything. He was an excellent analyst. I can only repeat what a colleague of mine— an old lady who is now 75—said recently at a lecture she gave in California. She said she wanted to pay tribute to her analyst, C. A. Meier, for having given her such a long rope. This was one of his most impressive characteristics. He would never really tell me what to do. He was a very passive analyst, not at all prone to reacting.

RH: You know how you sometimes meet a person you feel really understands Jung—maybe that depends largely on the person. In your experience, would you say that Meier really understood him better than others did?

TF: For sure, Meier was a dyed-in-the-wool Jungian. He was not just Jung's analysand, like the many others from Zürich and around the world—he was Jung's Crown Prince. He was for Jung what Jung had been for Freud.

RH: Really? Even more than von Franz?

TF: For Jung, Meier was the Crown Prince. And as for von Franz— to put it bluntly, she was just used by Jung. He made her translate his Latin and Greek quotes. So she was used to a large extent—and Barbara Hannah was the chauffeur. Everyone had his or her own function around Jung. He was a master at exploiting the transference.

RH: He would do that with women.

TF: But also with men. Meier succeeded Jung at the Federal High School of Technology and had to represent him in the outside world. Meier did the traveling when Jung got old—lecturing all over the world. He wrote the textbook on Jungian psychology.

RH: The textbook?

TF: Yes, the four volumes on Jungian psychology that have come out in English only in the last ten years. These four volumes represent the fundamentals of analytical psychology.

RH: As an analyst, do you feel Dr. Meier was important to you?

TF: Absolutely. He was biased in the way the Zürich school has always been biased. In his introduction to his book on the psychology of the transference, Jung says that he was always glad if the transference was mild. They were not interested in transference and not at all interested in countertransference. At least they wouldn't speak about it. Perhaps they thought about it. Meier and I had a falling out at the Clinic, and what went wrong, I think, was that neither of us was aware of the transference and countertransference between us. This is what I tried to show in a more general way in my article "Oedipus in Gethsemane."

RH: Do you consider that the most important piece you have written?

TF: For me, it is my swan song. I wrote it after the break with Meier, and it took me five years to get it down on paper.

JH: Was that your way of processing the break with Meier?

TF: Yes. I have always had a thing about homosexuality. As Hopcke has shown, the word *homosexuality* occurs only about 15 times in the 18 volumes of Jung's *Collected Works*—not even once per volume. And Meier was always against the homosexuals. He couldn't stand that. That's why he could not see the homosexual or homoerotic element in our relationship. We were neighbors, living two houses apart in Zürich. We were listening to the same music and had the same guests. We had everything together.

RH: Wait a minute, you were living that close together? You were neighbors?

TF: Yes.

JH: How much older was Meier?

TF: Twenty years. I went to see him just after the death of my father, which was an odd thing anyway, since my father was a banker and I was a student of philosophy, and I felt I could not be clear about what I wanted to do. I had decided—and told my father—that I would finish my studies, get my doctorate, and then take up banking. I suggested that he should start getting ready to help me get inducted into the profession. That was the morning of Easter Sunday, 1950. After lunch, he took a nap— and died. I had promised him that I would go into banking. And with this problem uppermost in my mind, I went to see Meier for analysis. And you can imagine what happened in terms of the transference.

RH: So that is the other issue you brought to him. You were blocked in your dissertation and you had just lost your father. Do you feel Meier became like a father for you?

TF: Sure. It was the transference. We worked together for six months—I was seeing him twice a week—and then, one Friday, he announced that he would be leaving the following Sunday for the States and would be gone for six weeks. He was not interested in the transference relationship. If you are interested in transference you don't do that to a patient—announce a six-week break the evening before. Well, he went— and by the time he came back I had finished my dissertation. [*Laughter*]

RH: Isn't that something!

TF: You see how irrationally analysis can work? The wisdom of Meier and his clever interpretations may have been right, but it was the transference—period—that made me write my dissertation.

RH: How did the transference help you write it?

TF: I think I had found an ideal guiding figure, and I was already secretly convinced that I would be an analyst. I felt quite ashamed to own up to that and tell Meier that I wanted to become an analyst. And the unconscious helped me by sending me a dream in which I saw Jung, and Jung looked at me and said: "I can see that you want to become an analyst"—and this dream I could not hide from Meier. [*Laughter*]

RH: So that was the dream that led you into your work?

TF: In the dream, Jung said he could see in my face that this is what I wanted—to become an analyst. He didn't say if he thought it was right or wrong.

JH: It reflected back to you what you were feeling.

TF: Yes. And I couldn't bring those feelings out into the world. So they came out in the form of a dream. And it was in the analytical contract that you had to tell your dreams to your analyst, so I told the dream to Meier and he said: "Well, maybe ... why not?" [*Laughter*] That was his way.

JH: But you finished your other studies first?

TF: Yes. I finished my Ph.D. and then I started at the Institute. I am one of those people. I would not trust a career history like mine in anybody else: being a schoolboy up to almost 30, and then becoming an analyst without having been out in the world and without having done anything. I don't think that is how it should be.

RH: So you went right from the Ph.D. to the Institute?

TF: Yes.

RH: I would think that if you were going to do that and you knew that this very important person, Carl Jung, lived right down the street, you would be rushing over to meet him. I would want to know him or try to work with him. None of that went on for you, right?

TF: No. But I was taken with his philosophy and the worldview he had. About a year ago a supervisee asked me a question about something in analysis. After I had answered, he looked at me and said, "I asked so-and-so and so-and-so the same question, and they gave me completely different answers." And I heard myself saying: "You know those two people, they are *psychologists*." I thought to myself, "What am I saying!" But I am quite sure that I am a philosopher. My basic impetus is philosophy, not psychology. And I am fascinated by these concepts—the archetypes and the idea that we cannot see the world in any other way than according to our senses and the way our minds are constructed. So we cannot possibly know the real world. That is a logical consequence of the archetypes, and I am intrigued by that.

RH: You were born in St. Gallen. How long ago was that?

TF: Seventy years.

RH: You went to boarding school?

TF: Only for a year. I was a very weak and sickly child. I had polio and two severe bouts of pneumonia—that was before the penicillin era. I almost died and could not move my left leg. So I was sent to the German boarding school in Davos—it was full of Nazis. It is ironic that Adolf Guggenbühl was sent there, since his family was one of the few families in Switzerland that was unconditionally anti-Nazi. His father was a publisher—he published the first book on the concentration camps, in 1935.

RH: You went to the University of Zürich for all your graduate education, including your Ph.D. You have been married for 40 plus years, have three daughters, three granddaughters, and a grandson.

TF: Yes. And my grandson is one of the few men in the family. He lost his father at the age of five.

RH: Were you in the first class at the Jung Institute?

TF: No, no. The Institute was founded in 1948 and I began in 1954.

RH: Who were some of your classmates that we might recognize?

TF: Adolf Guggenbühl. But he was not really at the Institute, and I don't believe he has a diploma, since he was a psychiatrist. So was Dieter Baumann, Jung's grandson, who is also a psychiatrist. They were the two psychiatrists among the students. There were no medical doctors at the Institute in the early days, and this caused a great deal of concern. You will find a passage in Stern's biography about how Jung scared away doctors. He treated them very badly. And the fact that the medical profession was rather anti-Jung—especially the psychiatrists—was due largely to Jung's attitude. Also at the Institute at that time were Jim Hillman, Marvin Spiegelman, Bob Stein, Sonja Marjasch and John Phillips. There must have been others.

RH: And yet Jung was encouraging people to become doctors?

TF: Yes, he was, but when they became doctors, he treated them very badly.

RH: Why did he do that?

TF: Because of the kind of person he was. During the war, there were some prominent psychiatrists who took the trouble to take the train out to Kusnacht once a week for a seminar with Jung (they couldn't drive because there was no gas). Jung would just laugh at them and treat them in the most unbelievable way. Finally, they had enough and did not come any more. And then there's his relationship to Bleuler—and all that stuff. He could have remained linked to the Burghölzli Psychiatric Hospital and linked to psychiatry in Switzerland, but he chose not to.

RH: Was he just arrogant?

TF: He had a very arrogant side. Someone would ask a question and he would say: "Of course! Why do you ask such a thing?" I have a lot of sympathy for Guggenbühl's statement that we have to see Jung as a psychological genius but that his personality had a side to it that was just small, Swiss bourgeois. That is why I am against all these biographies that try to make a saint out of him. It is just not true, and is strictly against his own concept of the shadow. Every human being has, in reality, a shadow—and Jung had a big one. If you had seen his body, you would have seen that he cast a tremendous shadow literally.

THE SHADOW

JH: Did you sense that Jung was comfortable with his shadow?

TF   I think to a certain extent he enjoyed it. And it was also a source of his suffering. The shadow makes you suffer.

RH: How does it make you suffer?

TF: The shadow confronts us with everything that is foreign to us, everything we don't want or that we hate. But out of the shadow also comes much that makes us and our lives valuable. Without shadow there is no creativity. We were talking earlier about Sabina Spielrein. There, Jung fell into his shadow—and made one of his most important discoveries.

RH: Have you found a good way to deal with your shadow?

TF: Ah ... what a question! [*Much laughter*] It connects with something else—another thought that I have been having increasingly. It is not so much the analysis that you go through that is important. Of course, that plays a part. But what I feel is that getting older makes a huge difference. I had always had the impression that my analytical fathers were much more shadow-integrated because they had been analyzed for longer than I had been. But now I don't think so any more. I think it is due to the process of getting older. When you are older, you can allow for much more shadow in yourself. You can allow for much less repression when the vital tension decreases. It is not so dangerous to let your shadow out. There is less energy and therefore there is less damage. [*Laughter*] You can afford to let it come out and be there—and people give you credit. Once you are an old man, you can do all sorts of things.

RH: So nature takes care of things?

TF: Certainly, at least to a certain extent. But to give at least a partial answer to your question: I believe that becoming aware of the shadow is already part of the achievement. Being aware means that you must make a conscious decision about whether or not you want to act out a particular part of the shadow. When you get into a conflict, you try to avoid it by repressing it. But if you manage to maintain the tension for long enough, the so-called "integration of the shadow" will take place. One can observe a similar phenomenon in mild cases of schizophrenia. I had a patient who was obsessed with the idea that he should change his job. He had already done this a few times, and it was clear that it would become more and more difficult for him to find employment. He would read the job ads in the newspaper, and when the nearby church clock struck 5 o'clock, or when a helicopter flew over the house, he would take it as a sign that he should apply for a particular job. I listened to this over several months, and one day as he was describing one such event to me, he added: "You know, I still have my spinning ideas." In time, he was able to put some distance between himself and his paranoia. Six months later, he was promoted to company director and we stopped the treatment. I imagine that merely through my listening he was able to free himself of his embarrassing secrets. The rest is taken care of by what Jung called "the self-healing tendency of the soul."

JH: Other people ...

TF: Yes, yes .... He was in treatment with a psychiatrist who told me on the phone that the man was incurable. He would not take his medication. And his delusion could not be corrected. I didn't correct the delusion. I just listened to it and let it be and then let nature take care of it.

RH: So what is the purpose of being in analysis then? Why not just let nature take care of everything?

TF: The analyst is like a midwife. Nature knows how to proceed in childbirth. But if the woman is over-civilized and has complexes and anxieties and fears and is cramped, then nature is blocked from doing its work. So the midwife has to tell the woman to relax, breathe in the right way, and so on. Then Nature can take its course.

RH: So part of the job of the analyst is to help people with nature?

TF: Yes, to allow nature to take its course. You may say it's a very optimistic idea that if you let things take their course, they'll turn out all right. But the probability that a child will be born with ten fingers and not eleven is incredibly higher than the other way round. So you have to let nature take its course. Then you have ten fingers. If you fiddle around with it, you may get something else.

RH: But if you let nature take its course, it does not mean that things always come out the way you wanted them?

TF: That's right. They come out not the way the ego wants, but the way the self wants. It's similar to dream interpretation. In interpreting a dream, there's a rule of thumb to follow: whatever happens in the dream is right in terms of healing and individuation. It is only what the *ego* does in the dream that can be either right *or* wrong. That's a very helpful rule of thumb.

RH: What about the person who says: "I think I will just let God take care of my life. I don't have to do anything."

TF: No, no. It's not that you don't have to do anything. There is quite a lot you have to do.

RH: What do you have to do?

TF: You have to follow what it—your life—wants you to do. The self doesn't do the job for you.

RH: Do you think things always come out right?

TF: No, I think they come out wrong very often. Take my experience of being kicked out of the Clinic. It was absolutely traumatic.

RH: One of the worst moments of your life?

TF: One of the worst. I didn't "let it happen" at all. I fought like mad. I went right up to the Federal Court—and I lost.

RH: Fighting C. A. Meier?

TF: Yes, Meier. We met for the last time in front of the Federal Court. Five years later, I worked it through and realized that my part in it was not realizing that my time at the Clinic was up and that I should look for a successor, withdraw to the background, and do something else with the rest of my life. I didn't see that at the time. So the self, in the form of Meier, took me by the neck and kicked me out.

RH: So even back then, looking at it in retrospect, Meier was acting on behalf of the self—though not intentionally.

TF: Absolutely! Not intentionally, but actually on behalf of the self.

RH: So your feelings about Meier now are not the same as when you were standing in front of the Federal Court?

TF: No. But when he was dying last November, an old friend of mine offered to bring about a reconciliation. I asked myself very intensely whether I wanted that, and I declined, saying that for me Meier had died ten years earlier. My relationship with him was in the past, and I did not want a reconciliation on a personal level. I know that he unintentionally did me a personal favor by kicking me out of the Clinic.

RH: Why didn't you want to see him personally then?

TF: He was dead for me. It was past.

JH: Because what he had been in your life no longer existed, because of everything that had gone on?

TF: To a certain extent—taken with a grain of salt—I would agree.

JH: OK, help me understand that then.

TF: I think there is always ambivalence. But by and large, I would say that that chapter of my life was over for me. I don't know how I will think about it five years from now. Perhaps I will regret that I didn't go for the reconciliation. But at that point it made no sense to me. Don't forget that this thing has another aspect beyond the personal. The Jung Clinic was destroyed by what he did. It is no longer a Jung clinic. It is now a branch of the Burghölzli Psychiatric Hospital. They are doing good psychiatry there, but they are not doing psychotherapy in the Jungian sense any more. None of the members of the Board is a Jungian any more.

JH: It sounds like there were two things going on. You referred to your personal relationship with Meier and the transference, which was somehow the catalyst that brought about this split that caused the Clinic to fall apart. The personal relationship got messed up, and that damaged the professional relationship. Getting thrown out pushed you ahead, but at the same time it destroyed a lot of other stuff that had been important.

TF: I have to acknowledge that I am 50 percent responsible for the Clinic's being destroyed. If I had been more aware of the background of this transference, and about my own situation both in the Clinic and in life—if I had realized that it was time to step down, then I think things would have taken another course.

RH: Perhaps you could have stepped down and appointed a successor.

TF: Yes, I could have. Theoretically.

JH: You mentioned the relationship between men, and there was something about it I didn't quite understand. One man is the mentor or father and the other is the son, and at some point the son grows up and is challenging the father, and it falls apart ...

TF: Think of the Oedipus myth. The outcome was that the son killed the father; and if you look at a book like *Power and Crowds* [by Elias Canetti], you see that fathers also try to kill their sons. The chiefs and kings are afraid that their sons will grow up and take power at their expense. There is this unconscious rivalry between father and son. That's why my paper "Oedipus and Gethsemane" is so important to me—because I think this was going on in the relationships between Breuer and Freud, Freud and Jung, Jung and Meier, and Meier and myself. God forbid that it should go further with my "sons."

JH: Are you saying that you were not aware of the competition between you and Meier?

TF: Yes, that was how it was. And it is interesting that the thing with Meier exploded with the issue of our daughter being involved in the Zürich riots.

RH: Really? Was that the issue that started the rift?

TF: Yes, we were together at a dinner party, and I told him that our daughter had been beaten up by a policeman, and his response was, "Whoever exposes himself to danger will get hurt."

RH: He was blaming your daughter, and that is what got you going.

TF: It made the pent-up pressure of the relationship explode. I was furious. It was not the reaction I expected from a friend. But this is how these things go. If you miss the personal transference, if you can't see what is in the background, where the shadow of this adoration of the analysand for the analyst is, you will run into trouble—and the extent of the resulting damage will be far-reaching. So from that little comment at the party, the shadow popped right up and took hold of the whole relationship, and now father is going to kill son and son is going to kill father, and you are off. My daughter had violated law and order and rebelled against the authority of the state, so her getting into trouble was her own fault. That was Meier's attitude. And I think he meant me. You boy, you obey! You are to obey the authority of the father!

JH: It sounds like you came out of that subservient role when you reacted personally to your daughter's involvement in the riots. You abandoned the value system you grew up in. You were saying: "My relationship with my daughter is much more important to me than whatever system I grew up in."

TF: I think that is one aspect of the whole situation.

JH: That triggered your split with Meier, since he was still in the authoritarian role with you, but you had gotten out of the role with your daughter.

TF: Thank you. I think you are right. And, of course, you can see an aspect of my anima in my daughter which made me break away from this imposing father figure who would not let me develop in my own way. It is the anima that meets you and challenges you and leads you into danger and crisis.

RH: I wonder also if there was a part of you that did not want Meier involved in the Clinic at all. You may have felt you needed him, but ...

TF: On this point you may be right.

RH: You wanted to do your own thing ...

TF: But he didn't interfere very much with the clinical side. He was interested in the research. He had a sleep and dream laboratory at the Clinic, and he spent a lot of the Clinic's money on it. He expected the Clinic to come up with more and more money, and the expense became increasingly an issue for me. It got addressed at a meeting of the Board. Meier had asked for a large sum of money for research, and I said that it was out of the question, that we could not afford it. But he simply said: "I *want* it." I told the Board that if they voted to authorize this expenditure, I would seek legal advice to determine whether such a demand was within the law. Meier then withdrew his demand. But then came the revenge.

RH: Your paper details how this very same dynamic went on in relationships between other men.

TF: Yes. Just after this incident, we had a meeting of the Swiss Society of Jungians. There, for the first time, the case of Sabina Spielrein was discussed. After that meeting, my wife and I went to the Swiss mountains for a hiking holiday, and on one of those hikes I started thinking about the whole thing. I asked myself why things hadn't gone wrong when Jung went beyond the transference point and got involved with Spielrein and Toni Wolff—despite the fact that these women were his patients. I realized that these relationships were heterosexual, and suddenly the penny dropped, and I saw Breuer and Freud, Freud and Jung, and Jung and Meier. And I said: "My God! It doesn't work because that other strand is homosexual." And it is much more repressed than the heterosexual. The homosexuality itself is the real issue, and it has to be repressed at all costs—which is why things take such a destructive turn.

RH: You saw this between Meier and Jung too?

TF: Absolutely.

RH: So they had a falling out?

TF: Yes. It was always concealed. I wrote about this in my paper "Oedipus and Gethsemane." Outwardly, they were still together. Meier was still the crown prince. He was still Jung's representative to the outside world, but their personal relationship had been broken since about 1957. Before Meier published his paper on projection and subject-object relations and transference, he sent the manuscript to Jung, who, like a schoolteacher, sent it back covered with marks in red ink. Meier said: "I will not have that." Again, a ridiculously small issue.

Constellation

RH: Can we talk about your notion of constellation? You say that constellation is the "becoming efficient of an archetype."

TF: The archetypes constitute the foundations of the soul. They are like sleeping dogs, and occasionally one of them wakes up. Or rather, one of them becomes active in the inner or external milieu. Another good image is a chaotic heap of iron filings on a sheet of paper. If we switch on an electromagnet under the paper, the iron filings arrange themselves according to a distinct pattern or structure. The magnetic field constellates the particles. Something in life switches on the current of the archetypes. The trigger can be the passing from childhood into adulthood at puberty. It can be the crossing of the mid-life threshold. The threshold into old age—or what I call the third half of life. It can be anything of that sort, or an outside event. During an association test, if the person being tested sits in front of the tester, he or she will get constellated. A tension is created by the expectation in the person being tested. Then the test takes its course, and the complexes are constellated. And you can see them in the course of the experiment in the delayed reaction times. You have this in analysis too. The analyst constellates the client, which means that the analyst prompts certain aspects of the client's character to come to the fore. That is why the Jung Institute in Zürich requires part of the training to be done with a man and part to be done with a woman. Totally different things are constellated. Not only because of the gender difference but also because of the character difference. And that's the constellation. You can see this in everyday life. If you have a married couple who get along quite well and the mother-in-law joins them on holiday for eight days and stays in the same house, you will see a new constellation. [*Laughter*] The word "constellation" comes from astronomy. It's the figure that a group of stars resembles. The stars don't actually create the figures, but we project the images into the sky and see things like the Big Dipper. The image is not actually there. It is only our projection. That is constellation. In fact, this conversation we are having right now is being shaped by the constellation between us. If I were being interviewed by someone else, there would be different questions, and I would certainly come up with completely different answers. Of course, this raises the question: Which one is the "real" me?

Dealing with the Unconscious

RH: What are your own practices for dealing with the unconscious? Do you have rituals or daily things you try to do?

TF: I don't think so. My only ritual, as far as I am aware, is to keep a written record of my dreams. When I have the time and energy, I keep a sort of diary in which I note down things that happen. The unconscious approaches us not only through our dreams, but through our daily life as well. Take my trouble with Meier. That came from the outside, and it was certainly constellated by the unconscious. So what happens on the outside is also meaningful and has to be taken into account. When I have some special experience in my practice or my family, I have to ask myself where it came from. What does it have to do with me? How am I responsible, not for what I do, but for what I am? How am I responsible for what happens to me?

RH: That work—do you do it mainly by yourself? Do you talk with someone else?

TF: I sometimes talk about this with people around me—quite often with my wife and also with my daughters. Not that I give out too many details about myself. I do not think it is good to tell your dreams to everybody. But you have to work them through. Then the *result* can be dealt with in relationships, but not the dream itself.

RH: What happens if you tell your dreams to too many people?

TF: I think you dilute the experience. Telling a lot of people helps you to get rid of anxiety. You are unable to stand the tension of a nightmare, for instance, on your own, so you tell it to somebody. It's the same sort of thing in the Catholic Church—you go to a priest for confession and you let off steam. That is also why I think it is not good for people to stay in analysis too long. There comes a point at which you have to stand your own ground, even if it means making a blunder that could have been prevented by seeing the analyst. In the "Light and Shadow" paper, I wrote about how I was struck by the way the analysts who ran the Jung Institute in the 1950s—who were the direct disciples of Jung—would go at least once a week to Kusnacht to discuss their dreams with the old master. Jung writes about it in *The Relations between the Ego and the Unconscious*. If you have a breakdown, you can pick yourself up in the regressive restoration of the persona. The alternative is to sit at the feet of a prophet—but this isn't a step towards individuation. If you are to individuate, you have to stop sitting at the feet of the prophet. Those analysts of the 50s were still sitting at the feet of their prophet. All his life, Meier wore a ring on his finger similar to one worn by Jung and smoked the same kind of pipe. He used the same kind of invoice with his patients as Jung had done. He even laughed in the same way that Jung did. And all of these people— Jolande Jacobi, Binswanger, Hannah, von Franz—they all went out at least once a month to talk with Jung and get his absolution.

RH: And you didn't do that with Meier?

TF: No. I stopped at a certain point. After I came back to Zürich from England, I saw him once in a while for a couple of years and then I stopped. What I can still do if I get into trouble with a client is go to a colleague and discuss the case. I am not unable to ask for help. But I think the responsibility is entirely my own. My colleague wouldn't say anything about my case anyway. He or she would listen and say that it was difficult, and then I would go home again and do my own thing. [*Laughter*] But talking to someone triggers the constellation, and when I go home I have the answer.

SPIRITUALITY

RH: Do you consider yourself a spiritual person?

TF: I think to a certain degree I am a spiritual person—but certainly not exclusively.

RH: Would you consider your spiritual life important?

TF: Absolutely! It starts in the morning. After breakfast I sit at the piano for a whole hour. That is my hour of bliss every day.

RH: What do you play?

TF: I play Bach, Mozart, Haydn, Chopin. I have just started with Debussy. I very often start in the morning with the preludes of Bach that I started learning when I was ten years old. Every time they seem new and fresh.

RH: You feel that is connected with your spiritual life?

TF: Absolutely. It is halfway between the spiritual and the sensual life.

RH: [*Laughter*] ... That's interesting.

TF: Why do you find it so amusing?

RH: I think it is great.

TF: That is work—it is not pleasure. Of course, it is full of pleasure. But it is mainly work that I cannot do in the evening because I am tired. Then it doesn't work.

JH: It sounds like it takes you back to yourself and centers you before you start the day.

TF: Yes, very much.

RH: It sounds like a personal ritual.

TF: It is, and you know someone else who had the same ritual?— Karl Barth. He used to play in the morning too—but only Mozart.

RH: Do you have a favorite piece?

TF: That changes. At the moment it is one of the posthumous preludes by Chopin which has a three-rhythm in the left hand and a four-rhythm in the right. It is hellish to play. [*Laughter*]

RH: Do you read Jung much?

TF: Off and on. After I have finished writing a paper, I read Jung and find out that he has already said the same things! [*Laughter*] There are certain papers of Jung that I read every few years. The main ones are: *The Psychology of the Transference* and *Answer to Job*; another is *Psychology of Alchemy.*

RH: What do you feel Jung meant when he said that he knew God and did not need to believe in Him?

TF: I think he meant that the psyche has, by its very nature, an image of God, the self. He also described some of the influences this image

69

may have on the individual. The self is what leads us through life and it helps us in a very natural way—also when we die. Jung *knew* that and found it superfluous to believe in something over and above that.

DEATH

RH: If you found yourself in heaven and you saw Jung there, would you want to talk with him, and what do you imagine you would talk about?

TF: I don't know in detail what we would discuss, but I would let him know how I feel about him.

RH: And what would you say?

TF: I would tell him I have enormous respect for his work. I am sure that his work was essential for my life and that it helped me get through life in a really meaningful way with a feeling of doing something meaningful. I needed it badly. I would tell him that his personality was not quite up to his work. But that is a human element and I cannot blame him for it. Look at all the great men—they were all monsters.

RH: Do you think Jung would actually hear that if you said it?

TF: I think so. And he would agree. Whether it's true is another question!

RH: What do you think happens at death?

TF: I think what happens is the end of a life.

RH: You see death as your body going into the ground, or being cremated.

TF: Yes, but my body is not me any more. My body is me before death. But after death, it is no longer me. My body will be cremated. My family will disperse the ashes somewhere around our home in the mountains.

RH: So there is no afterlife?

TF: Not for me. Not in that sense.

RH: In some other sense, then?

TF: Perhaps some of the pupils I have had, who now live on five continents, will practice the way I practiced. But in thirty years that will be gone too. I will live on in my grandchildren and great-grandchildren. The spirit of my grandfather is also around somewhere. One of our famous poets in Switzerland said that he had an experience when he was studying with Feuerbach, the philosopher. He said he suddenly realized that he thought death could well be the end. He wrote to a friend saying that accepting the idea that you have only one chance doesn't necessarily mean that you will become a bad person. When life is finished, it is finished. No repeat performances. You can't put everything to rights after the event. You have to think about what you do before you do it.

JH: That view places a great deal of responsibility on you as an individual.

TF: Yes. Lately I have had several periods of poor health. I have lost a lot of weight. My doctors were quite concerned. I felt weaker and weaker. I suddenly realized that if this is the end, it is acceptable. Life gets less and less and then it is no longer there. It is not frightening. Dying may be frightening, but not death. If you are suffering when you are dying, then death is the end of suffering.

RH: It sounds like you feel you have lived your life. Not that you want to die ...

TF: No, I do not want to die—but I think I could if I had to.

RH: You don't have any regrets?

TF: Oh, I do have a lot of regrets about things I wish I had done— and about a few things I wish I had not done.

JH: Are you saying that you feel this is the given condition for all of us?

TF: I have to bear the regret and the guilt. And if I try to get rid of it in one way or another, I think that would be cheating.

RH: It is like the shadow of life.

TF: Exactly. But I can't say: "It was just the shadow of life and therefore I couldn't help it." I have a strong feeling that I could have done something about it on several occasions. A good example is the Clinic situation: if I had been more aware of my real needs and of the needs of the Clinic, things might have taken a different course. That is something I regret.

RH: Let's imagine that this interview is the last shot you have to speak to the Jungian community in print. What would you like to say?

TF: We have talked about the function of the analyst and the notion of the analyst as midwife. Summing everything up, I would say to other analysts working with the psyche: "Let it be"—but not in the passive sense of just letting it go.

RH: That condenses your life and how you have learned to deal with the psyche ... just let it be.

TF: And the tension between the ego and self. The self knows exactly where to go, whereas the ego can be wrong, as we saw in dream interpretation. What the ego does can be either right or wrong, but the self is always right.

RH: Do you feel at 70 years of age that your ego is now better able to deal with the self?

TF: Yes, definitely. That may be an inflation on my part. I am somehow—rightly or wrongly—more at peace with myself than I was ten or twenty years ago. Again, this may well be an illusion. Who knows? [*Laughter*]

RH: How would you like to be remembered in the Jungian community?

TF: I would like to be remembered as someone who eventually calmed down after he had done some valuable things such as establishing and running the Clinic and giving lectures, someone who eventually found peace with himself and was at the same time able to share this feeling with some of his pupils so that they could take it with them.

RH: I attended a seminar with you in Zürich, and both then and now during this interview, I am impressed, Toni, with how open you are. You seem like a very open person.

TF: Yes, but that has to do with what I just said. I feel more at peace now and less tense.

RH: You mean the same thing would not have been said about you 20 years ago?

TF: No, I was very guarded—and I had every reason to be, because of my instinctual drives: power, sex, what have you. I would not have communicated these things to others back then. It has a lot to do with the 80s. It was very important that my daughters got going with their rebellion. Their rebellion was synchronistic, as it came at the right time for my own needs.

RH: Why are you less guarded today?

TF: I don't feel the need to be guarded any more. I *am* probably very guarded but I don't know in what ways because the resistance comes from unconscious mechanisms. [*Laughter*] The unconscious is unconscious. I may well be very guarded without realizing it.

RH: You don't seem that way, and how would anyone else ever really know that?

TF: Nobody would know. My wife and children would probably have something to say about that ... they may know. Otherwise, there are things about ourselves that we may never see, since we cannot exhaust the unconscious and will therefore never fully integrate the shadow.

RH: At the age of 70, do you feel that the unconscious is larger in your life or smaller than in earlier years?

TF: It is like the sea. It is immense. It has always been immense. Consciously, I am a bit less afraid of it. I have great respect for it and a feeling of awe, but perhaps a little less fear.

JAMES A. HALL, M.D.

James Hall, M.D., has had a distinguished career as a psychiatrist and a Jungian analyst, and is the author of seven works in Jungian psychology, including *Jungian Dream Interpretation: A Handbook of Theory and Practice* (Inner City Books, 1983) and *Hypnosis: A Jungian Perspective* (Guilford Press, 1989). He is a graduate of the University of Texas, Southwestern Medical School, and the C. G. Jung Institute in Zürich. A founding member of the Inter-Regional Society of Jungian Analysts, he served as its president for the first three terms and was also a Training Analyst for the society for several years. In 1992, he was disabled by a brainstem stroke, which left him with locked-in syndrome, quadriplegic and mute, but with normal sensorium and intellect. He is totally dependent on his wife, the visiting nurse, and his computer. Using a splint attached to his right index finger, typing one letter at a time, he uses his laptop computer, which emits a simulated voice, to stay connected to the world. Through e-mail, he manages to maintain a wide network of friendships, participate in professional organizations, and continue to contribute to the literature of Jungian psychology. He and his wife, Suzanne, have been together for 50 years. They have two daughters and a grandson. I have had a relationship with James via e-mail since 1998, and my heart is touched every time I receive a note from him and feel the vitality of his passion.

THE BLINK OF AN EYE
JAMES A. HALL AT 66

With the urge to action gone, I can think more clearly about the symbolic meanings of sexuality. You could say that I am more conscious of sex than I have ever been.

—James A. Hall

ENCOUNTERING JUNG

ROB HENDERSON (RH): How did you become interested in Jung?

JAMES HALL (JH): While looking over possible psychiatry residences during the summer between my junior and senior years in medical school, I found myself stranded for a weekend in Chapel Hill, North Carolina, between interviews at Duke and The University of North Carolina. At a bookstore, I bought some weekend reading, including a copy of Jolande Jacobi's *Complex, Archetype, Symbol*—selections from Jung's writings. It was the first time I had read a book that described life as I had experienced it. The clincher came during my second year of residency at Duke. In Dallas, I had become acquainted with Adrian Baumann, Jung's grandson, who was studying merchandising at Nieman-Marcus. From Adrian I learned that his brother, Dieter, a Jungian analyst/psychiatrist, was planning a U.S. tour. I wrote Dieter, inviting him to visit Duke as our houseguest and look over the psychiatry department and Rhine's famous ESP Lab. He did. Dieter impressed me very much. I decided then to become a Jungian analyst. When I told Dieter, he suggested I work with Rivkah Kluger and Marie-Louise von Franz. Later I was able to do this, and even work with Dieter himself.

RH: Did you ever meet Jung?

JH: No. Jung died a few years before I got to Zürich. I'm of the generation that was trained by those who worked directly with Jung.

RH: Do you have any favorite Jung stories?

JH: Jo Wheelwright tells of the time he went to Jung's house on Seestrasse for his appointment, and opened the door to see Jolande Jacobi flying down the stairs. As he stepped past her, all he could think to say was, "Good morning, Herr Doctor." Jo thought they had argued and Jung had kicked Jacobi out. They were both strong personalities. At the time I knew her, Jacobi was the sexiest 80-year-old woman I had ever met. Jo also tells the story of Jung standing outside, talking with a woman who refused to see the sexual implications of her dreams. As they talked, two birds flew between them and began to mate. It seemed synchronistic. Jung and the woman both laughed. Christopher Whitmont tells of his first hour with Jung. Dressed in his Sunday's best, Whitmont was led through the house into the backyard, where he was met by a sweaty Jung in his undershirt chopping wood—the perfect compensation to his own rigidity at that time.

RH: What did you learn about what Jung was like from your contact with von Franz?

JH: Von Franz frequently told stories about Jung, stories that made him seem more human. I remember her describing the first time she met Jung. They were discussing the dream of a woman who had dreamt she'd been on the moon. Von Franz took it to be "as if" she'd been on the moon, but Jung talked as though she'd really been on the moon. Von Franz thought, "Either he's crazy, or I am." It was her first experience of Jung treating psychic experience as real. Experiences we have in dreams are real experiences.

RH: What did you understand her relationship with Jung to be?

JH: Jung was important to her. Her life and work centered on Jung—perhaps too much. The only thing I disagreed with von Franz about was the value of group therapy. She, following Jung, felt that in any group people are less themselves. I had already had extensive experience with therapy groups and had found them a valuable aid to two-person analysis.

RH: What did you learn about what Jung was like from your contact with Dieter Bauman [Jung's grandson]?

JH: Dieter told me about Sunday dinners, which included "Aunt Toni"—Toni Wolff. I got the impression they had a negative effect on Dieter—perhaps on others as well. If Jung had simply had a discreet affair with Toni, I think it would have caused less trouble.

RH: What kind of father and grandfather did you get the impression Jung was?

JH: I don't think I formed any impressions on that point. All I can say is that I wouldn't want Jung as my father or grandfather. I'm not strong enough to hold my own against his kind of personality.

RH: If you could speak with Jung, what would you talk about?

JH: I would ask Jung what he thought of developments in parapsychology since [J.B.]Rhine, whose work, by the way, was very important to Jung in formulating his concept of synchronicity. Defining synchronicity as a subset of psi (or ESP) is under discussion by the Synchronicity Committee. This is a group composed chiefly of parapsychologists and Jungian analysts, founded several years ago by astrophysicist Victor Mansfield and me. I'd also ask Jung about his views on reincarnation, which divides Buddhists and Hindus from Christians and Muslims. I've been led to give it serious consideration through the carefully documented studies of alleged cases by Ian Stevenson, a parapsychologist/psychiatrist at the University of Virginia. In his autobiography, Jung mentions possibly having to return to human life if the questions that concerned him in the first life were not answered. In a conversation about the possibility of survival after death, von Franz told me that Jung believed that Toni Wolff reincarnated after her death in a young girl near Zürich. Von Franz said that for several years Jung followed the girl's development closely, even speculating as to why Toni would need to reincarnate.

RH: What was Marie-Louise von Franz like?

JH: She was the archetypal Jungian. I used to joke that she had a chrome-plated intuitive function. It was as if I could open her head, pour in two weeks worth of my dreams and she'd spit them back rapid-fire, all neatly categorized and related to my complexes and my individuation. There was little left for me to say other than how I planned to respond to what she said the dreams were saying to me. I call her approach "the structural interpretation of dreams." It's the subject of a book I'm now writing. She gives a virtuoso demonstration of this technique in the film series *The Way of the Dream*. The content of the series, by the way, is also available in book form. At the same time, von Franz struck me as a very vulnerable woman. Once, for a week, I was sexually attracted to her. That passed, but it matured into wanting to protect her. For a while I seriously considered adding her to my health insurance policy. I wanted to take care of her. A remarkable woman! To quote T. S. Eliot, "The wisest woman in Europe ...."

LIFE AS A JUNGIAN ANALYST

RH: What are some of the high points in your career as an analyst?

JH: Being allowed to see the heroic struggles of perfectly ordinary people. You'd never know such things from outside observation. People have to tell you about their subjective worlds. Of course, there are things that they cannot tell you, things that exist in their subjective worlds but are inaccessible even to them. Their dreams often tell you about such things— archetypal images, for instance. I think the current emphasis on transference/ countertransference (T/CT) obscures the perception of the archetypes. This is the main difference in emphasis between the two schools of Jungian analysts: the classical school and the developmental school.

RH: Which school has influenced you more?

JH: Andrew Samuels puts me in the classical school. I think he's right. My four Jungian analysts—those who trained me—were of the classical school. They had contact with Jung himself. Dieter Bauman was his grandson. Von Franz translated Greek and Latin texts for Jung.

PERSONAL MATTERS

RH: Can you tell us a little about yourself?

JH: I was born in 1934 in Gladewater, Texas, an oilfield town. I grew up 3 miles from town in the dreamy, mystical piney woods of East Texas. Summers, however, were spent with my maternal grandparents on their ranch in Tulia in the open, logical plains of the Texas panhandle. I graduated from the University of Texas, Austin, and Southwestern Medical School, Dallas. The bulk of my psychiatric training was at Duke University in Durham, North Carolina. I graduated from the Jung Institute in Zürich in 1972, working with Dieter Baumann, Rivkah Kluger, and Marie-Louise von Franz. I also worked with Edward Whitmont.

RH: James, I think I have your age wrong. You are not 72 but 67, right?

JH: I'm 68 till Feb. 13, 2003.

TYPOLOGY

RH: What do you make of typology?

JH: Generally, I have not found typology very useful, except in counseling couples. I rely more on dreams—a much more sensitive indicator. Jung himself, after his book on types, seems to have made little use of typology. Others find it useful, but it's too "thinking" for my taste. First you make a shaky inference about type, then you draw conclusions from it. When I wrote the first draft of *Jungian Dream Interpretation: A Handbook of Theory and Practice*, Daryl Sharp had to remind me to do a chapter on types.

RH: What do you understand your own typology to be?

JH: I think of myself as an introvert, though I have an extraverted persona. I think of introversion/extraversion as determined by one's locus of highest value, not the locus of most activity. When Jo Wheelwright first met me, he said I was the only extraverted Jungian—other than himself— that he'd ever met. Then he gave me the Grey-Wheelwright type test. I test introverted. On the Myers-Briggs inventory, thinking and feeling are close together as the second function. Sometimes one dominates, sometimes the other. My inferior function is definitely sensation. Being most unconscious, it manifests itself it two ways. First, I seem unable to organize my milieu, despite repeated efforts, in an aesthetically pleasing way. Secondly, I am fascinated by the sensation qualities of certain objects: a bolo (a large tear-shaped stone) I always wore, tsubas (iron hilts from samari swords—I have

28 of them), a cast iron aluminum unicorn head with a narwhal tusk, a forkula (an intricately shaped carved walnut oarlock on a gondola), and a netsuke miniature skull.

RH: My impression of you is that your thinking function is very strong.

JH: Up until medical school I might have shared your impression that thinking is my dominant function. Evidence: high school valedictorian, Phi Beta Kappa in college, graduated with high honors. But in medical school I fell firmly into the middle third of my class. That shook my confidence in my ability to think. I happened to mention this to von Franz, who said offhanded, "Oh, you think OK." On reflection, I realized that indeed I do. Nowadays I just think without thinking about thinking.

THE STROKE

RH: Would you describe what happened when you had your stroke?

JH: Briefly, just before it happened, I had nausea, which I attributed to too much scotch and soda. I was on my way to a college, where I was to supposed to be giving a lecture. Uncharacteristically, I got lost driving there. Just before the stroke, I had a ringing in my ears which didn't go away, so I stopped at a fire station, honked, and asked for an ambulance.

RH: James, what are some of the things that have kept you alive since your stroke?

JH: My doctors expected me to die immediately or to survive for only a few years. However, because of my near-death experience, I expected to live for 30 more years. What I am referring to when I say "near-death experience" is a dream/vision that presented itself to me about the time of my brainstem stroke in early 1991. I don't know whether to call it a dream or a vision, really. In it, I am drowning in a vaporous "ocean." There is a large, crouching, muscular male figure on what looks like a beach. I desperately "ask" this figure for help, but seem to communicate this request by telepathy. I ask to be allowed to live out my life with my wife, Suzanne. I say I can live another life in this lifetime, if I am allowed to live, that there is no need for another incarnation yet. The figure does not move, but suddenly I "know" that I will live 30 more years, to age 87. The sequence, whatever it was, then vanished. My next memory was of waking up, virtually quadriplegic, in an intensive care unit. Fr. Morello, my priest-friend, immediately thought the crouching figure might be Jesus, but it was unlike any representation I have ever seen. In my memory, the figure has taken on more the form of a gladiator, but I think that is retrospective. Might it have been the Jungian archetypal Self?

In any event, after it became clear that I would live, the greatest problem became finding something meaningful that I could do within my limitations. Larry, one of my sons-in-law, set up a computer for me and got me on the Internet, which was a godsend. Soon I was talking to friends in Switzerland, Canada, the UK, and all across the USA. My friend Patton Howell suggested we collaborate on writing the story of my stroke. We did and now we are seeking a publisher. I was nominated to be president of Isthmus Institute, an organization I founded along with three theology professors in 1982 to study the convergence of science and spirit. I served two terms as president. I now have many articles and five books waiting for me to write in the 21 years that remain of the 30 promised in my near-death dream.

RH: Having been such an active man all your life, you must have to dig deep into yourself to hold onto the will to live, given all the limitations you face. I suspect many people would simply surrender themselves to death. How have you been able to do this, and why do you feel others might simply die?

JH: It has gradually become clear to me that I have something to accomplish that can be done within my limitations. It's rather like my life is one small coral polyp in building an atoll. So I have no illusions about it having much impact, but at least it will be there if anyone cares to ferret it out. In recent years, the careful case studies of psychiatrist Ian Stevenson have led me to consider the possibility of reincarnation, so one of the ferrets just might be a reincarnation of myself. During my three decades as a practicing Jungian analyst/psychiatrist, however, I saw only one case that in my judgment suggested reincarnation.

RH: Why do you think it is that others sometimes give up when faced with the kind of physical challenges you are facing?

JH: I feel many persons identify primarily with what can be done only with an intact physical body—making love, skiing, golf, holding a job, etc. That's why my doctor asked me, about three days after my stroke, if I wanted to go on living in my condition. I could answer only with eye blinks—which he almost misread as my saying I wanted to die. Actually, as a result of my near-death experience in the emergency room, I had already decided that I wanted to live. I identify more with my mind than with my body, and my mind seems intact. My body is essentially a heart-lung machine to keep my mind (and my one typing finger) alive. Then, too, I have a sense of mission that gives me a reason to live.

RH: In his challenging book, *Answer to Job*, Carl Jung suggests that God has an unconscious, and that that helps to explain "why bad things happen to good people." Given your stroke and your Jungian training, how do you view Jung's claim?

JH: I have thought a lot about this …. I haven't yet made up my mind, though. Rather than say, "God has an unconscious," I prefer to say, "God exists in a dissociated state." Job says, "I will lay my hand upon my mouth and speak no more," but he also says, "I know that my Redeemer liveth." That is, he believes that there is a tendency in God toward order and justice, even if God is currently dissociated from it. In the story, God essentially tells Job that questions of morality, justice, and ultimately of good and evil are not the center of God's nature. In a sense, this is true. Good and evil are judgments from a human viewpoint. They are highly contextual and changeable. There's the story of a Chinese peasant who found a horse. "How fortunate!" said his neighbors. "Your plowing will be easier." But the farmer just said, "We'll see." One day while riding the horse, the farmer's son fell off and broke his arm. "How unfortunate!" said the neighbors, but the farmer just said, "We'll see." A few days later, officials came through the village conscripting young men for the warlord's army. Because of his broken arm, the farmer's son was exempted. The story goes on, but this is enough to illustrate the contextual nature of the opposites. In my own life, the women that I have loved the most have hurt me the most deeply. I think it is significant that in the Taoist *I Ching*, yang and yin represent many opposites—male/female, dry/ moist, penetrating/yielding, etc.—but never good/evil. Judgments of good and evil are made only from a human standpoint.

RH: As a spiritual person who is also deeply psychological, what spiritual and psychological resources have you found most helpful in sustaining your life and finding new growth?

JH: Right after the stroke—but not since then—I was helped by religious services. I was so grateful I had not just been thrown away. In the emergency room in Akron, an unknown priest gave me viaticum—the last rites—without asking if I was a Catholic or not (I was a Methodist then). During my three months in the VA hospital, I was visited regularly by an old friend, a Catholic priest. Finally, I converted to Catholicism—by no means because I agreed with all their teachings, but because, within the Christian tradition, they had dealt the most responsibly with the questions that concerned me the most. After I returned home, Bill, who had sold me insurance, brought me communion regularly, and I found this comforting. Then my priest friend read some of my writings, decided I was not really Catholic, and forbade Bill to give me communion. I think I represented his own unconscious doubts. Several other priests, including a bishop in another diocese (whom one of my friends consulted anonymously), felt that my priest friend had overstepped his authority. I am grateful, though, for his making me a member of two large denominations—ex-Methodists and ex-Catholics. After about 18 months, Bill brought by a new priest and resumed bringing me communion. My priest friend remained very friendly as long as he did not think of me as Catholic. I am very attracted to Buddhism, but I have chosen to follow Jung's advice and seek a religious solution within Western culture. My real spiritual support came from personal experiences and dreams. Dreams helped me overcome my extreme anger toward two former friends. In February 1995, I had what I can only call a spiritual experience, which lasted about two hours. It reminds me of Paul's experience on the road to Damascus, or Aquinas's experience late in life, which caused him to abandon his unfinished *Summa Theologica* as "only straw." I could easily put my experience in psychological terms, of course, but it doesn't fit well. It was the most transforming experience of my life—thus far, anyway.

RH: Can you share a little of what that spiritual experience was like in 1995?

JH: Yes, but I won't be able to convey the affect, the feeling that I had of being in the presence of something greater than myself. It seemed to radiate love. I could put it in psychological terms and call it a projection of the archetypal Self, but that seems inadequate and intellectualizing. Since the Self is theoretically the origin of my own ego, of me, I can only say that I feel unworthy. Here's a description I wrote soon after: On February 14, 1995, the morning after my 61st birthday, I awoke at 3 a.m. I had apparently gone to sleep with the TV on at Channel 2. I usually woke up at 3 a.m. and watched Channel 32. But before I could change the channel, a program on fairy tales came on on Channel 2, and I decided to watch it. There were four 30-minute tales, *Jack and the Dentist's Daughter (The Master Thief)*, *Rapunzel*, *The Goosegirl (The False Bride)*, and *Bearskin.* I have no idea whether the particular tales I was watching had anything to do with the experience that was going on simultaneously. I had Suzi call the station and ask about the fairy tales. They are from a series of ten films, "From the Grimm Tales," produced by Davenport Films, Delaplane, VA.

As I watched, a remarkable change began to take place in me. I developed a sense of certainty about things I had merely speculated about before. The major events of my life flashed before me. I saw them as attempts to teach me something. I felt the best way to express the nature of reality as we can know it was the familiar yang-yin symbol of a black "fish" with a white eye and a white fish with a black eye coming together to make a complete circle or totality.

Perhaps the most impressive change was in my feelings. I had gone to bed having written a furious letter to two members of the Jung Institute Board. I felt that the Board, for unknown reasons, was trying to restrict me to associate membership (no vote, no meetings), when I felt as qualified as any of them for full membership. The feeling of fury was now completely gone. I *felt* that I wanted to do nothing aggressive against *anyone.*

The experience changed my attitude about many things—God, Christianity, history, analytical psychology (at least the direction I see it heading in). I saw my life as falling into several archetypal patterns—Orpheus and Eurydice, the Isis-Osiris-Horus myth, and the pattern of the gradual internalization of the anima in one version of Offenbach's fantastic opera *Tales of Hoffman.* Furthermore, I felt as if I had been in the presence of some personality that I called 'god'—in contrast to God. This 'god' resembles the Tao as I understand it, which I associate with the Japanese (Zen) aesthetic principle of *wu-wei*, the waterway. Water always seeks the lowest level and does not put itself forward. That is why I write 'god' with a lowercase "g." I toyed with writing "I" in lower case, too, to indicate the post-experience I, but the computer automatically capitalizes lowercase "I"s when a space is inserted after them. So I settled on uppercase I. The *feeling* of 'god' that I experienced was a combination of two things: what I understand of the Tao *plus* a sense of personality.

I felt that the experience was so vital that I *should* write about it. Immediately, the form I should use was apparent—tell my life story in great detail, even the embarrassing parts, looking at all events as if they might be "the left hand of 'god'" sent either as tests, hints to me or *through me* to others, or as unearned *rewards* (*grace*). I assume that I am not unique and that the same is true for everyone. I am overwhelmed with awe at whatever intelligence could coordinate such a world. 'God' seemed uninterested in *what* I did but was exquisitely interested in *why* I did it. There was also the intuitive truth of an expression or phrase that sounds almost alchemical—*the greater the preceding contraction, the greater the resultant expansion.* There was a definite *belief* that we exist in order to *learn* and that in this process, death (the near drowning of "I" in my 1991 near-death dream or vision) is nothing to a part of us, the crouching figure on the "shore." Life is a spiral evolutionary process. The unfolding of one substance four times, as Jung depicts it in his *Aion* diagrams, goes on endlessly repeating itself on different levels.

There was a definite physical sensation that lasted about three days. I was elated (inflated?) for perhaps a week. After that, there remained the thoughts and the change in me. I soon realized that my fear of death had decreased, but my curiosity about it was now greater. Before my active imagination "conversation" with a mummy in the Vatican museum (back in my Zürich days), I had always preferred cremation. But then I switched to embalming. Now, suddenly, I realized that I might again prefer cremation. It really did not matter. Within a few hours I realized that my orientation had changed subtly from nostalgic yearning for my idealized childhood to an expectation of what the future might bring. The thought occurred to me—am I crazy? A good paranoid schizophrenic can find meaning in anything, even in the license plates of passing cars. I was reassured by recalling a remark by my favorite artist, Salvador Dali. He wrote, "The only difference between Dali and a madman is that Dali is not mad." "I" was not crazy. The experience felt exactly like Jung's description of the movement of the personality from the ego toward (but not to) the Self. The Valentine's Day experience—my birthday is Feb. 13—caused me at first to feel inflated, special. But I talked about it with two people whom I trust. They didn't reduce it. I seemed to be thinking faster in an intuitive way. The moment I posed a question an answer seemed to form.

Once before, in the early 1970s, I had experienced something similar. It lasted 6 weeks, but with intention I could keep it going for about 6 months. It happened in a group meeting with guru Muktananda, whom my analyst friend Arwind Vasavada knew in India. I expected this experience to fade within a year. It hasn't in 5, though there have been no further "intense" experiences. I am calmer, less angry, less concerned with what others think of me, of death. I'm more focused.

RH: Have you learned anything about prayer since your stroke?

JH: I pray, but I pray less in words, more in images, more in intentions.

Death

RH: Jung suggested that people need to come to their own understanding of life after death. I imagine he felt this would help people live their lives with more passion and meaning. With your near-death experience, have you come up with your own understanding of life after death?

JH: Yes, I have, Rob. But my near-death experience merely gave me greater confidence in what I already believed. I think we do survive death, but not in the sense we usually imagine. Put somewhat theoretically, I believe the archetypal Self in each of us survives death. And since the ego, the "I," is a specialized organ of the Self, one could say that it, too, "survives" and can be reconstituted for special purposes. In *Memories, Dreams, Reflections*, Jung gives what seems to me an example of this. After the death of his wife, Emma, Jung saw her in a dream. But he knew it was not Emma herself but a "portrait" that she had "commissioned" for him. In *Dreams and Death*, von Franz cites the last reported dream of a woman, which occurred a few hours before the woman (who was fearful of death) actually died. The woman dreamt that there was a lit candle on her windowsill. She sensed that when the candle went out she would die. Then the candle flickered and went out. There was a moment of darkness. Then the burning candle reappeared—but on the *outside* of the window. I think death is something like that. Beginning in 1882, a considerable body of research began to accumulate on the survival question. Nowadays, however, the question is somewhat out of vogue in psychical research.

THE UNCONSCIOUS

RH: What have you found for yourself to be the best way to work with the unconscious?

JH: Dreams.

RH: Jungians place a high value on becoming conscious. With all that you have been through in your life—your education, your personal analysis, your work in psychotherapy, and your stroke—at this point in life, do you feel more conscious than you have ever been?

JH: At this point in my life I feel that I am more *myself* than I have ever been, more "individuated." "More conscious" is a different question entirely. You see, I think unconscious contents rise to consciousness as symbols (the first half of Jung's transcendent function). They are then "worked through," and after this they do not necessarily stay "in consciousness" but become what philosopher Michael Polanyi called "tacit knowing," knowledge that shows itself in actions but cannot be explicitly stated. But tacit knowledge underpins all our conscious actions and perceptions, so in that sense I suppose I am more conscious now. Toward the end of his book *The Self in Transformation* (HarperCollins, 1977), Herbert Fingarette describes the case of a woman that illustrates what I mean. The women entered psychotherapy because she felt an irrational anger toward a female friend. After successful treatment, she was asked if she still got angry with her friend. "Yes, I do," she admitted, "but it doesn't *bother* me now." Apparently, the tacit meaning of the friend had changed. Before my stroke, I had had, since adolescence, an extremely high sex drive, which gave me much pleasure but also led me into situations that caused great pain to others as well as to myself. The stroke made me impotent but, mercifully, simultaneously took away my sex drive. I can still have sexual feelings and enjoy memories of my previous sex life—but I am not "driven" in regard to sex. With the urge to action gone, I can think more clearly about the symbolic meanings of sexuality. You could say that I am more conscious of sex than I have ever been.

SEXUALITY

RH: That's very interesting, James. I can tell you have given all of this a lot of reflection. Some feel that sexuality wanes as we get older, with less desire and ability to engage in sexual activity. Some see Viagra as a solution to sexual problems for older men. Adolf Guggenbühl-Craig claims that sexuality contains important symbols for a person's path to self-realization. What value have you found in being aware of these symbols for your own growth at this age?

JH: I have always looked upon sexual images in dreams and fantasies as related to *coniunctio* symbols. Perhaps now, with no external sex life, I examine them even more closely. Recently, I had a dream involving a dead friend that had strong homosexual overtones. This made no sense on the objective level. I took the homosexual overtones symbolically: I started reading a book that friend had given me earlier (one that he had written himself), and found in it much material that was relevant to a book I plan to write.

RH: How do you think Jung viewed sexuality?

JH: I think Jung viewed sexuality as a "god," an autonomous archetypal force that, when activated, cannot be denied. One simply has to come to terms with it. The only freedom the ego has is *how* to negotiate a compromise. Jung's childhood dream of an enthroned phallus with a single eye gazing upward could mean that sexuality yearns to move upward into the conscious world. In Greco-Roman mythology, the ultimate expression of god was not Zeus/Jupiter, but Zeus in sexual union with Hera in the "*hieros gamos.*" In Egypt, a similar idea is expressed in the image of the sexual union of Isis and Osiris. It was strong enough to overcome even Death. During his 1944 near-death experience, Jung had a Kabalistic vision: he was in the garden of pomegranates at the marriage of Tipharet and Malchuth, Christ and the world. In his personal life also, Jung found sexuality important. He resisted a relationship with Toni Wolff until psychological and parapsychological phenomena indicated that it was part of his individuation. This was, apparently, the rare attitude of Emma, Jung's wife. Von Franz told me that for a time they met together to analyze their dreams. That must have been something! In my own life, sexuality has led to both the highest high and the lowest low.

RH: What is your view of masturbation?

JH: Masturbation fantasies are very important because one can fantasize about anything while masturbating. I would ask new patients about such fantasies during the initial history-taking phase, before transference and countertransference set in. It would be inappropriate to ask about it later on. Interestingly, the fantasy often changes just before orgasm.

RH: Masturbation has been understood over the years as the cause of so many and various medical and psychological conditions. Hardly do we ever read anything positive about it. Yet most adults masturbate, and it often remains a secret. How do you react to this?

JH: The belief that masturbation causes medical problems is simply mistaken. I know of no studies or case reports that support that theory. Masturbation is healthy in the absence of suitable heterosexual partners—as is the case with men at sea or in prison. It is healthy if it is a rehearsal for heterosexual contact, unhealthy if it is used as a substitute for (or in avoidance of) such contact. In any case, heterosexual vaginal intercourse—reflecting the archetypal *coniunctio* of opposites— seems to be the goal. Some analysts argue that homoeroticism might be the goal. But I have heard dreams from exclusively homosexual men that suggest that their underlying drive is toward women.

RH: James Hillman is the only one I know who has written anything about masturbation. He claims that Aphrodite has been excluded from most areas of life and pornography is one area she is allowed to live in. And that is one reason for the immense popularity of pornography. What is your reaction?

JH: Hillman is right but incomplete.

RH: What do you mean?

JH: Hillman does not explore sufficiently the archetypal aspect of masturbation. In one of the creation myths of ancient Egypt, for example, masturbation is pictured as the original creative act. Originally, Ra is alone. Through masturbation, he creates Geb (Earth) and Nut (Sky). They in turn have Shu and Tefnut, who beget four children: Isis, Osiris, Set, and Nepthys. From the interaction of these siblings arises the whole Osiris cycle, the central myth of ancient Egypt. Hillman deals only with Greek mythology.

RH: Does this mean that when a person masturbates, he or she is engaging in an archetypal process? If so, why has masturbation always been seen as bad?

JH: Masturbation is seen as "bad" for two reasons—one legitimate, the other defensive but understandable. First, once conscious order has been established, *any* further direct contact with the collective unconscious is a threat to the existing conscious order. Secondly, masturbation obscures a "deeper" image, the *hieros gamos*, divine wedding, the union of Zeus and Hera, of Christ and the world. Jung had such near-death experiences while recovering from his 1944 heart attack. Jung describes them in *Memories, Dreams, Reflections*.

DREAMS

RH: How do you work with your dreams?

JH: I honor them, as I do the opinions of a best friend. I am writing two books that will answer your question thoroughly. The first deals with what I call the structural interpretation of dreams. The second shows the importance of dreams in my own life. I no longer feel that any dream interpretation is complete.

RH: In your wonderful book, *The Unconscious Christian* [Paulist Press, 1993], you mention how dreams often prepare a person for his or her next stage of life. Do you recall any dreams or fantasies in your life that prepared you for your life since the stroke?

JH: Not since my near-death "dream" and my waking experience, previously described, on Valentine's Day 1995. Oh, I've had lots of compensatory dreams—one, for example, convinced me that a man I'd always considered a friend really wasn't. Reviewing his *recent* actions over the last 5 years, I have concluded that the dream was right. And again, a series of dreams made me aware of my repressed anger toward two people. Becoming conscious of it made it possible for me to conceptualize it. No— there haven't been any dreams preparing me for a further sea change in my life. But I anticipate that such dreams will come when I am near death. If my wife of 45 years predeceases me, I think dreams will help me prepare for life without her.

RH: Your many writings on dreams have been very helpful. Dreams are difficult to research, but I know you feel dream research is important. Why do you feel it is important?

JH: Dream research is of two types, neither of which has much clinical usefulness. The first type, carried on in dream labs by scientists, is really research on brain processes, the substrate of dreaming. The second type is content analysis of the dreams of a class or category of dreamers, for example, "college males." Both types of research are intellectually interesting but they are of little value when dealing with the dreams of an individual, which is what counts for therapy. "Dream groups" vary in quality. The best format for them that I've seen is that developed by my friend Montague Ullman, a non-Jungian psychoanalyst of the American "culture" school [*Appreciating Dreams* (Sage, 1996)].

JUNGIAN PSYCHOLOGY AND THE FUTURE

RH: You have had some bad things done to you by the Jungian community. What have you learned about the Jungian community from these experiences?

JH: I have learned that the Jungian community is just like any other collective. It is rife with politics and power struggles. Among Jungians, as among others, rumor is often accepted as fact. For example, another analyst once collaborated with me on writing an article, until he heard rumors that I had had problems with professional ethics. Another time, a paper I submitted to one journal was turned down because I had "a history of ethical transgressions." There was only one episode. Two women that I had been close to filed the same complaint simultaneously with five separate professional societies of which I was a member. Only one society exacted a penalty: a five-year suspension. Another threw out one complaint and issued only a reprimand for the other. One woman had been a patient of mine briefly 15 years prior to her complaint. The other was a candidate when I was president of the society. I was never her analyst or supervisor. Though painful and costly, this experience has taught me much. Ethics can easily be misused. Our procedures should be reexamined.

RH: Carl Jung died in 1961, and I know he has been a very important person in your life. What do you see in the future for Jungian psychology?

JH: Early in my first Jungian analysis with Rivkah Kluger, I dreamt that I was in her kitchen sitting across a table from Adrian Bauman, one of Jung's grandsons. Rivkah was cooking a meal for us. Suddenly there was a loud pinging sound. A steak knife had spontaneously shattered. When I picked it up, it became "Jung's sword," the sword of a giant. Standing on tiptoe, I could barely keep its point from touching the floor. Near the hilt, a large piece of the sword was missing. Someone said, "It's a shame the official guardians won't let us repair it." Shortly before her death, I requested a mutual friend to ask Marie-Louise von Franz, my major analyst, about another matter. Von Franz spontaneously recalled that dream and said, "Tell James that the defect in Jung's sword is parapsychology." This set me thinking. I'm not sure that "the official guardian," the International Association for Analytical Psychology, represents Jung's thought. Post-Jungian thought has focused on the two-person analytic interaction, on transference-countertransference, on infant development. This is but a small corner of the large sketch Jung roughed out. In 1993, von Franz, who was one of the founders of the original Jung Institute in Zürich, and several other analysts resigned from the Institute because they felt that it no longer represented the central thrust of Jung's work. They then established a new institute in Kusnacht. I feel this was a momentous event in the Jungian movement, which has not yet been fully appreciated. I agree with von Franz that Jung, like Lao-Tsu, is an epochal man, the kind seen only about every 2,000 years.

RH: How would you like to be remembered by the Jungian community?

JH: I seldom think of this. To quote Jung, "I am not my own historiographer." Besides, my life is a work in progress. The best is yet to come.

The idea of suicide, understandable as it is, does not seem commendable to me ... as long as life is possible, even if only in a minimal degree, you should hang on to it, in order to scoop it up for the purpose of conscious development. To interrupt life before its time is to bring to a standstill an experiment which we have not set up. We have found ourselves in the midst of it and must carry it through to the end. [Anonymous letter, July 10, 1946. *C. G. Jung Letters, Vol. 1: 1906-1950*, Princeton University Press, 1973, p. 434.]

—C. G. Jung

JOHN BEEBE, M.D.

John Beebe, M.D., was born in Washington, D.C., and is a graduate of Harvard University and the University of Chicago Medical School. He has maintained a private practice in psychiatry in San Francisco since 1971, and became a Jungian analyst in 1978. In 2002, he completed a two-year term as President of the C. G. Jung Institute of San Francisco. He is the founding editor of *The San Francisco Jung Institute Library Journal*; the co-editor of *Psychiatric Treatment: Crisis, Clinic, and Consultation* (McGraw-Hill, 1975); and editor of *Money, Food, Drink, Fashion, and Analytic Training* (proceedings of the Eighth International Congress of Analytical Psychology, 1980) and C. G. Jung's *Aspects of the Masculine* (Princeton UP, 1989). He is the author of *Integrity in Depth* (Fromm, 1995) and has recently edited the proceedings of the 2002 North American Conference of Jungian Analysts and Candidates, *Terror, Violence, and the Impulse to Destroy: Perspectives from Analytical Psychology* (Daimon, 2004), which he helped to organize. I first met John in his cozy office on a peaceful winter afternoon in San Francisco in 2000, not long after he had turned sixty, and we have continued to correspond over the ensuing years to produce this interview.

• 5 •

AT HOME WITH HIMSELF
JOHN BEEBE AT 67

The Self violently resists developments that are encouraged along
lines that are not natural to the person in question, indicating
that for each of us the Self has its own ideas.

— John Beebe

ENCOUNTERING JUNG

ROB HENDERSON (RH): How did you become interested in Jung?

JOHN BEEBE (JB): In my first year at Harvard, as an undergraduate, I
took a general education course (Social Sciences 4), which brought together
cultural anthropology and depth psychology. It was taught by Clyde
Kluckohn and Henry Murray. In class, Professor Kluckohn tended to make
fun of Murray's serious interest in Jung. (Henry Murray had been analyzed
by Jung in the 1930s.) Nevertheless, *Modern Man in Search of a Soul* remained
on the required reading list. That was my first formal exposure to Jung's
writing. In another class, I became friendly with a sophomore, Bill
Wertenbaker, and through him I met his mother, the writer Nancy Hale,
who had just completed her novel *Heaven and Hardpan Farm*, a comedy of
psychological manners modeled upon the Jungian inpatient facility that
Beatrice Hinkle had maintained in Connecticut. (I later learned that Nancy
Hale had been one of Dr. Hinkle's patients there.) The best scene involved
a war between the extraverts and introverts.

As can happen when you are very young, especially if you have a strong
mother complex, as I did, I became even closer friends with Bill's mother,
Nancy, than I was with Bill. I spent a lot of time with them at their house
in Folly Cove, Massachusetts, in the summer of 1957. Nancy was the first
fiction writer with any reputation that I had had the chance to get to know

personally. At that time, I planned to be a writer of fiction myself. Nancy and I had wonderful conversations lying on adjacent granite rocks, sunning ourselves in Folly Cove. But it was the psyche, not the writing of fiction, toward which our conversations turned. Nancy told me about her analysis with Beatrice Hinkle in the 1940s, which had cured her writer's block.

By that time, I had begun volunteering at the Metropolitan State Hospital Children's Unit in Waltham, Massachusetts, along with a number of my undergraduate classmates. Robert Coles, then a psychiatric resident, would meet with us on regular basis to discuss our experience "hanging out" with the young inmates, so I had already developed a certain openness to psychological thinking. My own mother had been in psychiatric treatment when I was very young, and I had heard quite a bit about the psychotherapeutic process from her. But it was Nancy Hale who linked the psychological with the Jungian in my mind and made me feel that psychiatric treatment could foster the creativity—rather than just address the symptoms—of the psyche. In the year that followed, I began to realize that it was that process, and not the process of writing, that really fascinated me.

In the summer of 1958, on my nineteenth birthday, I returned to Folly Cove for just one day to confess to Nancy Hale that I had decided to become a psychiatrist, not a writer. She pointed out that my life as a doctor would be one of great self-sacrifice, citing, as an example, an old beau from her teenage years, who was now in San Francisco. He had worked so hard in the early days of his practice, she told me, that he had come down with tuberculosis. This doctor turned out to be Jo Wheelwright, one of the founders of the C. G. Jung Institute of San Francisco, where I would later receive my own analytic training.

But who's to say when my preparation for Jungian analysis began? As a fifteen-year-old scholarship student at the Lawrenceville School, I developed a pretty intense transference to the assistant housemaster of the Dawes House, who had gone to Harvard and worked in the Counseling Center under Henry Murray. When I began analysis with Joseph Henderson in 1973, I found that Joe had attended Lawrenceville as well, and that an earlier assistant housemaster of the Dawes House had been his mentor. There, perhaps, the synchronistic trail ends: The man holding that job in Joe's day was none other than Thornton Wilder, who, a few years after Joe's graduation, published his first novel, *The Bridge of San Luis Rey*, which was all about synchronicity!

So, though I was a young man, coming, psychologically speaking, out of nowhere, I had, even before I got to San Francisco, managed to cross significant paths traveled earlier by the two Jo(e)s—Wheelwright and Henderson—who were the founding fathers of the C. G. Jung Institute of San Francisco. Once in San Francisco, I became friends with a young psychiatrist named Tom Kirsch, and it was Tom who referred me to the Jungian analyst John Perry and who later encouraged me to apply for training at the Jung Institute of San Francisco. Tom was very helpful in connecting me with the Jungians.

JUNGIAN MENTORS

RH: What impact did Jo Wheelwright and Joe Henderson have on your life?

JB: Do you mean in my actual contacts with them, aside from these synchronistic anticipations I just described? Well, between them, they incarnated the extraverted and introverted aspects of being a Jungian analyst for me. They were invaluable role models for my own functioning in both modes. Jo Wheelwright had gone to Harvard, as I had, and was active in such organizations as the Group for the Advancement of Psychiatry at a time when I was training to be a psychiatrist and was gradually moving into my identity as an analyst. He made that new identity legitimate from the standpoint of the establishment. I never worked with him analytically or in clinical consultation, but we got to know each other out of a natural affinity. My friendship with Jo started in the waiting room of my first analyst, John Perry, with whom Jo shared a suite of offices. Jo loved to chat with John's patients (and those of Joe Henderson as well) while they were waiting for their sessions. Around that time, Nancy Hale came to San Francisco for a visit, and so it came out that we both knew her, and that he was the beau she had told me about. That's how we became friends years before I started training at the Institute. We were the same psychological type—in the superior ego function, at least. I loved to hear him teach Jung's theory of psychological types because he spoke so much to my own experience and delivered his lectures in the disorganized yet unconsciously purposive way in which I too spoke. Finally, in the mid-1970s I had a dream in which he tagged me in a game in which a number of Jungians were participating and said,

"You're it!" After that I began to lecture on psychological types around the country!

Joe Henderson, on the other hand, had gone to Princeton, the school my mother had wanted me to attend. He represented the introverted intuitive path I had left behind when I separated psychologically from my mother. A danger in that heroic separation was the abandonment of my connection to the unconscious in favor of an overachieving extraverted adaptation. It took me longer to find my way to Joe (he was my third analyst), but when I finally got to work with him, he made a decisive difference in my life. Joe showed me that there was a masculine way of connecting to the unconscious; I didn't have to abandon discrimination or my adaptation to outer reality to stay in touch with myself. Joe held me in analysis for over twenty-five years as I found a way to claim the introverted intuitive territory that had once belonged to an engulfing, "borderline" mother. He showed me that analysis could be done with grace—not hysterically, intrusively, depressively, narcissistically, or masochistically (the rather floridly unhappy ways in which my mother had deployed her introverted intuition). Joe made the way of the introverted intuitive seem ever so much less threatening to me, which eventually enabled me to see the value in my mother's standpoint. In the end, he catalyzed a real rapprochement between her and me that changed my relation to the inner world as well as to the numerous introverts who sought my services as an analyst. So, if you follow Jung's idea that mental health is adaptation to outer and inner realities, the two Jo(e)s did a great deal to foster my sanity—and my happiness—in my profession.

FILMS AND THE UNCONSCIOUS

RH: Like Joe Henderson, you have often reviewed movies from a Jungian perspective. What advantage do films have in portraying the unconscious?

JB: A movie can present the unconscious to us as an image that seems to emerge from the flow of life. Consider the final scene of *Queen Christina*, the 1933 Garbo film directed by Rouben Mamoulian. Garbo's unmoving face becomes a living masthead on the prow of the ship bearing her character to exile: as the person disappears from our concern, the actress becomes an archetype. The effect is uncanny and numinous—a personality memorialized so as to become eternal in the imagination. There are other unforgettable images in the history of art—the Amarna sculptor's model for a bust of Nefertiti comes to mind—that suggest the way process pauses to become content as the unconscious dreams itself into our minds. What gives film its edge in showing how the unconscious creates sudden moments of arresting insight is its ability to play stillness off against movement. After the advent of the close-up—the innovation that became the signature of the medium—the focus of movies became the juxtaposition of human stillness with human movement. Setting up that dialectic is the concern of the unconscious as well, so it seems as if film has managed to capture not just the imagery but also the style of the unconscious, the way the unconscious goes about fulfilling its own uncanny purpose, to make us at home with ourselves.

RH: You say that the unconscious has the uncanny purpose of making us at home with ourselves. What does it mean to you to be at home with yourself?

JB: The simple answer is: *everything*. I often say that the commonest reason people come to psychotherapy is that they can't live their psychological lives anywhere else. I see it as my duty to allow them to make themselves at home when they come, if I can. And I have found that those who find a home in my consulting room do extraordinarily deep work with me. You'd be surprised how often the room shows up in my patients' dreams.

In a wonderful, strange documentary called *Lightning over Water* by Wim Wenders, the great American auteur director Nicholas Ray is shown near the end of his life talking to some film students about a scene in a movie he'd made with Robert Mitchum in the 1950s, *The Lusty Men*. It is an interesting scene that is about his hero's getting into a home. In terms of story, what is shown is offhand; Mitchum ambles up to a house he's found and, I think, just goes into the basement, but the image conveys the encounter with the possibility of a home. Like much of Ray's work, it is very powerful. Ray told an audience of Vassar students that his vision for that scene was informed by his understanding that the top concern for people in the United States right after World War II was getting a home: the big news in 1946 was the housing shortage. With an eye on the box office, the filmmaker had chosen that image because he wanted to convey an emotion the audience could get into!

For years, the greatest suffering in my own life was not having the right physical home. Beyond that was the enormous problem of feeling at home in my body. But even deeper was the difficulty of being at home with who I am psychologically. I can see why it was difficult for me. A lot of people, on first meeting me, find my inability to talk easily at the feeling and sensation level at which most conversations begin a bit off-putting, and still more can't understand me when I open my mouth and try to share my own perspective about things. But when they finally discover that I am just being my intuitive-thinking self, they sometimes become fascinated, because I represent an alternative they haven't considered. I suspect that a "transference" in analytic situations often develops in a similar way. But nothing is really transferred from earlier experience, because this is a new relationship of comfort with something different from what one is used to, a relationship with different standards from those that reigned in one's original home. And it is a relationship that depends, ultimately, on the analyst's being at home with him- or herself, however different he or she is from what the analysand initially expected.

THE SELF

RH: Do you have some ideas about how we defend ourselves against the Self? How do you understand this dynamic?

JB: My ideas on this subject can be found in several places, but particularly in "Primary Ambivalence toward the Self," an article that appeared in *The Borderline Personality in Analysis*, edited by Nathan Schwartz-Salant and Murray Stein in 1987, and in my "Comment" to the Symposium on Borderline Patients, which appeared in the *Journal of Analytical Psychology* in 1993. In the latter article, I postulate that in addition to defenses *of* the Self (a clinical theme developed by Michael Fordham, who wouldn't have capitalized the "S"), there are defenses *against* the Self. These are what the older literature discussed as attitudes taken up by the ego that are negative toward the Self—starting with the opinion that our dreams have no meaning or that our feelings are something to rise above. Such an openly negative stance toward the unconscious is still a relatively straightforward psychological attitude—although in the person who really takes it up, fate replaces psychology because the progressive integration of consciousness that we call individuation requires that we listen to the Self, and, as Jung so beautifully expressed it in *Aion* (para. 126), when the "inner situation is not made conscious, it happens outside, as fate."

More insidious, and more common in our psychological age, is the attitude of the person who recognizes fully how nourishing the experience of what analytical psychology refers to as the Self can be as the ultimate well of all psychological life, but who nevertheless is ambivalent about accepting that nourishment. I think that's a response some people learn from their earliest caregivers, who may themselves be ambivalent about the kind of Self their baby is bringing into the world. Since all developing individuals must draw upon others to confirm and consolidate their self-experience, a split attitude toward the Self can develop as early as in infancy. One part of the developing personal self continues to derive some of its ongoing existence from its source in the deeper transpersonal Self. The other part of the self has noted very early on that this time and this place are not particularly friendly to the designs of the Self. It has internalized the attitudes of caregivers around it that would subvert large portions of the Self's apparent agenda. For instance, the incarnating personal self may have picked up that its environment does not want a particular innate characteristic to develop, for example, an ego stronger than the family thinks a girl should have, or, in either sex, a predominantly homosexual orientation.

If, from within, the Self continues to push for one of those taboo designs, the developing personal self, seeking to square itself with the values of the environment, may start to defend against the Self. Then we may see an ambivalence develop in which one part of the self likes very much to have the Self energizing it, and another part doesn't like that at all. That ambivalence is enough to put *all* access to the Self in a paralyzing double bind and produce the "borderline" condition. Under that spell, the personal self is so deprived of its energizing morale that the person is allowed to become only marginally alive, psychologically speaking. I sometimes suspect that this is the situation in the unconscious when patients begin to quarrel with me, just when I am encouraging them to do something that might make them thrive.

In practice, such defenses *against* the Self are hard to distinguish from defenses *of* the Self, which also resist attempts to get the person to thrive, but for a different reason. The Self violently resists developments that are encouraged along lines that are not natural to the person in question, indicating that for each of us the Self has its own ideas. That's one reason I place such emphasis on Jung's theory of psychological types: I do not want to get the pattern of potential individuation wrong when, in my extraverted intuitive way, I start encouraging people to be what *I* think might be good for them. Actually, I think the severe self disorders that go by Otto Kernberg's popular rubric of "borderline conditions and pathological narcissism" involve complications and distortions of self-experience occasioned both by defenses *against* the self and defenses *of* the self. Sooner or later, every analyst comes up against the reality of these defenses, which are at the core of every psychological problem that conceivably might be presented to an analyst, and so we have to have a Jungian defense analysis just as we already have a Freudian one, but using somewhat less psychoanalytic language.

I consider it our job as analysts to help our clients understand the attitudes that they have learned to take up toward the Self. These defensive attitudes, which are the content of the personal or small-"s" self, have much to do with how persons access the capital-"S" transpersonal Self that Jung discovered. As I have indicated, such defenses are dramatically evident in the negative ways that therapists, and other people who would like to help the person gain access to the natural energies of the Self, get treated. It's important to understand, too, that ambivalence toward the Self can surface after a period of venerating it. There is a natural way of accessing the Self, which, when first encountered, is well nigh irresistible. Siddartha Gautama, Jesus, and Muhammad all had the gift of making the Self accessible even to people who ordinarily would have been disposed to defend against it. The story of Jesus brings up the ambivalence that may then ensue. The gospel accounts of his trial, taunting, and crucifixion convey the terrible reality of the contempt people are capable of displaying toward the Self when it attempts to incarnate and make a difference.

Homosexuality

RH: You have been open about your homosexual orientation since you first applied to the Jung Institute of San Francisco to become an analyst. As a Jungian, how do you understand your homosexuality?

JB: I understand my homosexuality as a natural expression of the Self for me. I must say that the pressure from within to accept and integrate my sexuality in exactly and only the ways that seem fitting to it has been very helpful to me as an analyst in distinguishing a person's real self-experience from what I would call the propaganda from outside as to what that self-experience ought to be like. Obviously, that individuation has helped me overcome collective homophobia, which has been recognized as the problem it is only in my lifetime, though in good enough time to confirm my own inner conclusions. Ironically, that confirmation of my feelings has made me trust them enough to resist the much more subtle disavowal of my self-experience that I've sometimes been exposed to in the name of a gay-positive thinking. In other words, throughout my life I've had to resist collective ways of understanding and realizing my sexuality that would have violated the spirit of it, and that has toughened my resolve as well as my ability to listen to the Self, and this has made me a better analyst.

RH: What would you suggest to a man or woman who is struggling with his or her sexuality and wondering if he or she might be homosexual?

JB: There is no one answer to this question. I'd have to talk with the individual to know what I would say to him or her. But speaking generally, I believe I would encourage anyone who is "struggling" with homosexual feelings to take them seriously. To take homosexual feelings seriously is not necessarily to take them literally, but to give them weight. There is a cultural prejudice built into a term such as "gay" that the images and affects that move us toward homosexual relationships cannot and should not be taken seriously, even if we live them out. When I started training, I found the same prejudice in classical Jungian writings, which held that homosexuality is a *puer aeternus* activity, and it can't be a serious orientation because it evades the "true ground" of sexual relatedness—the union of male and female opposites. I have noticed, however, that *puer aeternus* type men who are basically heterosexual but incapable of settling down with a woman are often helped by taking seriously one of their homosexual attachments. It may be only a crush, of the kind they would not ordinarily speak about, but if they take it seriously, it can become a bridge to responsible marriage with a woman and parenthood. To take something seriously does not necessarily mean to consummate it physically, but to consider that one might, and that it may be important and valuable to do so. It's certainly not to shrug off the homosexual feeling or to try to "outgrow" it. Rather, it is to try to grow through the experience of holding the feeling and considering its relevance to oneself with an attitude of openness to its potential to enhance one's life.

There's an aspect of integrity to this. Integrity, as John Kekes has written, implies honoring one's commitments even when it is difficult to do so. And that's a big part of individuation, in the sense Jung uses the term. If we, on the psychological path, are really committed to integrating the feelings and images that come up, then we have to honor them in some way even when they don't fit what we imagined our lives would feel or look like. So we can't simply ignore our homosexual feelings and images on the grounds that we're "not homosexual." It would seem that our moral individuation forces us to challenge a good deal of traditional thinking that would (1) make that basic psychological step "unthinkable," and (2) attack any attempt to link the homosexual parts of our life stories to the other narratives that govern our lives. But that may be why the relatively small number of individuals who end up "coming out" as gay (in the serious meaning of that word) have become so important to the mainstream. They exemplify the integrity it takes to stand up for our feelings as something to be taken seriously, a psychological value that isn't restricted, in its practical relevance for individuation, to homosexual feelings.

RH: How do you understand the feminine in relation to your homosexuality?

JB: I would hope my homosexuality hasn't come at the expense of the feminine. When I started analysis, the prejudice within the Jungian community was that a homosexual man was someone whose anima had never detached from the Great Mother. Therefore, the anima couldn't do its jobs of connecting him outwardly to a proper feminine love object and inwardly to the Self. Not only, then, did he remain unmarried socially, he missed the inner marriage as well and was "stuck" from the point of view of individuation. But I don't think that happened to me. To be sure, I had to work through what used to be called a narcissistic anima. Today, I would call her my "opposing personality," a feminine introverted intuition that was modeled on my mother's introverted intuition and at the same time fought against her in her own cognitive mode. My mother had been what Edward Edinger has described as a psychological trespasser. She tried, like many an anima woman, to preempt my relation to the unconscious when I was young. I used to think that "it takes a woman to fight a woman like that." But what a woman came to my rescue from within! I once had a dream that I had my mother on one arm and Barbra Streisand on the other: my mother was making a scene and Barbra, not to be upstaged by anybody, was giving my mother hell! Streisand would be the opposing personality, what a Freudian might describe as my identification with the feminine aggressor.

As an effect of my mother problem, in my youth I had both an identification with the false-feminine narcissistic anima and a big deficiency in the true anima, which carried my neglected inferior function of introverted sensation. Before my analysis, all I could do was take pains to cultivate my persona so that not too much of this showed! In my analysis, I was given the opportunity to cultivate my true anima, and the eventual result was a real development of this more authentic relatedness to myself—which, in the outer world, showed in an ability, finally, both to win my father's respect and to hold my own with my mother without becoming so oppositional to her. Another result of the analysis upon the development of my anima was revealed when, at the age of forty-six, I fell in love with my present partner, an introverted sensation type man. At that time, I dreamed that a woman colleague of mine, an introverted sensation type analyst, met the man I was interested in and really liked him. And so I found that my anima had progressed past my mother and was now represented by a discerning professional colleague.

So this is why I don't think my homosexuality has come at the expense of the feminine. At this time in my life, the anima seems to be on good terms with my choice of love object, and interestingly it has been my fate to live in a time when the collective anima can feel good about it too. I guess anima development in my case has had a lot to do with accepting my homosexuality and taking it seriously. I feel the anima has deepened the quality and value of my homosexuality for me as well as for others. And, as the figure of my colleague in my dream (a woman who is also a dear friend) may perhaps convey, the anima has also won my gratitude. Certainly a positive attitude toward the anima has helped me to enter into some very deep friendships with women, which I particularly enjoy at this time in my life.

TYPOLOGY

RH: How do you understand the eight combinations that make up Jung's system of "psychological types"?

JB: Are you ready for a long answer? By "combinations" you must mean the terms for the different "function attitudes" that Jung derived by combining his notion of basic "attitudes" (extraversion and introversion) with his idea of discrete "functions" of consciousness (sensation, thinking, feeling, or intuition) through which, in each of us, these attitudes are deployed. If you accept that his four functions of consciousness can all be expressed through either an extraverted or an introverted attitude, it becomes clear that eight types of psychological consciousness result: extraverted sensation, introverted sensation, extraverted thinking, introverted thinking, extraverted feeling, introverted feeling, extraverted intuition, and introverted intuition. Each of these function-attitudes represents a different "type" of consciousness available to the ego and, as such, becomes subject to ego development. Once the ego is involved, one given type of function-attitude may become more or less differentiated than another. But all of them develop out of the original self, that originally undifferentiated but nonetheless intelligent matrix of judgment and perception out of which all ego-consciousness emerges.

Consciousness, for Jung, is an achievement—there he agrees with Freud, except that Jung thinks that the disposition to become conscious *in a certain way*, that is, to develop a particular function-attitude in preference to any other, is really a predisposition that is already present at the start of life in each of us. All of us, according to this view, have an innate tendency to develop an ego in which one of the eight types of consciousness will be dominant, will become, as Jung then calls it, the "superior function." And all of us have the complementary tendency to have one function-attitude— the inverse of the superior one—that develops only very slowly out of its original unconsciousness or embeddedness in the dynamics of the Self. That unconscious function-attitude, which Jung calls the "inferior function," is beyond the ego's control. It is for each of us the site of our inferiority complex, if we have one. The inferior function as the inverse of the superior one means that if the superior function is extraverted, the inferior function will be introverted, and vice versa. It also means that a thinking superior function will be complemented by a feeling inferior function, and vice versa. A superior function of sensation will be balanced by an inferior function of intuition; superior intuition is complemented by inferior sensation. I call this pairing of inverse superior and inferior functions the "spine" of personality, because it defines the relation of the ego to the unconscious.

In addition to the various functions of consciousness in their more or less differentiated states, Jung notes that the ego has, and is characterized by, its "will." The superior function is very much able to follow the ego's will; indeed, it is often symbolized in fairy tales, myths, and our dreams by the figure of the hero. And as every hero in mythology is associated in some way with a god or goddess whose purposes the hero serves, one can often identify a particular driving archetype behind the drive of the superior function. This is not to say that the same divine figure will be found behind every person who leads with an identical superior function. The differences between people of the same type are just as striking as the differences between people of different types. One man will impress us with a heroic, superior extraverted thinking that is positively Zeus-like, whereas another man, whose extraverted thinking is just as differentiated, will be positively Dionysian in the way he takes command of a situation—Mick Jagger comes to mind.

If you take Jagger as an image of an extraverted thinking man, you will immediately see beyond the sex, drugs, and rock and roll the sense of a career that has been especially well planned and thus able to prevail over four decades. I read in an interview a few years ago that Jagger asked the young rock star Rob Thomas to write a song with him. It made sense: Thomas had written the lyrics to "Smooth," which won a Grammy for Santana the previous year. Another old-timer, Willie Nelson, had recently sought out Thomas's services. But Jagger went so far as to have someone call Thomas's agent a day or so before to say he would be calling, so Thomas wouldn't think it was a prank when he called. Now that's thinking ahead, directing the other person's thinking, which an extraverted thinking type loves to do. Extraverted thinking is the function of consciousness that carefully blueprints everything in advance. In an artist with integrity, such as Jagger, that superior function lives in creative relation to the inferior function, which in Jagger's case would be introverted feeling. We know that in Jagger's creative work as a singer, he has shown from the beginning a real love of African-American blues artists, and his own voice duplicates their articulation of introverted feeling with affectionate fidelity. The part of him that can appreciate blues singers is, I think, his own highly developed inferior function-attitude of introverted feeling, which like the inferior function of other men, tends to be associated with the anima. A personification of her might be "Brown Sugar," the title character in one of his most famous songs.

I have found that the integration of the trickster into the anima most often comes at midlife and is the key to releasing the enduring creativity of the inferior function, whose anima or animus outpourings have otherwise a thin, too idealized, even whining quality. Every one of Jung's eight function-attitudes appears in every psyche, where it is associated with an archetypal figure. That archetypal figure will have its own history of development out of the unconscious, and it may still be contaminated, or have come to associate itself more consciously with one or more other archetypes. So we can observe in one extraverted thinking man an introverted feeling that is visibly "inferior," carried by an anima that is contaminated with shadow elements that haven't been integrated, whereas another extraverted thinking man may have introverted feeling that is associated with a much more differentiated anima. I see in Jagger—the artist—an anima that has incorporated the trickster and has become more autonomous, creative, and resilient.

RH: My dominant function is extraverted thinking and my auxiliary is introverted sensation. The tertiary is extraverted intuition, and the inferior function is introverted feeling. How would you understand the strengths and weaknesses with which I would be living?

JB: First of all, remember that you have extra*v*erted, not extr*o*verted thinking, despite the efforts of spell-checkers and dictionaries to conform Jung's notion of extraversion to parallel introversion, ignoring the Latin root of the word. I prefer Jung's spelling, because the "extra" reminds me of "Extra, extra, read all about it," the egregious tendency of extraverted thinking to spread its own point of view as widely as possible. Whereas introverted thinking winds up, often enough, speaking only to itself (and not knowing when to stop), extraverted thinking is often quite gratuitous, forcing others to flee.

My father, an extraverted thinking type army officer, was always alienating me by giving me an "add on" bit of advice as to what to do. The tragedy of his life was that he didn't make the rank of general. He loved to deploy people in different directions. He too had an auxiliary function of introverted sensation; before their divorce, my mother was always saying to him, "Don't be so damn technical." But he was capable, as she never was, of very long hours of work and meticulous planning, and he was very studious. He wasn't imaginative and he wasn't very good with extraverted feeling, although he certainly aspired to be kind. Unfortunately for me, he had a great deal of unconscious envy of more original thinkers than he, and he could be depreciative of them. On the other hand, he deeply respected the ethic of care, and he had a quite sensitive introverted feeling, which matured as he grew older. His biggest problem, I think, was that his was the same typology as the American collective—ESTJ (extraverted thinking with auxiliary introverted sensation)—and he belonged to that "greatest generation" that came into its maturity at a time when America had become inflated from having survived the Great Depression and won the Second World War. He participated, through his typology, in the collective inflation, which made it hard for him to see when his country's thinking, and his own, was wrong. He was very intelligent, but his insistence on the collective point of view could make him seem stupid, particularly to me as a young man trying to differentiate his own introverted thinking. (I, of course, participated in the later inflation of the 1960s counterculture, so critical of everything associated with the establishment.)

My father's image of a good citizen was that of someone who kept his lawn neat. I once heard him exclaim, at the edge of a golf course, "Egad, that's the worst thing I've ever seen! That man walked on the green with metal cleats on!" I suppose that was his auxiliary caretaking introverted sensation. But he articulated it in a one-sided way, so it came out sounding unfeeling. I would say the great pitfall for the extraverted thinking type is the tendency to believe that only collectively principled rationality is valuable. That's a very assailable position, as just about every intellectual has been telling us these past thirty years. But after enduring, throughout my own maturity, such a long critique of the values of the Enlightenment—an extraverted thinking, introverted sensation project if ever there was one—I find an increasingly soft spot in my heart for the American Founding Fathers and for my father. He had an eighteenth-century turn to his mind that I've come to value. (His favorite writer was Gibbon.)

Lately, I've come to value the eighteenth century more than I would have thought possible when I was younger. I would advise any person with your extraverted thinking/introverted sensation typology to take up the literature of that century. There seems, in fact, to be a renewed interest in that period just now. Alexander Pope's translation of *The Iliad* is now back in a paperback edition, and if you read Pope's preface to that once best-selling translation, you can see what individuated extraverted thinking with introverted sensation can do. There, tertiary extraverted intuition is allowed to play, and a highly animated introverted feeling gives the prose its soul. There is even a lively respect for the irrational tricks introverted intuition can play with meaning. Pope also understands how to use the shadow of oppositional introverted thinking to resist easy definitions, and he has a positively demonic extraverted feeling that undermines easy sympathies and shifts loyalties in complex ways, both cruel and kind at the same time. With this kind of Augustan development, achieved by Pope, the Neoclassicist, by merging his own gifts with those of Homer and in the process making himself the first writer in English to live by the sale of his books, extraverted thinking seems anything but pompous and shallow.

I think your own project, Rob, of making a space for the Jungian-analyst mind (and your incredible patience with the process of getting so many of us intuitive fish in your net) is a similar one, of merging with others' minds to open up your thinking, and giving full play in the humble role of interviewer to your own tertiary and inferior functions. I think that is an excellent way to overcome the limitations inherent in the collectively sanctioned strengths of your type. Another extraverted thinking interviewer who has done this with outstanding success is Bill Moyers, who almost single-handedly reintroduced spirituality to our American collective's rational discourse.

SPIRITUALITY

RH: How do you understand yourself as a spiritual person?

JB: Ever since the events of September 11, 2001, I, like all Americans, have felt terribly undermined by the intrusions in our lives from people with "spiritual" motivations, so I wouldn't wish to trumpet a spiritual drive in myself lest I sound, and become, similarly inflated. As a close reader of Jung, I'm of the opinion that spirit most authentically enters psyche through the shadow; that is, not through the parts of ourselves of which we're proudest, but the ones of which we have good reason to be ashamed. As an extraverted intuitive man, my own most remote function-attitude, typologically speaking, is extraverted sensation. Certainly others experience my unconsciousness about extraverted sensation as demonic. People would say of me, when I was young, "You're hell to have in the house." That's because

I am quite uncoordinated and geographically challenged, to the point of undermining others in physical experiences that involve the sharing of space. I am likely to misjudge distances between others and myself—I've mostly given up dancing, which I love, because I tend to crowd the dance floor in an inconsiderate way.

And yet some of my most intensely spiritual experiences have occurred while dancing—moving the body in space is a hallmark of extraverted sensation. Not long after I turned thirty, upon breaking up with a man I'd lived with for four years, I went out and danced like the devil. And when I was finished, I had connected with not just my anger, but also my determination to stay alive to myself. I have never abandoned that commitment to my own vitality in the subsequent thirty-five years. I feel I owe to that dance of release my capacity to hold my relation to myself within a long-term relationship, and that has served me well in my subsequent romantic history: one thirteen-year relationship, followed by a very productive hiatus in which I was single for several years, and then a true partnership that is going on twenty years.

And sexuality, which seems to defeat so many people of my type (Bill Clinton?), has been an incredible source of spirit to me, although there I have had to bring in my introverted sensation anima to contain the experience. The psychological formula I have developed to explain this paradox is that the anima (in my case, introverted sensation) deepens the integrity of the psyche by serving as the bridge from ego to Self. The resulting integrity "holds" the demonic shadow (extraverted sensation, in my case), according to the fairytale model so archetypally rendered in the Disney movie, of Beauty dancing with Beast.

I have found in my own case that to the extent that Beauty—my introverted sensation anima—really holds Beast—my demonic extraverted sensation function—the potential of the demonic to become *daimonic* (i.e., a source for the infusion of spirit and the development of character) is released. That point is rather imperfectly rendered in the Disney movie (and also Jean Cocteau's classic version) as the *transformation* of Beast, supposedly a change for the better that is always something of a letdown to viewers because it doesn't ring true archetypally. According to a poll conducted in France after Cocteau's *Beauty and the Beast* was released, children were overwhelmingly critical of the transformation of Beast into a handsome prince. Greta Garbo, after viewing the film, said, "Give me back my Beast!"

The children and Garbo liked Beauty with Beast, just as the little girls who have Disney images of these figures on their bedroom walls do today. So my anima has learned to bring her integrity to bear with the beastly part of my psyche, which, like the beast in the tale, is kind and cruel at the same time. I have found that when that demonic side of myself is held with integrity by what I can only call my compassion for myself, the very problematic extraverted sensation has become the channel for my most intense experiences of spirit—giving body to my love of life, of others, and even God.

I suppose these days I most often encounter the spirit over a good dinner. I'm known for consulting the *I Ching* about a specific extraverted sensation problem many would call trivial, but I would not—the choosing of a wine for dinner. Often people who have dined with me end up recalling the wine I chose for months or years after, because it served as the physical medium through which we were brought into genuine relatedness. That people would feel this way about something I provide in the area of extraverted sensation feels, to me, like the grace of God. I suppose the *I Ching's* feat mirrors, in a faint way, what Christ achieved at the wedding at Cana when he succeeded in transforming water into wine to save the party. But in my case it's through the shadow of gluttony that the helpful spirit of shared communal pleasure enters. I am grateful that at this time in my life, I have become sufficiently at home with my complexes to allow something like this to happen.

One lives as one can. There is no single, definite way for the individual which is prescribed for him or would be the proper one. [Letter to Frau V., December 15, 1923. *C. G. Jung Letters, Vol. 1: 1906-1950*, Princeton University Press, 1973, p. 132.]

— C. G. Jung

Power that is constantly asserted works against itself, and it is asserted when one is afraid of losing it. One should not be afraid of losing it. One gains more peace through losing power. [Letter to Mrs. C., November 3, 1958, *C. G. Jung Letters, Vol. 2: 1951-1961*, Princeton University Press, 1976, p. 463.]

— C. G. Jung

JOSEPH L. HENDERSON, M.D.

Called the Dean of the San Francisco Jungian Analysts, Joseph L. Henderson is one of the most respected Jungian analysts in the world. Born in Elko, Nevada, he graduated from Princeton University with a degree in French Literature and later received a medical degree from St. Bartholomew's Hospital in London. He is the author of numerous published works. His most well-known book is *Thresholds of Initiation* (Wesleyan UP), published in 1967. He also wrote, at Jung's own invitation, one of the five chapters in *Man and His Symbols*. These and other of his works are documented in *The Shaman from Elko*, a *festschrift* published by the C. G. Jung Institute of San Francisco in 1978 in honor of his 75th birthday. He and his late wife, Helena, had one child, Elizabeth. This interview took place in 1999, just prior to Joe's 96th birthday, on an invigorating late summer afternoon at Joe's home north of San Francisco. It was his day off—even at 95, he was seeing several patients a day.

• 6 •

WE WILL KNOW WHERE WE ARE WHEN WE GET THERE

JOSEPH L. HENDERSON AT 95

> What is going on in the unconscious is interesting to me, but it doesn't have the same sense of "becoming." I am much more filled with a sense of "being." Life does not surprise me as it used to. I think life is just the way it is, and I am the way I am …. It seems I have done enough exploration, and I am now more content with just being who I am.
>
> —Joseph L. Henderson

WORKING WITH JUNG

ROB HENDERSON (RH): Describe Jung as you knew him.

JOSEPH HENDERSON (JH): Well, when I knew Jung, he was in his early 50s. He was a very vigorous man and very tall. One of the things that doesn't show up in any of his photos that I know of is how tall he was. He had a very striking appearance and his energy was very apparent from the way he looked, the way he talked. One got the impression of a man who was more than ordinary in vitality and presence. People often said that he came across to them as a kind of Swiss peasant because of his size and his physical presence, but at the same time one knew that he was also a very intellectual and very spiritual man, so the combination of those two made him extraordinary.

RH: You had several years of analysis with Jung. As his patient, what kind of analyst would you say he was?

JH: A Jungian analyst—that is all I know. I can't describe him as anything else. I had other analysts, of course. I had Dr. Baynes and Dr.

Rosenbaum for short periods of time, and even Toni Wolff, his mistress and colleague. Jung's analysis is the only kind I know well. I can't compare it with anything else.

RH: How many times did you meet with Jung?

JH: The year I worked with him regularly, I met with him three times a week and in the spring term twice a week, and then I had one hour with Dr. Baynes, who was his assistant.

RH: Do you think Jung had any drawbacks as an analyst, and if so, what were they?

JH: Well, you see I have no criticism of him as an analyst because I was his patient and I took him as I found him, and if I had wanted to lie on the couch and talk about my early childhood, I would have missed what he was best gifted to give. At times, I did think it would be nice to have a comfortable analyst whom I could talk to freely about whatever came into my mind, and go to sleep if I felt like it and not have to relate to him. But you couldn't be in the same room with Jung without relating to him because he was a dynamo. He would stride back and forth, talking and gesticulating, except that every now and then he would sit down and become very personal and very direct, and that was all inspiring and sometimes difficult. [*Laughter*]

RH: If Jung were alive today, would you choose him if you were going to go to an analyst?

JH: Well, of course I would. [*Laughter*] No, that's a silly answer. There are plenty of people I enjoy talking to very much. He wouldn't be the only good analyst in the world for me.

JUNG'S PERSONAL LIFE

RH: How do you think Jung handled the tension of having both a wife and mistress?

JH: Remarkably well, considering the difficulties such a dual relationship is bound to have.

RH: Why do you think it has been so difficult for many people to understand and accept Jung's relationship with Toni Wolff?

JH: Many people have moralistic prejudices against such a relationship. But the people who knew this couple well all came to respect the special character of the relationship, as did Emma Jung herself.

RH: You have lived almost 96 years, and I am sure you have a lot of stories that you remember of Jung. List just a couple of them that bounce right out as you think of him today.

JH: Stories .... I will have to think about it a little while. I have many memories of him, but stories, I don't know. I just don't know where to begin.

RH: Well, maybe something will come to you as we go on. There are those who feel that Jung was just a crazy mystic who did very strange things. How do you react to that?

JH: Well, I have heard that said about him, but it has never been said directly to me. People have always been quite interested in anything I have to say about Jung. And if that question ever comes up, the answer is that from what I saw of him, his persona—his outward appearance— was very much that of a conventional Swiss bourgeois gentleman.

RH: I had the opportunity on two occasions to meet with Franz Jung [C.G. Jung's son] before he died and spent some time at Jung's house when I went to Zürich a couple of times. I often wondered, in talking to Franz, what it must have been like to be one of his children. Do you have any insight into that?

JH: Well, I think it must have been quite difficult for them. The girls apparently felt that he didn't give them much attention. He paid more attention to Franz, and they used to call him "Franzi's father." The girls themselves told me this—and Jung himself told me once that he felt he hadn't spent enough time helping his children with their education. But I don't think that was it at all. I think it was that he didn't have quite enough time to be an ordinary father to the girls. But he did with Franz because he thought it was extremely important for a man to have a good relationship with his father. In general, it is detrimental for children to have a parent who is a big personality or a genius.

RH: Earlier, you described Jung as a spiritual person. Did you get that impression when you first met him? Or, would anyone get a sense that this was a very spiritual kind of man on the first encounter?

JH: Well, not when you first met him, no. He was full of humor and jokes and had an enormous laugh that filled the whole house. He was a very animal man. He was not a spiritual man in the sense that you would ordinarily think of spirituality. There was nothing mystical or pious about him at all.

RH: Did you go to Jung's funeral?

JH: No. My wife was there since she had been doing some work with von Franz. She called me up and told me of his death, and I gave a little talk on the radio about him, but I never thought of going over there to attend the funeral.

RH: What did your wife have to say about the funeral?

JH: She found it very dull. I think this was true for all the people from outside of Switzerland. For the people immediately around Jung, it was probably quite meaningful, but it was very conventional and the speeches were not at all on the level that Jung himself represented.

JUNG AND JOHN FREEMAN

RH: We all know that when Jung was asked if he believed in God he said that he didn't have to believe in God, that he knew God. I have asked every single person that I have interviewed what they thought he meant by that, and I would be interested to hear your reaction.

JH: Well, my reaction is that Jung's statement should be understood entirely in the context of that film interview with John Freeman. Jung was very suspicious of Freeman because Freeman had a reputation for tricking his subjects into telling him things that they didn't want to reveal. So Jung was quite guarded as Freeman tried to get him to talk about himself and Freud, for instance. The letters between him and Freud had just come out and

Freeman thought it would be interesting if Jung would talk about them, but all Jung would say was "No, no interest, no interest whatsoever." He was not going to allow Freeman to trick him into talking about himself and Freud because that would open up a great turbulent discussion, such as had been going on for years, and Jung thought it was unprofitable to keep talking about it.

So when Freeman started talking about religion, Jung felt he had to put his answers in terms that Freeman would understand from a very materialistic point of view. Freeman had interviewed a number of other famous people—the series was called "Face to Face"—and Jung was one of them. Freeman wanted Jung to reveal himself in a personal way, and so he brought up the question of religion and asked if Jung had faith. Somewhat on the defensive in reaction to Freeman's approach, Jung said no, he didn't need faith because his own experience of religion was not based on faith, it was immediate. That is all he meant.

RH: That is good. I had never heard that before. You need to understand the interviewer in order to understand why Jung said it that way.

JH: Exactly. Freeman interviewed a number of other people and in each case he tried to get the person to reveal things that they couldn't possibly discuss in a venue like that. For example, he asked Edith Sitwell, the poet, why she never married, and she replied, "That's none of your business, young man." It took a rather strong person to stand up to this guy. He was later appointed as Britain's Ambassador to the United States, but before that he had served as editor of the *New Statesman* and *Nation*. Jung rather liked him, actually, because he was completely outside of Jung's world. Freeman had almost no knowledge of Jung's psychology, but he was interested in Jung. And so, when Jung agreed to collaborate with other Jungian analysts on a book—which came to be published under the title *Man and his Symbols*—he asked Freeman to be present at the discussions between the contributors and publishers prior to the publication of the volume.

Jung asked if I would write one of the chapters, and so I, along with the other contributors, was requested to meet with Jung at his house in Kusnacht in September of 1960. There was some uncertainty about whether the meeting would take place or not, since Jung had been ill—

in fact, he had to be brought back from his vacation in an ambulance—and so we didn't know whether the book deal would come through or not. Jung said, "Anyway, perhaps you all will be writing it and I won't have much to do with it." But he wanted John Freeman to be there to act as a sort of bridge between the writers and the publishers. The representative from Doubleday and other people were there.

We sat down at a table in Jung's living room and talked, and Jung sat upstairs in his study and didn't come down at all, but he was concerned about whether we would be able to come to an agreement without fighting. Of course, there was no question about it—we all got along perfectly well, and von Franz was there as a kind of mediator along with John Freeman. Well, John Freeman was then chosen to write the introduction to the book—and this was a very good idea, since it was written by someone completely outside of the Jungian world. It was his insightful impressions as a layman of Jung and Jungians that made the book such a popular success.

RH: Speaking of that book, how did you feel when you were asked to write one of the chapters? Did that feel like an honor?

JH: Well, yes, of course it was an honor. I was very happy to have him choose me to write a chapter, but it was also rather difficult. For one thing, there was quite a bit of expense involved. I had to take time off from my practice to go over there and be present at that meeting with the publishers. As contributors, we were paid only about $2,000, which was not a great deal, considering that I lost income while I was away from my practice and there were traveling costs—so it was not the easiest thing in the world to do. As soon as I got down to writing the chapter, however, I was very happy, since the project gave me an opportunity to formulate my ideas more clearly and to do something for Jung at the same time.

RH: Why do you think Jung chose you out of all the people he could have chosen to write one of the chapters?

JH: Well, according to Freeman, Jung felt I was one of his followers that he could trust more than all the others.

RH: Why do you feel Jung trusted you?

JH: We had known each other for a long time and had many friends in common.

THE CULTURAL UNCONSCIOUS

RH: You have written about the cultural layer of the unconscious, which I have always found very interesting. Can you just briefly share with us what its origin and function is?

JH: Well, I wrote a paper about it, which was published in the *Journal of Analytical Psychology*, and so my answer is in that paper. I talked about it originally in a lecture I gave at the International Congress in London in the 70's or early 80's. There was very little discussion. Nobody showed the slightest interest in my idea that there is a cultural unconscious as well as a collective unconscious. So I thought, "Well, that's okay. Nobody is interested in it, but that doesn't matter. I don't have to please everybody." But I went on exploring that area because I felt that it was inherent in Jung's own work that there was a cultural unconscious as well as a collective unconscious.

Now, the cultural unconscious has been accepted to a large extent. However, there are certain statements that Jung made, which I quoted in my paper, that show that he really understood that there is a cultural unconscious—and very clearly. But nobody that I knew at that time paid any attention to it. It was all collective unconscious or personal unconscious—but I felt that there are three areas: the personal, the cultural, and the collective, and they are not the same, although they can and do interact. It became clear to me, in my work with patients, that when I was interpreting dreams, I was interpreting the personal conscious and the collective unconscious, but sometimes what seemed to be the personal unconscious was really the cultural. As for instance, when a child or young person is learning and there is a parental feeling about the teacher, the reaction is not personal alone. It is also cultural, because that person who is the teacher has a cultural orientation, which comes forward, so even on the personal level, there is also a cultural aspect.

Many of the things that Jung described as personal were really cultural. I am trying to think of a good example. Take the difference between a child whose parent has a well-defined religious attitude and another child whose parent does not. The child of the religious parent would sense the parent's religious orientation. The child may not necessarily be lectured about it, but he or she will develop the attitude that religion is a vital thing. It comes from the parent. The child knows how that feels because of how it is with the parent. Maybe the parent— or the teacher—is an artist, or has an aesthetic attitude. That attitude can come through to the child quite easily. And this is true of social attitude too, as some parents are so politically minded that they can't think of anything else, and the child or young person is affected by that whether the parent says anything about it or not.

Besides the cultural unconscious, I have tried to define four cultural attitudes: the religious attitude, the aesthetic attitude, the philosophic attitude, and the social attitude. I wrote a paper about it, which has also been published in my collected papers, *Shadow and Self.* In the paper, I tried to show that I got this idea from all the people who attended Jung's seminars. When I looked around at the members attending the seminars, I would realize that here one of them had a religious attitude, and one of them had an aesthetic attitude, another one had a social attitude, and yet another had a philosophical attitude—and there they all were, sitting together in the same room. I realized that that's what society is made up of. It doesn't mean that the religious attitude is formally a religious attitude, or that the person with the aesthetic attitude is an artist, or that the one with the philosophic attitude is a professional philosopher, or that the one with the social attitude is somebody in politics—not at all. It was not based on what they do, but on their attitude. In my discussion of the attitudes, I also spoke of the possible "psychological" attitude, which is new in our times, and I felt I saw it well represented in Zürich at the Jung Seminars.

CULTURE AND SEX

RH: Speaking about culture, how do you feel our culture has been impacted by Jung's ideas?

JH: Well, I don't feel I can really answer that question because the term culture is too general. I have no idea how Jung affected culture in general. I only know how he affected certain aspects of it. Certainly, he has had an enormous impact in the psychotherapeutic world and in the world of psychiatry. One could almost say that psychiatry has not been the same since Jung, maybe because of what he brought to it in the way of understanding—and that is also true for psychology. He was one of the major psychologists of his century. So I think of him as having had a big impact on that aspect of our culture. But, of course, there are many people who are not interested in that because they have a different orientation. In general, I think Jung's psychology went through various stages of acceptance. At first, certain people were fascinated by him and others thought he was a crazy misfit. And some felt he was just a bad boy, and Freud was the father. Then gradually, as he became better known, people began to make him into a kind of saint, or whatever they wanted him to be. He had some kind of magic and would often be a magician. In fact, he told me that some English psychologists once came to see him and wanted to work with him, and after a while he said they couldn't continue because the English psychologist wouldn't do magic.

RH: Again, a little bit on modern culture. All the recent stuff with President Clinton revealed—at least to me—that we are still hung up on sex. Do you feel our culture—maybe it is our society more than our culture—but do you think we are still hung up on sex?

JH: Well, on the surface Clinton is an example of what Jung called the *puer aeternus*, the young man who feels he is especially entitled to have whatever he desires, preferably with a mother behind him who makes sure he gets everything he desires. This attitude may lead in one of two directions. If it leads in one direction, the young man become a homosexual; if it leads in the other, he becomes a Don Juan. It seems as though Clinton went in the direction of the Don Juan, the one who can't resist any opportunity for seduction. Such a man is not nearly as interested in the sex as he is in the act of seduction. That is the characteristic of the Don Juan. It is what gets him into so much trouble.

Mozart's opera, *Don Giovanni*, contains the perfect representation of the Don Juan type, because it portrays Don Juan as a fascinating seducer who drops every woman as soon as he gets her and goes after another one. The women who have been dropped—and their followers and their friends—find this so terrible that they all band together to denounce him and tell him how awful his actions are and what an offense he is to society and so on. But this doesn't affect the Don Juan type one bit. After listening to all their tirades about how awful he is, Don Giovanni goes right on just the same as he did before, seducing Zerlina, the servant girl, or whoever happens to be around. Don Giovanni sings a beautiful aria when Zerlina first encounters him. She is just a servant girl, but he tells her in the aria that he intends to treat her with all the honor and respect he would give to a princess, and thus the audience is given to understand how utterly impossible it is for women to resist him. Early on, he kills the father of one of the women he seduced. This man was the Commendatore and he was well known, so there is a statue of him in the garden. In the final act of the opera, the statue of the Commendatore comes to life and comes down off its pedestal to denounce Don Giovanni, and Don Giovanni says, "Well, what have I done?" He still doesn't get the point, so he is sent down to hell. I wouldn't dream of suggesting that this is an exact description of Clinton in every detail, but I would only say that it expresses something of his personal complex and also the overly judgmental attitude of the people who condemn his actions.

On the Snake Dance

RH: I noticed in looking through some of the things that you have written that fairly early on in your career you went to the Hopi Indian Reservation and you wrote something on the snake dance. Did I get that correct?

JH: Well, I did a little paper on the snake dance ceremony, but I don't even know where it is. I haven't seen it for years. It was while I was in analysis with Jung. I was studying medicine in England, and my father was ill and probably close to death, and so I needed to see him for the last time before he died. I came out and spent some time with him, but he got much better during that time, so I was able to leave and go down to the Southwest, where a group of friends had asked me to come with them to attend some of the Pueblo Indian ceremonies. We attended a Zuni ceremony and then we went to the Hopi Snake Dance. I was very fascinated by the Indians and by the wonderful religious content of this ceremony, so when I went back to London, I gave a talk about it to a small group of Jungian analysts that met in London once a month.

RH: Do you have any impressions of the ceremony? You actually saw the snake dance. It must have been very impressive.

JH: Yes, many impressions. You see, the ritual and the myth go side by side. The myth tells of a youth called Tiyo who goes out in a hollowed-out log canoe on the Colorado River through the Grand Canyon and down to the sea, "wondering where all the water went," he said. And when he got down there, he found a beautiful woman who seduced him, and he had a wonderful time with her through the night, but when he woke up the next morning she was an old hag, and he couldn't stand her. Also, he was afraid, because she was the wife of the sun. The sun would come down and kill him if he found him there. So he got away as fast as he could. Then Spider Woman, a little spider who sat behind his ear, said, "You must go to the snake people, and when you get there, you must pick up one of the snakes, and don't be afraid." He was afraid, but he picked up a snake anyway, and it turned into the Snake Maiden, Tcuahana, whom he married. She became the mother of the Snake Clan—so their ancestors were snakes.

The members of the present day Snake Clan all have this ceremony in remembrance of the ancestors. The snake dance is a way of communicating with the ancestors. The clanspeople talk to the snakes and are very careful not to hurt them because they are their ancestors. It is as though they have been taken over by the snake archetype. They become quite beside themselves in a kind of trance-like state, and they are helped along by members of the Antelope Clan, who tend to them while they perform the dance. The most difficult part of the ceremony is the part where they dance with the snakes in their mouths. The dancers hold a snake in their mouth and the Antelope priest holds his arm around their shoulders and deflects the head of the snake with a feather. Sometimes, they get bitten, but very seldom. It is very impressive, because it makes you realize the extent to which these men are in the power of the archetype. That would have been something that Jung would have understood completely as an activity at a deep level of the collective unconscious. The snake would stand for the collective unconscious. The ceremony helps the dancers to relate to the collective unconscious without being devoured by it.

RH: That is very powerful. That's a nice way of saying it. I've never heard it said quite that way. What is your view on medication and how it is being used today in psychotherapy?

125

JH: I prescribe medication sparingly. In cases involving borderline states or psychosis, I refer the patient to a psychopharmacologist.

On Jo Wheelwright

RH: You may or may not be aware—your daughter was aware—that we interviewed the Wheelwrights. We had a simply wonderful time. They both spoke very highly of you and your relationship with Jung.

JH: He [Jo Wheelwright] died, you know.

RH: I was aware of that, and I was going to ask you how you felt about it—about Jo's death, I mean—and how you'd describe Jo Wheelwright and what he meant to the Jungian community.

JH: Well, Jo and I met in London. We went to the same medical school, and during those years I married an Englishwoman, and he and Jane lived there with their children, and so we were friends from that time on. Then, of course, we ended up in San Francisco. I stayed in New York for two years after I left England. Jo then came straight to San Francisco and did his internship at the City and County Hospital. Then I came along, and we formed a group of people that had been in analysis with Jung. We called it the Analytical Psychology Club. We didn't aspire to become a professional society to begin with. There was, however, one Jungian analyst here, Dr. Elizabeth Whitney, who had been my first analyst, before I went to Jung.

At that time—1927—there were no Freudians at all in San Francisco, and no other analysts of any kind. So my experience—and I think Jo's also—was that we came to Jung without any preliminary indoctrination by anybody else. So we were "natural" Jungians, so to speak, and all the talk about the difference between Freud and Jung fell flat with us because we had no interest in Freud. We found what we needed with Jung, and didn't bother with Freud any more than Jung did after he parted ways with him. We, of course, always recognized the importance of Freud as a historical figure and as the founder of psychoanalysis, but the founder of psychoanalysis was not the founder of Jungian psychology.

Jung's psychology came out of Jung and not out of his contact with Freud. That is a fact that is not generally known. Most people today talk about it as if first there was Freud and then there was Jung, as if there wouldn't have been any Jung if there hadn't been Freud. That is perfect nonsense, as is very well demonstrated by Sonu Shamdasani, a Jungian writer in London, who gave a seminar here just this last week in which he makes that point—that Jung was never originally a Freudian. Jung was a psychiatrist who was inspired by Pierre Janet, the French psychiatrist, and William James, the American psychologist, and by others outside of Freud's circle. This is not generally known. So Jung would have been a psychologist and a psychotherapist whether Freud existed or not. Jo and I both agreed on this, especially having known Jung as we did. He was, after all, our teacher and something of a father figure. I think he was more of a father figure for Jo than for me—I already had too many fathers.

RH: What did your relationship with Jo mean to you?

JH: We had a lot in common. I liked the quality of his lifestyle and his interest in French literature, which was also an interest of mine. We were both of the same vintage, you might say, in our college years. He was at Harvard and I was at Princeton, and we had many friends in common. We also had the experience of Zürich, and one of the things we thought might be nice to have was a society that would be more homogeneous than the Zürich group. There were a lot of things going on in Zürich that were rather disruptive and somewhat constricting, and we hoped we could form a somewhat different kind of society, where there wouldn't be so much shadow projection going on.

RH: Jo was quite a character, wasn't he?

JH: Well, he was a very extraverted man and I'm an introvert, so we had to deal with the things that go with that difference, such as the difficulty in understanding each other, but there was also the attraction of the opposites. We both felt that it was very important that if we had differences, we should work them out and not just project them. He understood that so well that it made it easier for me to be myself and not feel like I had to be an extravert, which I couldn't be anyway. Dr. Baynes in England and Jo were both extremely extraverted feeling-type men, and this is very unusual in psychological circles, but they both had a strong influence because of that.

RH: You refer to yourself as introverted. What are some of the things about you that are indications of your introversion?

JH: I enjoy a good party, but I am always looking forward to coming home and being by myself.

RH: What are some ways you have learned to deal in an extraverted society as an introvert?

JH: Living in Europe as long as I did truly convinced me that an introverted way of life could be considered normal. As a boy growing up in a country town, I suffered greatly from feeling that my introversion was abnormal. Now I can live in the U.S. much more comfortably, even in the midst of our extraverted urban lifestyles.

RH: Of all the things you have written, which—at this point in life—do you feel best about?

JH: Well, the one on initiation. That was my basic thesis, and the thing that I feel that I am best known for. I spent ten years learning how to write that damn book!

RH: What was so difficult about writing that book?

JH: Writing has never been difficult for me—I was a journalist before I got into psychology. My difficulty in writing that book was with myself. I had to confront my deepest weaknesses and let my talent mature.

DREAMS

RH: I remember asking Dr. Guggenbühl, when I spoke with him, how he stayed in touch with the unconscious, and he said the unconsciousness just kept trying to stay in touch with him. Can you share with us a little bit about how you do that and have done that over the years—staying in touch with the unconscious and working with your own dreams, or what your practices have been in working with your dreams?

JH: I learned in Zürich to interpret my own dreams. I learned especially one summer when I was in great doubt as to whether I should continue with my medical career. I failed an examination in pre-medical science. I had to take pre-medical science because I hadn't studied that at college—this was at the University of London. Well, I failed my exam. I had an archetypal dream that seemed to indicate that maybe I was barking up the wrong tree—I shouldn't be a doctor at all. I dreamt that an eagle came down and killed a beautiful white horse that was running along the shore of a dark sea, and the next day I failed the examination. I saw the white horse as my natural self and the eagle as intellectualism coming down from above trying to make me a scientist. The eagle represented for me the danger of pure science. But the next night I had another dream in which I saw a round, black fish on the bottom of the sea with a vulnerable spot on its back, and a snake with a red head came up and bit the fish and did away with it. That was a good thing in the dream. Presumably, the bottom of the sea represented a deeper level of the unconscious, the opposite of the eagle from above. In other words, if I could get to a deeper, more essential level of the unconscious, I would be able to balance the two things—the eagle and the horse of the first dream.

I wanted to talk to Jung about it, but Jung was off for the summer. There was nobody analyzing in Zürich that summer, and I managed to see Jung for only one or two hours before he went off. So I sat down in my hotel room and figured out what I was going to do—decide whether to go on with my medical work or not. I started writing down my dreams, and I found that my dreams were telling me exactly the same things that my analysts would be telling me if they had been there. In addition to that, I made a painting, which summed it all up as a kind of mandala. That took me three weeks. I talked about my dreams a bit with a friend, and then I saw Jung again when he came back from his vacation, and by that time I had somehow decided that I should go ahead. It was the dreams and the ability to interpret my own dreams and the painting that completely changed me and made me feel that I could go ahead with the work.

RH: Have you, over the years, kept dream journals and written your dreams down every day?

JH: Oh, not every day. I write for short periods of time nearly every day, and then I don't write for two or three months. I don't keep a daily record, but I remember my dreams every day, because I always have a great many dreams. But I couldn't possibly write them all down. I write down what seem to be the most important ones.

RH: You have many dreams all on one day? How many? Four or five?

JH: Yes—well, more like two or three that I remember. I have difficulty understanding my dreams, like anybody else. We will have trouble with dreams unless we sit down and write out our associations.

RH: One author claims that dreams are God's Forgotten Language. Do you feel dreams come from God and that He is the Dream-maker in our lives?

JH: I don't know where dreams come from other than that they are spontaneous products of the psyche.

AGING, DEATH, AND THE AFTERLIFE

RH: Why are you still seeing patients at this point in your life?

JH: I still enjoy my work and I like getting to know new people.

RH: What does it feel like for you to be this old and living in our society?

JH: It feels fine.

RH: At the age of almost 96, how do you view death now? What do you feel happens at death?

JH: I am very interested to find out. [*Laughter*] I have no idea what it is like. I mean, I do have many ideas, but I don't think any of them are even close to what it will really be like. I feel most comfortable with the idea that I won't know until I get there. It is like the Navajo painting, "Where the Two Came to the Father." It is a depiction of the story of twin brothers and their initiation. Leaving their mother, Changing Woman, they seek the pollen path, which will lead them to their father, the Sun, who provides them with weapons to kill the monsters of fear and inertia. On the way, they encounter many obstacles, but then they receive encouragement from a benevolent goddess, Spider Woman. They take heart and, reaching the pollen path, they say, "We will know where we are when we get there!" This is what I feel about initiation or any rituals that are concerned with the archetypal pattern of death and rebirth.

RH: If I were to put a title to this interview, would that be a pretty good title—"We Will Know Where We Are When We Get There"?

JH: Yes, that would be fine.

RH: Do you believe in life after death?

JH: Well, I have always felt that there was something beyond death. I have never thought of death as a total end. To me, that is a materialistic way of thinking about life and death. There are plenty of materialists around who do think that there is nothing more to life than eating and sleeping and death is the end. That doesn't feel natural to me, but I don't have any idea what another life in another lifetime would be like. I feel better if I don't try to imagine what it will be like.

RH: After my father died about 30 years ago, one of the things I was really moved by was how he has returned several times to my life in my dreams. Your wife, Helena, died three years ago. I was wondering if you have learned anything particularly about death as a result of her death and from dealing with her loss?

JH: Well, I felt simply that she went on her way. She was in a convalescent hospital for the last 5 years of her life, and so her death was a release for her and also for me. Although I went to see her every day and she came home on the weekends, she didn't really have a full life from the time that she went into the hospital. It was, you might say, a case of terminal depression. She was always so very affirmative about our relationship, and the last thing that she said to me was, "I love you." After her death, I saw her in her long white dress, the kind she used to wear when she danced or read poetry on this deck here. She was a dancer and a poet, and she used to dance when she read poetry, and she would wear a long, Grecian-type dress. So in my dream I saw her in that dress, walking out of the convalescent hospital. She had a very beautiful walk—and so she just went on her way. I dream about her quite often. My life and of course my feelings are always centered around her, and she comes up in my dreams quite a lot.

RH: So she still is very much alive for you?

JH: Yes, but she is also very far away. She is not in my life any more. I don't think about her every day or anything like that, but every now and then the thought of her comes up, and I am always glad when I feel a pang of grief, because it makes me feel closer to her. There is a picture of her over there on the wall taken while she was doing English folk dances. She was trained as a ballet dancer in London, and that little picture there is a prize that she got for one of her dances called "Country Mirth," and that little thing on the left is an example of the programs that we gave every summer. The people came and sat on the lawn, and the dances were performed on the deck out here and this was the dressing room, and that larger picture is of an opera ballet of [Gian-Carlo] Menotti called *The Unicorn, the Gorgon and the Manticore.*

RH: There are a lot of people who would say that Jung has been helpful to them in middle life. I suppose we could say that this is the third part of life for you, rather than middle life. Have you found Jung's ideas in any particular way helpful in this phase of your life?

JH: Well, in this phase of my life, the ideas of Jung have become so much a part of me that I wouldn't think of them as being helpful or not helpful, since they are just a part of me. But certainly I think of him as the psychologist of the second half of life. And I began my own analysis with him when he was entering into the second half of his life. I was only 26. To be with a man who was in the second half of life and who accepted it and could live as he did was a great inspiration to me. It was a great introduction to life, and I didn't feel he was strange or frightening being that much older than me and closer to death, since his attitude was so positive. He was saying to me one day, "Do you know I have to think about death every day?"... and I thought, "Wow!" [*Laughter*]

RH: Do you feel you are in the third part of life?

JH: I think I am in the fourth! [*Laughter*]

RH: Have you found any of Jung's ideas helpful in the fourth part of life, then?

JH: Well, yes. I think what is helpful to me is to feel that I am less and less dependent on the contents of the unconscious. What is going on in the unconscious is interesting to me, but it doesn't have the same sense of "becoming." I am much more filled with a sense of "being." Life does not surprise me as it used to. I think life is just the way it is, and I am the way I am, and I don't need to keep telling myself that if I worked harder I would know more or be more spiritually enlightened or something like that. It seems I have done enough exploration, and I am now more content with just being who I am.

RH: In terms of your own individuation, looking back at your life now, what have been some of the most important times?

JH: Well, I just told you one—realizing that I could work with myself towards a better understanding of who I am and what I was meant to do. And presumably out of that came the idea that I was meant to be a doctor and an analyst. But apart from that, I would say that the development of my cultural attitudes has been the other big thing in my life, besides the initiation archetype and the feeling that I am going through the death and rebirth experience of analysis on the one hand, and then understanding the importance of a viable relation to the culture on the other.

RH: Talking with you has been a fascinating experience. Having read most of what you have written, I can safely say that I never really got a sense of who you are from reading your writings, but I certainly got that sense today from talking with you. Do you feel that people don't really know who you are, even though you are so well known in the Jungian community?

JH: Oh sure, they don't. How could they? People always say really nice things to me, if they know me, and many of them who have read my books feel they know something about me, so it is a question of whether the person they think they know is a projection or whether it is really me. So I am always glad to see them and to let them see who I am, so they don't have to bother with projections.

RH: If you were to meet Jung after you die, and he inquired as to what had gone on in Jungian psychology after his death, what are some of the things you would tell him?

JH: I would say that I wish he could have lived long enough to see the end of the Cold War. I think it would have given him new hope for the future of his influence in Europe, especially, but also around the world in general. The present advances in communications technology have brought his psychology to public awareness to an extent undreamed of before, and I think Jung would be glad to know that.

RH: How would you like to be remembered in the Jungian community?

JH: Well, as somebody who enjoyed being with people. I really do enjoy people, and I would hope that the Jungian community remembers some of the work I have done with people to make living with themselves enjoyable in many different ways—I don't mean in silly ways (though even they have their place). I will be satisfied if people remember me as someone who didn't take psychology too seriously, as someone who, through psychology, found many reasons to be joyful.

I am deeply obliged to you for having remembered my fateful 80th birthday. I am glad at last that I have been able (though not through my merit) to spare my wife what follows on the loss of a lifelong partner—the silence that has no answer. [Letter to Laurens van der Post, February 28, 1956, *C. G. Jung Letters, Vol. 2: 1951-1961*, Princeton University Press, 1976, p. 292.]

—C. G. Jung

Dear Professor Freud,
I accede to your wish that we abandon our personal relations, for I never thrust my friendship on anyone. You yourself are the best judge of what this moment means to you. "The rest is silence." [Letter to Freud, January 6, 1913, *The Freud-Jung Letters*, p. 540.]

—C. G. Jung

RUSSELL ARTHUR LOCKHART, PH.D.

Russell Arthur Lockhart obtained his bachelor's degree from the University of Southern California (USC) and his master's and doctorate degrees, both in human psychophysiology, from USC as well. In 1974, he graduated from the C. G. Jung Institute of Los Angeles, where he served as Director of Analyst Training from 1979 to 1982. Since 1974, he has been in private practice. He has served on the faculties at the University of California in Santa Barbara and in Berkeley. He was a research psychologist at the University of California, Los Angeles, and Director of the Psychophysiological Research Laboratory at Camarillo State Hospital. He is the author of *Words as Eggs: Psyche in Language and Clinic* (Spring Publications, 1983); *Psyche Speaks: A Jungian Approach to Self* (Chiron, 1987), and *Secrets of the Undergroundtrader,* with Jea Yu (McGraw-Hill, 2003). Currently, he has two books in progress: *Gleanings From the Dreamfield* and *Hints & Helps for Short-Term Traders.* Born and raised in Los Angeles, he and his wife Frankie have been married 44 years and have four children. My first contact with Russell occurred in 1973, when he shared with me his work with cancer patients. We met again in 1982, when he presented the inaugural series of The C. G. Jung Lectures at the C. G. Jung Foundation of New York. Since that meeting, he and I have maintained an online correspondence, which evolved into the following interview.

LISTEN TO THE DREAMS

RUSSELL ARTHUR LOCKHART AT 65

> I have learned that dreams are sensitive to wayward organic processes in the body long before anything appears in the clinical picture. But not necessarily. Dreams can ignore as well as attend, and this is an intriguing issue to me—this difference.
>
> —Russell Arthur Lockhart

ENCOUNTER WITH JUNG

ROB HENDERSON (RH): How did you get interested in Jung?

RUSSELL LOCKHART (RL): I first encountered Jung in a box of Communist books lent to me by a neighbor in 1951, shortly after my thirteenth birthday. I was quite the young Trotskyite at the time, and this neighbor—a man who seemed to spend most of his time in his underwear (which is what I thought a Communist *was* when I was younger)—took on the role of my mentor in "revolutionary" ideas. In that box, I found Jung's *Modern Man in Search of a Soul.* How it got there I can't begin to imagine, but I was a dutiful "mentee" then, as well as a very hungry reader as now, and devoured this book at about the same time as I read Salinger's *The Catcher in the Rye.* I didn't know what to make of Jung at all, but the book struck a strange chord, to be sure, as evidenced by the fact that while I was always returning the Communist stuff, I never did return the Jung book. So I guess one might say a bit of "Hermes' thievery" set me on the Jungian way, even if I did not know it at the time. Perhaps some of my "adversaries" will find this "explanatory."

But the more self-conscious journey began with a dream—a nightmare, really. It was in the spring of 1963. I was twenty-four, sailing through my experimental psychology doctoral program. I was a "golden boy," who had no troubles, a wonderful wife, a rambunctious two-year old, and a new little one. I had already done my research, I had talked about it at meetings around the country, I had university job offers in hand. All that was left for me to do now was finish writing my dissertation.

I hadn't ever been *stopped* much from doing what I wanted to do—except before college, when I had to abandon a tennis career because of calcification in my arm, or a bit later, when one day in my junior year, I inexplicably woke up and *knew* I had to change from medicine to something else, and chose experimental psychology without the least idea why. But try as I might, I could not get going on my dissertation. Every time I would sit down to write, I would get sick, nauseous, cold, and—worst of all—*fearful*. The fact that Lockhart was having *problems* was a source of considerable jesting on the part of my friends and colleagues. But after battling this inability to write for some months, I realized that it was no laughing matter to me. I decided I needed some time out, and so I resolved to take a leave.

The night before I was to communicate this to my chairman, I experienced one of those life-altering dreams. In this dream, I was in a desert area. On the horizon, I could make out the outline of the buildings of my university (USC-University of Southern California). Suddenly, from the left, an enormous wave rose up and came crashing toward me. It had the look of one of those Japanese prints with finger-like waves reaching out. Just before it hit me, the whole scene went into stop-motion. I was still in this image as I woke up, climbed out of bed, and began pacing up and down. I couldn't get out of the dream and my terror escalated dramatically. My wife Frankie woke up and saw me as white as a sheet. Finally, the image faded, but I continued, frozen in fear. It was just after three in the morning. Frankie called her analyst and reported my condition. He called a colleague and arranged an appointment for me a few hours later. And that's how I ended up at what J. Marvin Spiegleman has called his analytic "cave."

How I loved that office! And that man! Like a first love, there's never anything quite like one's *first* analyst. Despite Marvin's constant references to working with me being like "pulling teeth" (after all, I was a terribly skeptical "scientist" at the time), it took only six months of teeth pulling to transform that threatening wave into a surge of creative energy that not only broke through my writing block, but connected me to a long-lost artistic side buried since early childhood. *But more than that!* Marvin led me to the *reality of the psyche*, which has been at the center of my life and work ever since. For that I can never thank him enough. And he taught me as well what a burden this can be, for it was this very thing that produced a break between us—the bursting of a world. Only many years later did I realize that I had also learned from Marvin that it is not a question of "fault." It is a question of "fate." That, in brief, is how I came to Jung.

ON BEING A JUNGIAN

RH: How did you decide to become a Jungian analyst?

RL: I had been in my personal analysis for some years and had made the transition from working with Marvin Spiegleman to working with Hilde Kirsch. Becoming an analyst had never crossed my mind. At the time, I was teaching and doing research at the University of California, Santa Barbara. At one point, I went to one of those weekend conferences, at which one of the speakers happened to be Harold Stone. During one of the breaks, quite unexpectedly he said to me, "Russ, why don't you become an analyst?" It was one of those remarks that seemed as if I had been preparing for it without knowing it—the feeling of "rightness" about it, the sense of "timeliness" about it. I got pretty excited about the idea over the next few days. Then I had my appointment with Hilde. I said, "Hilde, I've decided to apply for the analyst training program." She looked at me for the longest time with those "owl" eyes of hers, and finally said, "Don't be stupid!"

Well, this took all the wind out of my sails, and the whole idea seemed to collapse. At that point, I did feel pretty stupid—and of course there was no end of chatter from the witchy anima chorus about "who do you think you are?", "what makes you think you have the stuff?", "what an inflation," and the whole show. And, of course, at that point there was nothing to it except that thread that Hal [Harold Stone] had thrown out and on which I had eagerly started to climb into the air. Not much ground there, nor attached to anything either!

Only then did I start to have a series of dreams, which clearly suggested that the path of analyst would draw forth from me aspects that would otherwise "fly away with the wind." So, after a time, I told Hilde the dreams and why I thought they supported, not my ego investment (which wasn't all that deep in any event at that time), but the possibility of developing something in me that would otherwise be lost forever. Again: a long silence, her owl eyes penetrating me sharply; finally, a slight "nod," even a trace of a smile. I was on my way! That woman could be so *numinous* at times.

I have to say that my formal training as an analyst had little, if anything, to do with the sort of analyst I became. Most of the essential experiences that *made* me an analyst occurred elsewhere. One of the most important of these was a many-years-long seminar on Jung's then-unpublished *Zarathustra* seminars. Sometimes weeks were spent on mining the depth of a single line. The psychic intensity of these weekly sessions was what *cooked* me into being an analyst—what catalyzed my real development as an analyst. It was nothing less than an alchemical process—a direct transmutation by the manifested intentionality of something "other." These experiences certainly colored my attitudes about the *training* of analysts and played a huge part in what I tried to accomplish in the training of others. I will always value this "cooking," just as I will always regret that I was not successful in ensuring its perpetuation in the world of Jungian training.

It is not difficult to experience the palpability of the *other* I refer to. For example, in a small group, simply go round and round in a circle doing nothing more than speaking aloud an image from a dream—no interpretation, no analysis, no associations—just the image. The image will call forth another dream image from someone else, now spoken aloud in turn. Round and round this way. After a time, because as I was told in a dream, "a dream wants a dream, a poem wants a poem," one begins to feel the manifesting presence of something "other." This "other" is the result of the images as "energy vectors" forming first a sense of spatial enclosure, then a sense of incarnational presence. This, I believe, is the "being" quality of the *imagination* that Blake described—here experienced in a small community. What it begins to bring forth is of course unpredictable; most certainly, its implications cannot be reduced to past knowings. The reason, I believe, is that it has much more to do with the *future* than with the past.

RH: How would you describe yourself as a Jungian?

RL: There are two questions here, so I'll respond to the obvious one first: What sort of Jungian am I? What this question calls to mind is a meeting many years ago in my home office. There was Murray Stein, Linda Leonard, and several others. Murray had gathered this bunch together to plot out the book he wanted to bring out, an *American* version of Jungian analysis and the Jungian analyst. In a fit of hubris, I volunteered to do the chapter that would be called "The Jungian Analyst." It was something I thought I had a lot of passion for and ideas about. I had been Director of Analyst Training for some time at that point and felt eager to try to say something useful on this difficult question. Well, I worked and worked on that chapter. I wrote at least a hundred pages! I finally ended up in total frustration and threw it all in the fireplace and watched it burn. And then I told Murray he would have to find someone else to do it. Tom Kirsch came to the rescue.

Quite early on in my first years of analysis, even before I was much aware that there were *Jungians* as such, Jung had become a reality in my experience, in dreams, in visions, and in the sense of the living "presence" I felt in his writings. While I have had many Jungian teachers, it is this "interior" Jung who has been my mentor, and it is this Jung to whom I feel something like "allegiance." Nothing in my training as an analyst, nor anything in my many years in and out of various Jungian collectives, professional or otherwise, has ever supplanted or altered this central fact of my experience.

Let me tell you a dream to illustrate what I mean. Not long after I became an analyst, I fell into a period of fairly deep disillusionment with what I had experienced of the professional world of *being* a Jungian analyst. The disparity between what I had experienced as realities in my analysis (most particularly with Hilde Kirsch, James Kirsch, and Max Zeller) and what I was experiencing in the "outer" world of *being* a Jungian analyst, among other analysts, was so large as to be nearly intolerable. Of course, I knew consciously that this disparity was entirely to be expected—it was nothing unusual—and my expectations of anything different were based on idealizations that could not possibly be realized in the real world of people functioning in the way institutions and collectives have to function. I *knew* that. That was obvious.

Still, it bothered me so much that I began to experience a strange awareness that I really did not "belong" in this "Jungian" world. The dreams that I was having seemed to support this, but in my analysis these dreams were taken as injunctions to remove all remaining idealizations and projections of *Self* onto Jungian collectives. To help you appreciate fully this developing feeling of "not-belongingness," I have to tell you an early childhood dream, one of those repeating dreams that so often forms a leitmotif of one's fate. In this dream, I would be walking down the street and looking at each house in turn. *Every* house looked like my actual childhood house at the time. Every time I would go into one of the houses, I would hope fervently that *this* would be the one, that this would be *my* house. But in all those dreams across the many years of childhood from about the age of 3 until I was about 8, I *never* found my home.

So, naturally, I expected to find my home in the Jungian world, just as I had expected to find it in tennis, and in medicine. And I was beginning to have forebodings that this too was not my home. At a certain point, I had a series of three dreams that very plainly indicated that I must leave this "home." But I dug my heels in and said, "No! I will not leave. I will find a way to *make* this my home." It was then that I had one of the most powerful dream experiences of my life. In this dream, all the analysts were arrayed in a circle. Each had hold of a rope, and all the ropes were knotted together at the center of the formation. The circle of analysts was moving through a meadow, both moving across the meadow and turning at the same time. From the air it would look like a spoked wheel, turning and rolling along. It took a lot of concentration on everyone's part to make the "wheel" do this. Then someone whispered in my ear that he was going to cut my rope. I told him to go away. Louder this time, he repeated his threat. Again I told him to leave me alone, that this was hard work. Then as he repeated his threat a third time, he came down with a large sword over my shoulder and cut my rope, just as he had said he would. I tumbled to the ground while the circle of analysts continued on its way, seemingly oblivious of what had happened. Standing over me in my somewhat hapless condition, Jung looked down on me and said in an angry voice, "Why won't you understand?" Totally puzzled, I looked up at him and said all too weakly, "Understand what?" Whereupon he repeated back to me the three dreams I had recently had in their entirety.

I was stunned and sat bolt upright in bed. Experientially, I was engulfed in flames. My skin was stinging worse than it had ever done from any sunburn I'd ever had (and as a redhead and a Southern California beach kid, I had had some pretty bad burns in my life). My chest was under so much pressure I thought it would burst. Surely I was having a heart attack. I could hardly breathe. I could not get out of this state. It seemed clear to me that I had to act in response to the dream, and so I sat down and composed a brief letter of resignation to the local society of analysts of which I was a member. I took this letter to the post office and only then, when it was in the mail, did the fire subside.

I guess from this experience one can see what sort of analyst I would come to be. First, there is the fact of having dreams that are frequently more real and compelling than anything I experience in my waking life. Second, there is that strong sense that mere consciousness of a dream's meaning is *not* enough, that consciousness must lead to *choice,* and choice to *action.* These two aspects are always at the core of "what sort of analyst" I am. There is simply no way that dreams and *their* intentionality can take a back seat to any other dimension of my experience. Even so, I have all too frequently not been up to seeing this all the way through. My failure and my failings as an analyst almost always stem from my persistent efforts to discount these core realities, to try and force them into second place, almost always under the pressure of that lifelong attempt to "find home."

I was persuaded not to resign. This pattern would repeat itself in both small and large ways over the years: my investing time, energy, and love in the business of being an analyst and—where my passion seemed to be most intensely focused—the *training* of analysts, only to end up intensely frustrated—or worse, and having to leave, resign, or break apart in one way or another. I am satisfied that my work for more than a quarter of a century as an analyst and teacher has been good work. But I also know this: my recurrent attempts to "find home" in the Jungian world in the ways I have attempted have been *wrong* in some elemental way.

Essentially, it has taken me all these years to listen deeply enough to the Jung of the dream when he cut me away. To those whom I have hurt by this intransigence and its fallout, I have apologized, or tried to, and do so again here. I am no longer a member of any society of Jungian analysts, no longer engaged in the training of analysts, no longer in contact with Jungian analysts (except for those very few who have remained steadfast in their genuine friendship). I *have* come home to the dream again, and am now living out what it means to be "cut away," what it means for the dream Jung to know so well the dreams I had, what it means to experience once again his fury at my not understanding. I *am* beginning to understand. I am not yet prepared to say much about where this is going because I am dwelling in it now. Perhaps I will do so in a book I am working on, which I have titled *Gleanings from the Dreamfield*, in which I am trying to tell the story of my life through the lens of a baker's dozen of dreams, including some of the ones I've mentioned here.

The "cutting away" is ongoing—and unsparing. Recently, I discovered I had a condition known as "silent" heart disease, silent because there are no symptoms. The usual outcome of this disease is a heart attack—often fatal. Fortunately, this condition was discovered before that eventuality came to pass, and it was treated with quintuple bypass surgery. Both of my parents died quite young as a result of heart-related problems, so I've "known" intellectually for some time that I am "at risk." Still, the shock of the discovery of my heart condition led me into a labyrinth of reflections, the likes of which I had never known before. One outcome of this "soul searching" was the decision—more like a decision "presented" to me than one rationally made for myself—to close my office, essentially, the formal end of my work as an analyst—this, too, now cut away. So, that's the sort of "Jungian" I am.

ABOUT JUNG

RH: What are your two favorite stories about Jung?

RL: One of my favorites is the image of Jung, the great man, telling his dreams to his gardener. This image played a part in the sense of *eros* I have worked on, where "telling" one's reality is such a crucial aspect of generating *eros*. And when *eros* is generated, then creative possibility becomes imminent. So the *act* of telling one's reality to another is central. Failing to do this destroys the possibility of intimacy and deep connection to another. The same is true, of course, in relation to *community*.

Another story I like about Jung comes from a dream. Is that permitted as a source of stories? In this dream, I am with Jung in Zürich and we are at a movie. The movie is some sort of high drama and as the film gets really intense, Jung starts to snore—very loudly! I nudge him with my elbow to wake him so he won't embarrass himself. As he wakes up, I explain why I woke him. "Nonsense!" he explodes. "*Where* I was is what is important!" This dream was actually very instructive to me. For a period of time, I would have my analysis with Hilde Kirsch at 6:00 a.m.! Periodically, she would doze off. From this dream I learned *not* to disturb her. Invariably, after a few minutes she would wake up, and she would tell me where she had gone or what had visited her in this impromptu nap. These experiences were enormously valuable to me, and they often crystallized *synchronistic* experiences between us. Jung's comment that *where* he had been was what is important has "haunted" me now for many years. The "locale" of the unconscious, its geography, its space-time qualities—all these have been objects of my reflection now for many years and serve to form something of the sense of the work I do as an analyst.

RH: What do you feel the world, perhaps even the Jungian world, has not understood yet about Jung?

RL: More than forty years ago, Jung wrote a letter to Sir Herbert Read, the art critic and poet. Some years before, they had had a falling out over Jung's rather negative assessment of "modern" art. There is a paragraph in this letter that I believe contains the *essentia* of Jung's deepest sense of the meaning and purpose of dreams. This paragraph, I believe, also contains the answer—well, *my* answer anyway—to your question. Here it is:

> We have simply got to listen to what the psyche spontaneously says to us. What the dream, which is not manufactured by us, says is *just so*. ... It is the great dream which has always spoken through the artist as a mouthpiece. All his love and passion (his "values") flow towards the coming guest to proclaim his arrival. ...What is the great Dream? It consists of the many small dreams and the many acts of humility and submission to their hints. It is the future and the picture of the new world, which we do not understand yet. We cannot know better than the unconscious and its intimations. *There* is a fair chance of finding what we seek in vain in our conscious world. Where else could it be? [To Herbert Read, September 2, 1960, *C.G. Jung Letters, Vol. 2*, pp. 591-592.]

Everything I have worked on as an analyst has had to do with this paragraph. Everything I hold of value in Jung's psychology is in this paragraph. Much of modern analysis and analytic training has become rooted more in developmental approaches and utilizing transference and countertransference methodologies in conceptualizing the nature of the psychoanalytic enterprise. I do not find my home in these developments, although as you now know, not finding my home in something is endemic with me. Still, as valuable as these new developments in psychological work are and have been and will be, they are essentially oriented toward what I call "completing" the ego. I do not find that they address the question that hounded Jung: *what* is the completed ego *for*? Jung's paragraph provides many hints and, in a sense, I *do* find myself at home with the intimations embedded in what Jung says there. That is, if one works through love, value, and passion and, most of all, *acts* of humility and submission to the dream's hint, a welcoming *eros* will be created for the incarnation (=making *real*) of the "coming guest." It is this, says Jung, which we seek in vain in our conscious world. I do not find much of modern psychology working in this direction or with this value or with this passion or with this sense of the "great dream" Jung speaks of here.

FAMILY

RH: What was your family like?

RL: Oh, my! How does one answer such a question in a short space? My earliest memory of my parents is this: I was in the car and they were bringing bags of groceries out of the market. When they went inside to get more bags, I rummaged about in the bags they had left in the car and managed to find a carton of eggs. When they came out, they found me dropping eggs one after another out the window onto the sidewalk. I must have been about 3 or so. I was having fun and laughing, and what I remember most about this scene is that when they saw me dropping those eggs, they both started laughing too! That captures my general feeling of my early years—it was as if the god of humor was always close by.

Coming home on an airplane many years ago, I was half-heartedly watching a movie called *Honeysuckle Rose* starring Willie Nelson. In the midst of this film, I suddenly became very tearful, and then I suddenly found myself really sobbing, to the point where it became noticeable to the passengers around me. In addition to the music and singing in the film, I could hear other voices singing, and it was *these* voices that were bringing on the tears. I did not know what to make of it at all. Some days later, I was visiting my parents and told them about this experience. My dad started laughing (he laughed a *lot*) and said that I must have remembered his singing to me when I was just a baby. He would hold me and sing to me, singing along with Hank Williams and other country singers *as a way to cure his stuttering.*

Now that was indeed a surprise, because I had not known he had stuttered. This whole incident taught me a great deal about being "open" to experience of all kinds without prejudice because you just never know what's going to open your psyche up to you. I love that image of him singing to me.

RH: What did your father do?

RL: My father was a "bookie," in addition to his other work as a foreman at the old Arden Milk Company in Los Angeles. He spent a lot of time at the racetrack and he would take me along. This is how I got to know all the jockeys in those days. They were "Eddie" and "Johnny" and "Willie" to me, and I was "Rusty" to them—with my red hair. I remember the day Citation became the first millionaire horse and how my dad and I *danced* together at the finish line as our favorite horse came home. I would say that moment marked the peak of my childhood and the sense of togetherness with my parents.

I was entering adolescence, and childhood was coming to an end. But it was another experience that marked the end in a most definite way. Not long after Citation won, my Dad was being hounded by Mickie Cohen, the head of the "mob" in Los Angeles. Mickie wanted to organize all the bookies, and my Dad did not want to be "organized." (I guess I learned that from him!) Mickie was threatening my father and us, so my Dad turned to the police for help. My Dad knew several people in the police force—they were all his clients. I remember them being around a lot in those days—in fact, I learned to play poker from them. Well, I was on my way home from school—running (in a hurry to get home and work on a telescope I was making, or something in my darkroom, or a project in my chemistry lab—I don't recall)—running flat out across a field. I tripped on something and fell with my right hand landing full force on a broken Clorox jug. As I grow older, the scars from this injury become more and more visible—white lines on my wrist and palm running up to my fingers. What I remember, besides the huge amounts of blood, was that my palm was opened very deeply and I could *see* into it. I do not remember being in pain; most likely I was in shock. But I do remember that as I continued to run home, I examined in great detail the inside of my hand.

When I got home, my mother was there, and I distinctly remember wanting her to see what I was seeing, so after she rushed me to the bathroom to start working on the wounds, I opened my palm to show her. At that point, she fainted and fell backwards into the bathtub. I couldn't get her to wake up and in the process of trying to revive her, managed to get a good bit of blood all over her. I then ran to the neighbors' house—where my communist tutor lived. I showed my hand to his wife and she managed to faint away as well. The last I remember was everything spinning as Rocco, in his underwear, picked me up. Rocco apparently scooped me up and put me in his car and rushed me off to the emergency room. I can't imagine what the emergency room people thought when they saw this huge Italian guy in his underwear carrying this hulk of a teenager with blood everywhere. Meanwhile, my mother got herself out of the tub and was rushing out of the house covered with blood, when one of the police detectives arrived. I was nowhere in sight. After piecing together the idea of where I likely was, off they went to the emergency room. Together with one of my Korean friends, I had developed quite a facility with accents. We were very taken with British accents, and we had great fun going into these accents at a moment's notice. So it was not surprising, I guess, although I was still in shock I'm sure, that when I saw my mother rushing up to where I was, I shouted out in my best Brit: "It's my bloody mother!"

Shortly after this, my mother apparently decided she had had enough of my father's being a bookie—she was the one who ended up taking the bets as they came in over the phone when my dad was at work, and there were a lot of them. So she concocted a plan. One afternoon, when my father got home, she told him that she'd made a horrible mistake: she had accepted a large wager on a long shot and had made no countermoves to offset it. The long shot came in and now they owed an astronomical sum—pure fabrication. My father was beside himself and took off. Later that night, he came home terribly drunk. My mother asked me to help her get him into the shower. So he's in the tub, and she turns on the water and he's lying there all wet but not moving a bit. In that moment, the juxtaposition of the images of my mother all bloody in the tub and my father nearly drowned in the tub hit with me a force I cannot describe. But in that moment, one world died and another world was born.

RH: I get the impression that your parents did not come down very hard on you as a child and that you had a close relationship with them.

RL: Well, as I entered adolescence, my parents adopted a strange form of "punishment" when they felt I had done something wrong or something they did not like. I have to say that in comparison with the horror stories one hears these days of child abuse, my early years were Edenic. My father's infrequent attempts to "lower the boom" on me invariably turned into scenes of comedy, as I would run to my closet, my father in close pursuit with my dog grasping hold of his trousers and growling ever louder. These attempts at punishment would end in great laughter all around, and in some strange way this had a more salutary effect on me than an outright spanking would have, I'm sure. But the later "punishment" was much more paradoxical: my parents would go into *silence*. These silences never became associated with humor as earlier punishments had done. Instead, they simply came and went, and I could never discern exactly what would bring an end to the silence. I mention this *silence* phenomenon because it would come to play a curious role in many of my dreams and associations, and in many of the difficulties I had with others. It has perhaps played a part in my emphasis on *telling* as a crucial element in *eros*; when colleagues have had problems with me, they have gone *silent*, and I have not heard about their feelings directly from them. I have always experienced these silences not as punishing (if that was the intent), but as *mysterious*. When my parents went silent, I went into reverie. And this has been my reaction to silence ever since.

TYPOLOGY

RH: How do you understand your typology?

RL: Well, let's get the diagnosis out of the way first. In the popular way of expressing one's typology, I would diagnose myself as an introverted intuitive thinking type. *Introverted,* because my experience is processed first by its relationship with my own psychology and only secondarily in relation to anything "outer." *Intuitive,* because my experience gets flooded with possibilities and potentials, while what is actually "there" does not seem to register very well. And *thinking,* because I find my experience naturally goes toward the relationship between things rather than the value of things. I tend to think of typological dynamics as a major factor in creating field effects between people, within collectives, even with objects. People are not the only ones to have typological characteristics. Much of the effective development of one's typology as well as the wise use of one's typology in relationship stems from the deliberate holding of the superior functions in abeyance.

A simple example: I look out the patio window and I "intuitively" see a deck there. It comes complete as an image with a certain charge. I may say to my wife, "I think I'll build a deck there." Now she already knows I have five hundred unfinished projects as well as several messes all over the place I've yet to clean up. Her instant "feeling" reaction is a very negative valuation of my plan. If she responds from this superior valuation, we are going to have a fight, or I'm going to go into a mood. The field effect is automatic and over determined. Fortunately, in more than forty years of marriage, and having been through this many times, the *wisdom* of the functions prevails. She holds her reaction in abeyance—even asks me more about what I see—and then as I rattle on, the image tends to lose some of its luster, I begin to remember some of the things I've not yet finished, I start to think about the image and see that actually it would not work as well as other plans, and so on. Soon I come to the conclusion that I don't need to take this on now and relegate it to the "future projects" pile. I say something to that effect. She smiles.

One must be aware that the types are not static categories. They are better conceptualized as energy vectors and always in some degree of dynamic motion. Through the unconscious mirror image of the conscious aspects, you have an energetic system of considerable complexity. There is nothing simple about Jung's typological theory. In analysis, I have always been quite taken with Gerhard Adler's idea of the "rotation" of functions. This notion has guided how I use my own typological energies in analytic work. His idea was that one should not always function out of one's superior function in analysis, but "rotate" the function in relation to the typological dynamics of the patient. For example, if someone I am working with is a pronounced "thinking" type, it won't do for me to try to relate through thinking—nor will either of us get on well if I try to relate through feeling. Adler's idea was that the analyst should "rotate" the function in such a way so as not to function out of the same or the opposite function, but out of the alternate polarity, that is, out of intuition or sensation. In a sense, these alternate polarities are shared areas of "objectivity" and serve well the exploration of more difficult aspects. So, over the years, I have had considerable practice functioning out of all functions as the need arises with different people. I'm not sure this is sufficient to give one a genuine impression of what is involved in this, but perhaps the idea is sufficient to set one mulling over the potential of typological dynamics.

Spirituality

RH: Do you feel you are a spiritual person? Is spirituality a part of your work?

RL: Well, the "Coming Guest" is certainly a spiritual image. And since the work I do as an analyst and in relation to myself is embodied in developing the ways and means of creating and engendering the "welcoming *eros*" Jung speaks of, I have no hesitancy in describing myself or my work as spiritual in that sense. However, I find spiritual resonance more in the arts, literature, certain religious traditions, modern physics, even continental cultural criticism, than I do in psychology. Psychology seems still too caught up in its own "of-ness": psychology *of* this or *of* that. There is considerable significance in Jung's using the *copulative* conjunction "and" in so many of his titles: psychology *and* religion, psychology *and* alchemy, archetypes *and* the collective unconscious, Freud *and* psychoanalysis. These are not accidental titles. *Of* tends toward hierarchical understandings and traditions; *and* tends toward *generation* of something "other."

RH: What do you feel Jung meant when he said, "I do not believe in God. I know"?

RL: Maurice Freidman calls Jung a modern *Gnostic*. The word itself comes from a Greek root meaning "to know." In particular, this sense of "knowing" means simply: "it is in my experience." Not as evidence for something else (as in the experiential requirement of empiricism), but inhering in the value of the experience itself. The shades of meaning inherent in the words that the root gives rise to, such as "cunning" (to know how to), "ken" (to be able to name), and "narrate" (to be able to tell), all point to something in one's experience that *enables* one *to do, to name, to tell*. So he "knows" God in that sense—that he can do, he can name, he can tell. And by this you know that he "knows."

For Jung, as for the Gnostics, "belief" is a process that *pales* in comparison with this sense of *knowing*. Of course, Jung's knowing can make absolutely *no* claim whatever on anyone else's experience. The Gnostic position is utterly *individual* in this sense. And, like the alchemist, one seeks confirmation not in the *collective* by sharing with or forcing on others (as is so typical of belief), but in the further reaches of the unfolding experience of the interior process. Where experience of the "other" is so powerful and numinous, *there* (in *that* geography of the psyche)—and this is the character of what Jung refers to—belief simply does not come into it. This is what I think Jung meant. In many ways, it is like a dream. You simply *know* the dream. Belief begins to operate when one tries to speak of the dream's meaning (and here you are probably a member of one of the modern psychotherapeutic or psychoanalytic belief systems concerning dreams) or value. But no belief can genuinely touch your *gnosis*, your *knowing* the dream. Subsequent to the dream, your belief system may powerfully effect what you *do* in relation to the dream. And to be sure, belief systems may render certain experiences impossible.

RH: How do you feel about the current state of mental health treatment, given managed care, stricter ethical guidelines, lower fees, and what some have defined as a consumer's market?

RL: Well, I just don't think that what Jung was after can be found in the precincts of these current developments. But then I consider myself to be something of a dinosaur in this regard. Those interested in working on behalf of the dream—and I mean the deepest soul work in this sense—may need to find other geographies in which to locate themselves. I'm not so sure I care any more what psychology does, where psychotherapy goes, what modern analysis becomes—as Mao said, "Let a thousand flowers bloom." It is only when these developments make soul work nearly impossible that I wonder how young workers in this field will find their way. I saw recently that a psychologist lost his license to practice because he referred a client to an astrologer. The rationale was clear. The licensing board deemed astrology a pseudoscience, and therefore the practitioner was violating both accepted "standards of practice" as well as "ethical guidelines." Now I'm not going to claim that astrology is a science, but then neither is art, nor the imagination, nor walking among the trees. In my work with the psyche, any and all of these things may be lines along which the soul needs to wend its often *irrational* way. So if the psychology licensing board says I can't send someone to an astrologer, then I have to say to the board: it is not your psychology I am practicing. I must be practicing something else. And, indeed, I think that is the case. The problem is there may be no name for it, no official home for it, no way to do it with official sanctions of "the state."

But I do not mind that. As I have written somewhere, dreams are *subversive* in nature, whether we are talking about the typical demands of the ego or the state. I have a project that I call "my novel." I've worked on it for a long time, without making a lot of progress—so much so that it is a joke—nearly. But the themes there have to do with what happens to the world when dreams *stop*, and what happens to states when they start taking dreams seriously. This all relates to a short story I wrote back in junior high school ("When Dreams Stopped"), based on a dream I had had. The teacher accused me of plagiarizing it! Perhaps that's why I don't seem to make much progress with "my novel."

INDIVIDUATION

RH: What is your understanding of the individuation process—the importance of struggling?

RL: To me individuation consists of two parts: what I refer to as *completing* the ego, and then the task of determining what this more completed ego is *for*. The first part is largely the work of disentanglement from living out the misplaced desire of others; the second part is largely the work of living more fully in relationship to the desire of the "Other" in you. Jung called this the Self; some would call it God; some would call it fate, or destiny, or karma. I like to call it "other."

To speak of "struggle" is difficult. So much struggle in the world these days is simply "to exist." Those of us who have the "luxury" of individuating in relative affluence must realize we are doing so riding on the struggles of billions of people whose main experience in life is finding a way to live another day. Even when the tasks of daily bread are no longer an issue, so much struggle these days is "to become what you are not." This has perhaps always been the case. But most certainly, the commodification of desire and the accelerating pace and ever-spreading range of influence of the process is making this a pandemic problem in our time. Jung might say you cannot individuate until you have struggled with the devil. Or drop the "d," and let's say you cannot individuate until you have struggled with the evil in yourself *and* in your neighbor *and* in the world at large. Jung said that individuation "gathers the world to itself." That simply brings you into the precincts of profound struggle. So, these two ideas belong together in very direct ways.

DEATH AND THE AFTERLIFE

RH: What is your view of life after death?

RL: Of course, this question can be viewed only from the biased position of "life." However, what modern physics is learning from the study of *multiverses* may be telling us that what goes on in this universe called "life" may bear little or no relation whatever to what goes in the universe called "death." I am sure of one thing: there will be plenty of *time* there. The whole question is totally opaque to me in terms of any "knowing," and that leaves "belief," and I don't find myself very occupied by this question. Other questions, yes. For example, how does near-death or brushing with death *change* the way one lives life?

My first brush with death came when I was 8 years old. I was on a hike and in doing something foolish, I tripped and began falling down the side of a mountain. I was rolling and tumbling and getting pretty bashed up. I was scared beyond dimension. Suddenly, a great huge owl appeared, and in a powerful voice said, "Grab the tree." Just then I smashed stomach first into a smallish tree, and I did as the owl said. I must have blacked out for a time, but when I returned to consciousness, I was wrapped around the tree, and I could hear my rescuers exclaiming. I was near the edge of a cliff and if not for that tree, I would now be dead. I did not tell anyone about the owl for many years, but the owl has since been a frequent visitor in dream and vision, and I don't mind saying I owe my life to an image! How did that *change* my life? For one, it played a large part in developing the *feeling* since that day that my life has been a *gift*. And like the Indian and the Pilgrim, I try to remain conscious that this gift *must* circulate and not become a Puritan "possession." The demands of life make it difficult to remember this, and for some reason it is so much easier to be a Puritan and to follow the ever-present pull of commodification of life itself. But I *am* trying, and I expect the *gift* of new life made possible by the unblocking of my heart arteries will lead to renewed vigor in circulating what I have to say, what I have to tell, if nothing else. Perhaps even completing "my novel" is in the cards!

RH: Speaking of life and death, your work with the terminally ill—with cancer patients—is fascinating. How would you summarize what you have learned?

RL: I have learned that sickness and disease always bring us close to the question of our death. I have learned that almost everything works against our taking up this question until something "forces" it upon us. I have learned that it is one's relationship with death, perhaps most of all, that is crucial in achieving what Jung meant by *depth*. Depth *is* death to the seduction of the surface with all its speed and rootlessness. Depth demands the singularity of choice, not the illusion of endless choices. And, death is the great singularity.

I have learned that dreams are sensitive to wayward organic processes in the body long before anything appears in the clinical picture. But not necessarily. Dreams can ignore as well as attend, and this is an intriguing issue to me—this difference. I have learned that sometimes where spirit had led, the body must now lead. Perhaps most of all, what I have learned in my explorations of dreams and disease can best be summed up by saying that the body too is a dream and that when the body is approached only from the *rational* side—as ineluctably necessary as this is—the body as dream and therefore the *purpose* of the body is often eclipsed. Just as we must ask what a "completed ego" is *for,* we must ask what a "healthy body" is *for.* These are parallel questions. If a "dream wants a dream" and a "poem wants a poem," clearly "body wants a body." We can understand this on many levels. We all know, for example, what it means for a body to "want" a body. We all know how such wanting gets commodified, from simple prostitution to body image as major industry. We may even understand or sense we understand the idea of a body "wanting" a *subtle* body. Just as one deepens into the mystery of a dream wanting a dream, a poem wanting a poem, the idea of body wanting body cannot be explored without considering the question of death. Our experience generally is that *we*—as ego in particular—do not want death; we do not want to explore death's desire. Yet death is such a *natural* part of life, how can we not?

DREAMS

RH: Do you feel dreams are God's forgotten language?

RL: No. Whatever meaning there is for the idea of dreams as God's language, it is hardly *forgotten*. Oh, to be sure *we* forget dreams. We may forget or not even know this sense of the *divine* in dreams. But *God* has not forgotten—whatever we choose to mean by God. The intentionality implicit in dreams has always been there, and I see no reason for it to change, and that intentionality is beyond our making. The dream does its work by "presenting" itself to your experience. After that, the ball is in your court, so to speak. In this, I have been much influenced by a little dream that said, "A dream wants a dream; a poem wants a poem." It's not unlike what Klee said when asked why he did not like to give lectures: because the audience listens with their ears and not their hands. While we are so wrapped up in our own desires, we generally neglect what the dream "wants." What *is* forgotten is what to *do* in relation to dreams, or even that dreams "want" us to do something in return. That is where the consequential forgetting lies.

That's how I like to work with dreams whether my own or others. What can one do to attend to the dream's desire? What sort of dream can you bring to a dream? Baudelaire said that the only proper criticism of a work of art is another work of art. That gets close to the sense of what my little dream "wants." This is the *erotics* of poetry *and* of dreams. It is not that dreams are the product of a dysfunctional erotic life; rather, they are the very *basis* of erotic life. Whatever it means to bring a dream to a dream will likely preoccupy me for the rest of my days.

RH: How exactly do you work with your own dreams?

RL: Well, of course, it's changed a great deal over the years. I dream less now. I no longer feel as if "I work on the dream" as if it were some object to my consciousness. More accurately, the dream works on me as object, if anything. But that's not quite right either. Perhaps as never before, dreams and I have become *comrades* in the deepest sense of that old Spanish word *camara*, "chambered together." Out of this *camera* comes a "picture" of what the dream leads me to *do*, for I've long since given up on the idea that consciousness is enough or can, as Jung said, "make a halt." I always experience something of a *task* arising from a dream, and whether it is the title of a paper (e.g., "Psyche in Hiding"), or a book (*Words As Eggs*), or making books by hand (*The Lockhart Press*), or learning what's written on the cave walls with the light of flames from my fingers (*Gleanings from The Dreamfield*), or trying to discern the "mysteries of the market" and their embodiment of the principles of Sacred Geometry (*Hints and Helps for Short-Term Traders*)—all of these things and many more are direct fruits, as it were, of what has been brought to me in dreams and which I have endeavored to make real and manifest in the world. So, perhaps I come full circle to speak of dreams as comrades—a word my old communist mentor was wont to use—the one who gave me Jung's *Modern Man in Search of a Soul* and set me on the road. "Comrade!" he would greet and call out to me. I do something similar now when a dream comes to visit, and we sit together *in camera* trying to discern what it is I must do. This *dwelling* together, to use Heidegger's wonderful expression, this dwelling in *negative capability* to add Keats' extraordinary notion, is the closest I can get in conveying a sense of "how I work on my own dreams."

WORDS AND ETYMOLOGY

RH: You have had a significant interest in words and their meanings. What prompted this interest and, in a nutshell, what have you learned about words and their importance in analytical work?

RL: Let's look at the word *community* that I used earlier. Of course, we all know what it means, and we could each come up with an acceptable definition. And then, of course, we could argue about our definitions. I like to approach this problem differently. I want the word itself to "speak" to me, so I can learn from "it." And since this orientation to words and language plays such a huge part in my way of working as an analyst, I need to elaborate just a bit on what got me on to this. It was a dream. (I hope it doesn't rub anyone the wrong way, my going into dreams so much—but that's how it is with me.) In my dream, a dream voice announced: "Do you not know that words are eggs, that they carry life, that they give birth?" Well, no. I don't think I had understood words that way before. But I experienced this dream as an injunction to do so. I often experience dreams as *tasks*, and this dream no less so. This dream was the source of my essay and book, *Words as Eggs*, titled in the language of the dream. Most of what I write has its origin in some dream—and so do the titles! That dream led to a long excursion into the *etymology* of words and how exploring words in this way often revitalizes and deepens one's relation to the word because the etymology invariably brings in *images* and *stories* one would not otherwise be aware of, if one used words and language in the usual way.

The word *community*, for example, *com-*, meaning "together," and *-munity* (from the Latin *munnus*), meaning "gift." Thus, central to community is the image of "giving gifts to one another." The Indians encountered by the early Pilgrims and Puritans understood this. So when they gave the pipe to the settlers, it was a gift that was meant to circulate. The Pilgrims seemed to grasp this idea, while the Puritans did not. To the Puritan, the pipe became "property" and was to be "possessed." So that when the Indian took the pipe back after seeing its circulation completed, the Puritan concluded that Indians could not be trusted—the origin of the famous expression, "Indian giver."

Much of our country's history could be written through the lens of this tragic failure to grasp the essential notion that *gift-giving* is fundamental to the generation of community. So, in terms of what I was speaking to above, I believe that *telling* the reality of one's psyche *is* a gift and that the circulation of such "truth telling" is a deep source for generating intimacy and community among people. Of course, everything conspires against it. As analysts, we are in a position to hear such truth telling as part of our daily experience. Naturally, such truth telling invites truth telling on the part of the analyst, otherwise the *eros* dimension of the relationship becomes distorted. The one-sidedness of truth telling in therapy is the source of some of its success as well as most of its failures.

MONEY

RH: Your article on money and its symbolism was very helpful to many people. What would you say to people whose money complex has a paralyzing hold on them?

RL: The history of money is the history of the *commodification* of whatever happens to be the engine of wealth creation at the time—whether it is land: what the land can grow, or what can be extracted from the land— or people: what people can do, or what people can be forced or induced to do—or inventions—or information—or weapons—or cures—or bodies—

or souls. At some point, everything falls under the sway of the commodification process, everything from the highest to the lowest "turned" into "money," everything "turning" in *relation* to money. It's the alchemists dream become nightmare! There is no escape. Everyone, from the world's richest person to the poorest peasant, is caught in the wheels of this process. The twentieth-century history of money could perhaps be written as a history of the commodification of *desire*. I believe the dream will be the last holdout to the devouring dynamics of this process. Because of this, I fully expect every effort will be made to control this current "source" heretofore beyond the reach of the worlds of power. The commodification process will attempt to appropriate the dream, whether as a byproduct of medications that effectively eliminate dreams, or by bringing the very idea of dream into relationship with money and power. Have you not noticed how "dream" has become the advertising buzzword? "Give us your dreams," says one advertisement quite bluntly. Of course, no one will *buy* a dream, although you can end up paying large sums for their interpretation! So, dreams come to you *freely*, and in some strange way, it is this very fact of the dream's "freedom" from the dynamics of money that makes the dream itself my answer to your question about the paralyzing effects of money. Because our dreams are *not* (yet) paralyzed by money, nor by the oceans of commodification we are all drowning in, they are our source for the way out of both the collective grip that money has on us as well as the personal binds that money has spun in our history.

An example. A company with branches in Israel and Germany was having internal difficulties. It was a young company filled with enterprising, bright, talented young people. All the plans were laid out, everything should have been working fine—but it simply was not. No end of consultants could solve the problems. Finally, the company brought in an unusual consultant, someone who worked only with dreams. He got the employees to gather for a weekend retreat with the proviso that the *only* things that they could speak about were the things that were in their dreams. An *odd* way to approach business problems, to be sure. One of the first dreams to be considered was just an image of a forest of beech trees. After much laughing and joking and snide remarks about how could this possibly help resolve the company's *real* problems, everyone was brought up short when someone asked what the word for "beech forest" was in German. It was only then, of course, that it hit everyone like a thunderbolt, and no one could escape the fact that *beech forest* was *Buchenwald*. And so, perhaps what lay beneath the company's contemporary character was a problem that would not go away, a history that could not be escaped so easily. These young people grew a lot in that weekend.

So if you are tangled up in money issues, realize that almost everyone else is as well. But you have a source nearby that is not—at least not yet: your dreams. Look *there* for hints and intimations on the way through.

While on this topic of money, let me tell you of one of my recent projects. Are you familiar with this quote from Jung?

> Therefore anyone who wants to know the human psyche … would be better advised to … bid farewell to his study, and wander with human heart through the world. There in the horrors of prisons, lunatic asylums and hospitals, in drab suburban pubs, in brothels, and gambling-hells, in the salons of the elegant, the Stock Exchanges, Socialist meetings, churches, revivalist gatherings, and ecstatic sects, through love and hate, through the experience of passion in every form of his own body, he would reap richer stores of knowledge than text-books a foot thick could give him, and he will know how to doctor the sick with real knowledge of the human soul. [*Collected Works*, 7 § 409]

What a training program Jung outlines here! I can't say I can check everything off on this list as part of my training. But I come pretty close. And most recently it is the Stock Exchanges that have occupied me in a particular way. My research in graduate school, both for my master's degree and my doctorate, had fundamentally to do with *time*. And without going into it in detail here, I can say that much of my work as an analyst has had to do with *time* too. And for as long as I can remember, I have been fascinated by the question of *time* in relation to the *synchrony* of events and especially the synchrony between the financial markets and historical events. In my studies of these things, it became clear that financial markets are a fine-tuned instrument for measuring large-scale human dynamics— such as the commodification of desire. I'll be writing more about this in the near future. What I am doing now, though, is a bit unusual for an analyst. I am spending several hours a day teaching traders the principles of Jungian psychology, which are proving to be extraordinarily useful in understanding not only the psychology of the markets, but the psychology of traders. Moreover, the markets themselves and therefore the psychology of the markets and the psychology of those in the markets are very closely governed by the principles of *sacred geometry* as well the *time* aspects of *astrology*. Not only am I learning a great deal about the human psyche in this way, just as Jung indicated above, but I am also able to bring together so many of the streams of my own process in very unexpected ways. I talk on such topics as: "Why the Markets are Psychological Phenomena," "The Language of the Markets and Its Sexual Nature," "Harmonizing Self and Other in the Markets," "The Uses of Imagination in Relation to the 'Stories of the Market'," and "The Esoterics of Number and Time." In case you can't tell, I am having a lot of fun with this.

Legacy

RH: You are retiring from your practice. Can you tell us why, and what it has been like?

RL: In the year 2000, in a routine physical exam, some "minor abnormalities" were seen in a treadmill stress test EKG. In exploring this further, it was discovered that all my major arteries were blocked—almost entirely. Still, I had no real symptoms. This is a condition known as "silent" heart disease, as I mentioned earlier. Very often, the first real "symptom" is a major, often fatal, heart attack. So, without much ceremony or time to consider, I was in the operating room undergoing quintuple bypass surgery. Clearly, this operation saved my life, and for that I am grateful indeed. As far as I could tell, there was no foreshadowing of this condition in dreams, intuition, or any other psychic experience. I have studied the relationship between disease and dreams enough to know that dream "warnings" are not invariable and that, in fact, the absence of dream figuration in relation to disease processes may serve another function entirely: *shock*.

My usual ways of "working" with myself are *silent*. Thus, even my body was *silent* in that it was not shouting out or even whispering symptoms of this impending "end." I couldn't help but think of my parent's *silence* or my colleague's *silence* when there were issues with me. And I couldn't help but recall one of the most compelling dream experiences of all. At the time of this dream, I was staying at Dunvegan Castle on the Isle of Skye, a guest of John MacLeod. He had invited me to participate in his annual *Arts*

Festival. Each year, he would invite an American to participate among the gathered poets and pipers. I had given a couple of talks there. One was "The Cost of Poetry and The Price of its Loss." I can't remember the title of the other. But I had finished with my presentations and was relaxed and enjoying my stay at this wondrous place. Then, this dream. I am in the Great Hall at the castle (unlike the actual castle). I am alone, standing at the great table and looking at the high walls. From ceiling to floor hang enormous tapestries. As I gaze upon each tapestry, I see that the history of this place is pictured there—all the historical figures, the battles, the celebrations, the ceremonies—everything. As I watch ever more intently, the figures in the tapestries begin to *move!* It's as if the entire history of the castle and its world becomes animated before me. It is truly astonishing. Strangely, there is an eerie *silence*—all this activity and no sound. As I watch, the motion of the figures begins to become swirls and whirlpools of color, all figuration is lost to these swirling pools of color that begin to whirl with increasing speed. Suddenly, out of these whirlpools of color arise, one after the other, enormous heads, males and females, obviously of ancient origin, Vikings or earlier; they rise up and sink back, replaced by a new one, faster and faster. Each appears as if speaking *to* me with great intent, *urgency* even—except no sound gets through, there is only *silence*. The scene goes on endlessly, until I awake and find myself standing at the open window of my room, leaning out as if looking to see someone in the night sky. For a time it was as if there was an afterimage of the dream figures in the sky itself, and the rising and falling continued for some time—all in *silence.*

Silence.

All these silences were doorways to *reverie* for me. And all these silences were experienced as full of portent, full of the irrational "knowings" (*tacit* knowledge) of the uncertain and unknown future. *Tacita* is the goddess of silence, and if she was present in these precincts of my silent dreams, my body's silence, and all these silences as a leitmotif in my life, it is her prompting that has always pushed me to *act* from these silences along the lines as best as I can glean from the reveries they induce.

It was not as if I "decided" to close my office and begin my "retirement." It was as if the operation "crystallized" all the subtle and irrational bits and pieces of this *tacita.* You know, I always felt that my work as an analyst was a perfect place for the realization of the historic motto of the Lockhart name: *Corda Serrato Pando*—"I Open Locked Hearts." The irony was not lost on me: my own heart had become *blocked* to the point of extinction. I *knew* I had to stop in order to make room for "something else." Just as I had written in *Psyche Speaks* in quoting Lorca's poem: "The rose was not searching for the rose. Motionless in the sky it was searching for something else." I was mindful that I had also quoted Rilke's call for "heart-work" now. It seemed clear to me only *after* the shock of the bypass surgery that while all that I had written in *Psyche Speaks*, I believe, characterized my work with others, there was something missing in relation to my *own* heart-work that now must inform what I do. That is why I stopped working—so that there would be time and energy for whatever that may be. Do not ask me what this is yet. I have hints and intimations, of course. But I'd best be *silent* just now.

RH: How would you like to be remembered by the Jungian community?

RL: Since I am no longer a member of any "official" Jungian community, I don't know about this question of being "remembered." To my adversaries there, I'm hearing the lines from Waylon Jennings' song, "Pretend I Never Happened." More seriously, I've always been taken with the epithet ascribed to Benjamin Franklin on his grave: "Benjamin Franklin—Printer." I have recently re-read *Words As Eggs, Psyche Speaks,* and most of my more recent writings to see how they "hold up" as a "testament" to where I have been and what I have done since I entered the "Jungian world" more than 40 years ago. There's not much I would change, nothing I would take back, nothing I wouldn't be able to stand on today. So there's that, and of course the writings to come, about which I am very intrigued to see how they will find their way into the world. But if, like Franklin, I had to reduce my life to one word, I guess it would have to be, "Russell Lockhart—Dreamer." Thanks, Rob, for your penetrating questions and for letting me have my say!

PATRICIA BERRY, PH.D.

Patricia Berry was one of the youngest ever to enroll at the Jung Institute in Zürich, which she entered right after receiving her undergraduate degree from Ohio State University. She also has a master's degree from St. John University in Santa Fe, New Mexico, and a doctorate from the University of Dallas. Active for many years in Jungian activities, she has served as President of the Inter-Regional Society of Jungian Analysts and President of the New England Society of Jungian Analysts. Her works are considered foundational for an understanding of archetypal psychology and have been translated into several languages. She is the author of *Echo's Subtle Body: Contributions to an Archetypal Psychology*, editor of *Fathers and Mothers*, and contributor to *Images of the Untouched* ("Virginity's of Image"), *Chiron: A Review of Jungian Analysis-1985* ("Some Dream Motifs accompanying the abandonment of an Analytical Practice"), *Mirrors of the Self* ("The Shadow: Agent Provocateur"), *Fire in the Stone* ("Reductionism/Finding the Child"), *Shadow of America* ("Light and Shadow"), and *Jung & Film: Post-Jungian Takes on the Moving Image* ("Image in Motion"). We visited with Pat in her lovely home office on a wonderful spring day in Cambridge, Massachusetts near Harvard Square in the summer of 2001.

• 8 •

SEIZED BY A PASSION

Patricia Berry at 58

Everything is shadow-marbled.

—Patricia Berry

Encountering Jung

Rob Henderson (RH): I read somewhere that your interest in Jung began when you were at Ohio State through something you had heard from James Hillman?

Patricia Berry (PB): His was the first voice I heard talking about Jung. This was a tape-recording of a talk Jim had given at the First Community Church in Columbus, Ohio, where the minister, Dr. Otis Maxfield, was interested in Jung. I did not attend his church, but I had a couple of memorable meetings with Otis Maxfield—so powerful that I decided to go to Zürich after Ohio State. I felt that if I were going to become a clinical psychologist, I needed as thorough and deep an analysis as anybody could possibly put me through. So I thought of depth psychology, and, of course, Jung. That is why I went to Zürich.

Jan Henderson (JH): So you went to Zürich after your undergraduate degree for the purpose of getting your own analysis?

PB: Yes.

JH: That was a big step.

PB: It was totally crazy! [*Laughter*]

JH: How long were you there before you decided to enter the training program?

PB: A long time. At first, I did not think much of the Institute. I was full of my American undergraduate self. The Institute had a minuscule library.

RH: Yes, I know which library you are talking about.

PB: I remember striding into that library and lighting a cigarette. (I smoked in those days—as so many people did.) "My God," I said, "at Ohio State at least we have libraries!" [*Laughter*] Just as I said that, I burned a huge blister in the palm of my hand. I had assumed that the Institute would be like a university, and classes would be serious academic studies of Jung's work. What I found instead were worshipful people telling stories. Of course, in retrospect I can see they were wonderful stories.

RH: Did you actually meet Jung?

PB: No. He had died four years earlier.

RH: But you would hear stories of Jung?

PB: That's what the classes basically were.

RH: What story stands out from that time?

PB: Well, of course there's the story about lightning.

RH: When Jung died, you mean?

PB: Yes. [*Laughter*]

RH: When you heard that story, what was your reaction?

PB: I felt it irrelevant—which is what I still think about synchronicity. I am not very magical, I'm afraid. It seems to me synchronicity is so much the way things operate, we needn't make such a fuss about it.

RH: Then, what are called synchronistic occurrences do not impress you?

PB: We Jungians, of all people, should know the world is interconnected. The one lecturer who did make sense to me at the Institute was Jim [Hillman].

RH: He was more academic.

PB: I could understand and learn from him. Other lecturers made so many intuitive leaps. I am intuitive too, but for some reason I was more into an academic animus in those days.

RH: What is an "academic animus"?

PB: I guess it is being invested in the intellect to a far greater extent than in other ways of knowing.

RH: I take it you feel you are not in that animus any more.

PB: Actually, I could use a little more of it. [*Laughter*]

RH: How would it help you now if you had a little more?

PB: I would be more articulate, clearer.

RH: Was James Hillman the most influential person in your life?

PB: He was one. Rafael Lopez-Pedraza was another. Clinically, Toni Frey was by far the most important teacher for me. Fordham and the London group had trained Toni.

RH: What was it about Toni Frey that was so important to you?

PB: From him I learned to hear everything as part of the psychological process. Nothing was incidental. Anything a patient said or did—this was at Klinik am Zürichberg—was relevant. Nothing was apart from the psychological process.

RH: What was special about Rafael Lopez-Pedraza?

PB: Embodiment. He was what he said.

RH: How did James Hillman help in your development as a Jungian?

PB: I learned symbolic thinking and developed an appreciation of psychic reality from him. I was inspired by his imaginative flights and leaps. And then, of course, personally, there was so much more. He ushered me into adulthood, really.

TYPOLOGY

RH: What do you see as your typology?

PB: Introverted intuitive. Every Jungian says that [*Laughter*]—except, maybe, Jo Wheelwright.

RH: Does typology mean something to you?

PB: It doesn't work that well for me. For some people it does. But I like it ideationally, because it asserts different modes of functioning, kinds of consciousness, perspectives. That's Jung in 1921—and such a wonderful contribution for that time. The trouble is that I don't like systems—any system.

RH: How would you describe an introverted intuitive?

PB: Internal, imaginative. I seldom orient in terms of facts and reason, but more unconventionally. I could call my process schizoid, but I'd rather call it "introverted intuitive."

JH: How do you put that together with living here in this environment in Harvard Square, which feels very extraverted to me? Not so much inside your apartment, but outside—the University, lots of people, cars ....

PB: Well, I love that too. [*Laughter*] I need extraversion. I like the real world. I like people. I like to sit in the Square and watch people. I enjoy parties and socializing. But I am also introverted. I can go weeks—months probably—quite happily without seeing anyone. What goes on in my own head is entertaining and fascinating to me. I can, of course, hide too—as I have with you, avoiding this interview. All that is my introverted side.

JUNGIAN ANALYSIS

RH: How do you see yourself as a Jungian analyst?

PB: I am Jungian in that I value the relativity of modes of consciousness, as in typology. I assume perspectivism. I value, above all, Jung's notion of the teleological perspective— giving credit to something and seeing what it is trying to do—like a symptom.

JH: What it is trying to tell you ….

PB: Yes. Or what is it trying to show or develop in the psyche.

RH: Can you give an example?

PB: Here is where I have trouble as an intuitive. The ideas are so much quicker (and vaguer) than concrete examples. Say, someone has a cold. Feeling cold? Needing what? Needing to be loved? Needing warmth? Needing some kind of nurturing? Needing to hide your head under a blanket? Needing to sneeze aggressively all over everyone? Giving credit to what the cold is expressing rather than trying to get rid of it is a purposive or teleological perspective.

JH: Instead of the medical model, which would help you get rid of the symptoms?

PB: Yes, listening to the symptoms and honoring what they are saying or doing.

RH: As a Jungian analyst, how would you deal with someone who actually has a cold?

PB: It is up to them how they deal with the physical side of the cold, whether they do or don't take cold medicines. But I would show sympathy for and see if the person wanted to explore feeling cold or down or abandoned or alone.

RH: Someone might say then, so you think talking about it that way will help get rid of the cold?

PB: Colds run their course. [*Laughter*] They go for a certain length of time, no matter what we do.

RH: Then why explore them symbolically?

PB: Not to get rid of the cold, but rather to appreciate what it is trying to express. The attitude that something has meaning helps the psyche feel heard.

RH: How do you know if the psyche has been heard?

PB: It stops throwing a fit. Symptoms decrease—or maybe increase, since they've got your attention. Things want to be recognized.

SHADOW

RH: What areas of Jungian psychology are especially important to you?

PB: The shadow—the notion that there is no right or wrong stance. And, always, shadows that complicate. That's a wonderful addition of Jung's to depth psychology and to consciousness in general.

RH: How do you deal with the shadow?

PB: I just try to be open about it. The shadow constantly relativizes the ego, whatever I think I am about. I usually hear about my shadow from somebody else. Someone says I am being stubborn. And I thought I was being ethical! [*Much laughter*]

RH: At this point in your life, when you hear someone say that kind of thing to you, is it a little easier to accept it now?

PB: At this point, I think there is not much that's simply 'ethical' or simply anything. Everything is shadow-marbled.

RH: Do you feel it is easier now to deal with that kind of stuff as you have gotten older?

PB: Much easier. I am no longer on my way up. It is when you are on your way up, I believe, that it is hardest to deal with shadow.

RH: So if you are not on your way up, where are you now?

PB: On my way down! [*Much laughter*] Shadows everywhere—and on to the valley of the shadow.

RH: You said you encounter your shadow mainly through what other people say about you.

PB: Feedback from the world, however that comes, yes.

RH: Not through dreams or active imagination?

PB: Dreams are always a matter of interpretation. You tend to interpret your dreams using the same constructs your ego is already identified with.

DREAMS

RH: Do you interpret your dreams?

PB: I do not write down every dream every night. But if I am going through a difficult period or if dreams are banging me over the head, then yes, I pay lots of attention.

RH: Do you think you can see the shadow in your dreams?

PB: I don't think anybody can. I do not trust isolated self-awareness. I differ from some Jungians in this regard. It seems to me so easy to get into introverted inflations. All alone in a tower with the Self? Naw! I believe we need world and feedback from others.

JH: Or at least getting out in the world and tripping a few times to see it.

PB: Yes. Too often new analysts wander off after graduation—particularly from Zürich—and don't join professional societies. This is one of the reasons the Inter-Regional Society has seemed to me so important. It connects individuals and groups that would not be connected otherwise. Those interconnections and the continuing education they provide are crucial for the field, as well as for individual health.

RH: How have you dealt with that yourself?

PB: In Zürich I was part of a clique, or subculture. When I got back to the States in 1978 and joined Inter-Regional, I found myself associating with persons who had been in other groups in Zürich. My group had hung out only with people who had the same analyst or who were friends with friends of our analysts. Now here in the Inter-Regional I was associating with a broader variety of people. To my astonishment, these others were perceptive and 'psychological.' How could this be, for they trained with so and so?

RH: Where do the people in your life come from who help you stay connected to the shadow?

PB: Colleagues, friends, any sort of relationship.

RH: How do you describe a friend?

PB: Somebody who perceives and loves you and will tell you really hard things.

ART, POETRY, AND PSYCHOLOGY

RH: Where do you find your energy in doing analytical work?

PB: Well, some of the patients I work best with are people in the arts. I have a painter, for example, who describes her world in a way that would not make sense to many people. To me, it is enlivening.

JH: Do you think it is because such people are closer to the symbolic?

PB: I don't know. I have a photographer who talks about *seeing*, not just looking, but *seeing* with his camera. I don't know that what he sees is so much the 'symbolic' as just what is there. But he frames what is there so we can see it. I think essentially that's what the arts do. They reveal the unconscious that is present.

RH: How do you like to work with an artist?

PB: I follow them.

RH: Would you have them bring you their works and you look at them together?

PB: Some people do bring things. Many don't, because they do not want to risk therapy becoming a criticism of their work. If there is any question, it is better that they don't bring their work, better that I just listen to their process. When I go to someone's performance, which I sometimes do, we have worked together a long time and have a secure relationship, so criticism is not a problem. They know I won't hurt them. How I work therapeutically with artists is most often quite practical. The more complicated the psyche, the more practical I get—like how to survive doing art, how to get the grant, how to show up every day and do the work. Forget that nonsense about your innermost soul. You've either got something on the page or canvas or stage, or not. [*Laughter*] I feel I know the escape routes and so can help people *not* take easy ways out.

RH: I see you have a practical side to you. Do you feel art has to be interpreted in order to have meaning?

PB: No. But it has to 'work' in an artistic sense. Of course, there is the question of who decides whether it 'works' or not. I listen to people who have studied the field—whatever it may be—to keep educating myself about what works—how, and how not.

RH: Are you an artist?

PB: Not really, but I did do a stint of performance poetry. I was on the Boston poetry slam team for a couple years, and represented Boston at the national competitions. To get good enough to do that, I had to learn a lot about communicating and embodying.

RH: Would you like to share one of your poems?

PB: No, but I'll tell you about them. One is about a stalker. It goes back and forth between the stalker and the woman being stalked. I have another that is in the voice of a rapist and victim, then wife-beater, etc. I like these poems that speak from alternate sides of an emotional situation. That is interesting to me.

JH: Because you have to convey them very differently so people can follow that you are jumping back and forth?

PB: It's that I enjoy developing my own emotional flexibility.

RH: That is where the artist and psychologist come together then for you?

PB: Yes.

RH: But there is a fear of being reduced.

PB: Yes. I have done a lot of public performances. Once in a while, a colleague witnesses something and says, "Gosh, I did not realize such terrible things happened to you." Whether or not something happened to me personally doesn't matter. One artist would never say to another, "Oh, I'm so sorry that thing that you made your poem about happened to you." To go to a performance and try to reduce it to the personal psychology of the performer feels to me an insult.

RH: I remember you wrote something back in the 70s about the artist being reduced. [See "Echo's Subtle Body," *Spring,* 1982, pp. 163-185.]

PB: That has been an obsession, I guess.

RH: What is the danger of reduction?

PB: Not appreciating the larger psychic reverberations.

RH: The rapist/victim poem must have been very powerful.

PB: Especially when I became the rapist.

RH: Do you feel there is something Jungian about a poetry slam?

PB: Yes. I am always trying to dig out what is underneath. For example, what does this rapist need so desperately from this girl? I try to get inside—as I would with a patient. If you have a stalker in analysis, you surely want to understand him.

RH: I wonder if your hesitation to expose your poetry in this interview would be a common thing for an artist to feel about bringing art into an interview?

PB: Jung said psychology is death to the second-rate artist. You need to expose your stuff. But there are also times to protect. If you expose something in the wrong forum (which would be the case here, I believe), it would not serve you. I have been hurt by colleagues reducing my work (actually my essays, too) to my personal psychology.

RH: Is that the shadow side of psychology?

PB: Yes, psychology as a science.

JH: Psychology as a science rather than an art?

PB: Yes. I am most interested in psychology as art—for example, what one can *make* with pathology. Making is art. Psychology as a science, however, likes to generalize, objectify, classify, categorize.

JH: To make it go away.

PB: Yes. Forgetting that the basic workings of the psyche are in its pathological workings too. Pathology is really quite brilliant.

RH: You know we spoke with Edith Wallace ["Visions Never Cease: Edith Wallace at 95," *Quadrant*, 2002], and it was interesting to see how she does her art. I don't think she interprets it.

JH: But she takes it to another level. After I read her latest book, I had a much better sense of who she was, and I didn't have it when I looked at her collages. There is a lot of her in her book.

PB: Edith is burning with the Self. She is one of those old-fashioned Jungians—so wonderfully real and alive. She is a different kind of Jungian than I am. But I love who she is.

RH: Have you found Jungian psychology helpful as you pursue artistic work?

PB: Jung himself was not particularly good with art. He did what a scientist is supposed to do. He tried to categorize. That is not what I want to do.

JH: He was using it to explain his journeys into the unconscious, and whenever he would draw or record something, he would use that to explain his theories.

PB: You mean in his paintings?

JH: Yes.

PB: I wasn't thinking of that. I was thinking of his criticism and essays on art.

JH: What do you want to do with art in your analytical work?

PB: It's not that I want to do anything, but it is how I perceive, or how I think about how I perceive.

RH: Do you use art in your analytical work with others or your work with yourself?

PB: I sometimes draw a paper before I try to write it, just to see it visually or dynamically.

RH: You *draw* a paper?

PB: Yes. I remember doing a paper in which I discovered that the structure was a series of superimpositions, one on top of another. It helps me to do things like that rather than to make a logical outline. I never could make outlines. I always had to write the dissertation first and then go back and make the outline. [*Laughter*] If I knew what I was going to say ahead of time, why in the world would I write the paper? [*Laughter*]

RH: How do you draw a paper?

PB: I just put down fragments of ideas without knowing how they connect or if they do. It is an unconscious process. I think people in the arts probably work this way all the time.

RH: Do you feel the unconscious is a source of creativity?

PB: Yes. But it is conservative, too. It is both. It takes some work to learn to use it creatively.

RH: Do you enjoy writing?

PB: Not so much any more. Right now, I like teaching—so long as I'm exploring something new. I am beginning to feel myself aging. Everything is getting worse. My body does not work as well as it used to. But I like teaching new stuff. I taught a course last semester on film. I used films to explore the psychology of the filmmaker, the film, the period. The focus was the psyche of all those things. It was way too much—but interesting and tons of fun.

RH: Is that your current interest?

PB: Yes. Using film so people can see for themselves, instead of my writing or speaking about something only in words.

RH: That sounds like it picks up on your interest in images.

PB: Yes. Image is, as Jung said about symbol, its own best expression. I am much more with that now, that part of Jung.

SEIZED BY A PASSION

WOMEN IN JUNGIAN PSYCHOLOGY

RH: As a woman in Jungian circles, with all the history of women who surrounded Jung (and most of them were single—and you are a single woman), do you feel a connection with those women, or there is something about Jungian psychology that hits a woman in a certain way?

PB: There are a large number of single women among my friends and Jungian colleagues. Perhaps Jungian analysis and a lifetime of Jungian work makes for a strong character. Many of these women are outstanding. And many don't seem to need relationships of a more intimate sort—or they have already lived that.

RH: Do you think there is something about Jungian psychology that fosters that in a woman?

PB: I don't know, because I myself *do* tend to need relationships. But those early Jungian women, those founders—that was another thing. I'm thinking of the women who took up Jung's spirit, wrote the early books, took the notes at the seminars, and helped spawn the Institutes.

RH: Do you feel you are following in their footsteps in any way?

PB: I don't think that way. But you know someone who did impress me in Zürich was Jolande Jacobi. No, not her. I meant von Franz. Von Franz was so much who she was. She would sit up there on the lecture platform with her legs splayed, her dirty fingernails, and hold forth with such passion and sparkle—it was truly exciting. She *was* the psyche. For a young woman of 23, like myself, it was inspiring, if not life-altering, to be in the presence of such a woman. You see, at that time in Switzerland, women could not even vote. Yet here was the strongest individual I had ever witnessed, also the most respected at the Institute, and she couldn't even vote.

RH: That is amazing.

PB: But for my own analyst I sought out Pip Pope, who was more fashionable and wore stylish clothes and nice scarves. But as an individual— my goodness, von Franz!

RH: Why would you confuse Jolande Jacobi with Marie-Louise von Franz?

PB: I don't know. Jacobi was also a very strong character. But I was most impressed with von Franz.

RELATIONSHIPS

RH: How do you feel about relationships? You said you can go for weeks without seeing anyone. You seem to be a strong woman.

PB: As I get older, I get more and more appreciative of relationship. That has been happening over the past ten years.

RH: You say that Jungian psychology, if you stay with it, as you have for so many years, builds strong character. How does it do that?

PB: I don't even know if it is true. Do you think it is true?

JH: Yes, I think so.

PB: Maybe it is the focus on the Self—looking inward rather than looking to others, which is the very thing I do not like about it. Maybe this is the good side of that interior focus. It develops a world of resources within oneself. As I said, however, I am biased in favor of relationship. So you have me in a contradiction here. [*Laughter*]

RH: If you were to consider marriage again, would you need a lot of space?

PB: Ironically, I would probably need less than I used to. In my family of origin, everyone was independent. I was independent, my brother, my parents. Basically, it was one of those WASP, everyone-do-their-own-thing-and-don't-depend-on-each-other kind of families. It was perfectly natural for me to go off to Switzerland on my own. My development has been to learn to value relationship more and independence less. When I get scared, of course, I become quite dependent. [*Laughter*] For me, the growing edge has been to become more relational.

SPIRITUALITY

RH: Are you a spiritual person?

PB: I am one of those Jungians who call themselves spiritual but not religious. I am not a member of a church, but have great appreciation for what happens in religions and what religions are about.

RH: How important is your spirituality?

PB: The mass is spiritually important. Religious rituals are important. The mysteries are important.

RH: How does spirituality find expression in your life? I do not necessarily mean publicly, but privately.

PB: Trying to be in touch with myself, authentic, knowing there are always things beyond me and more important than I am.

RH: Is God a part of your life?

PB: Sometimes I use the word God; sometimes I think in terms of destiny or fate. With clients I often look for what this person is meant to be or do—his or her final form—in an almost Aristotelian sense. This is all God-stuff to me.

RH: Do you ever feel that God is present when you are doing analytical work?

PB: Certainly the mystery is there. I just need to be with it as well as I am able.

RH: Then what is your issue with the church or organized religion?

PB: My childhood experience of organized religion was that it was a breeding ground for hypocrisy. I am suspicious of talk about goodness. It is too easy to become righteous and lose shadow. I certainly do not believe it is unfortunate that churches or religious institutions exist. But I don't feel pulled there myself. At this point in my life, if I were going to participate in organized religion, it would probably be Buddhism.

RH: What part of that speaks to you?

PB: The quietness, the notion of suffering as a given, learning to let go, getting in touch with and appreciating, but not grabbing at life, not taking myself so seriously.

RH: Do you have any spiritual practice that you have found helpful?

PB: I just try to get centered, to let go of things, to feel when I am frightened, to be true with myself. That takes moments of sitting down and being still, stepping outside the spin.

RH: How do you do that?

PB: I sit or lie on the sofa or bed and let go and drop until I land.

RH: Do you do that on a regular basis?

PB: Whenever I feel the need.

RH: Then you don't have any regular practices.

PB: Oh, I do! I get up every morning and check my e-mail. [*Laughter*]

RH: Do you think there is something Jungian about the Internet?

PB: I certainly hope so. [*Laughter*] The world is more connected in literal, obvious ways than was the case in Jung's day. That's quite exciting to me.

MENTORS

RH: Who have your mentors been?

PB: No one for a long time! [*Laughter*] But I have had teachers who were important for me at the time I was studying with them.

RH: Who are some of these?

PB: Louise Cowan, who taught literature at the University of Dallas, was formative for me. Toni Frey was important, as I said earlier. Some mentors have been people I have never known personally—William Faulkner, for example, and many other novelists and poets. I don't do mentors in real time much.

RH: Why do you think that is?

180

PB: It's similar to my not doing Jung. I don't like big personalities. I have seen too much shadow—big, glowing personalities have big, glowing shadows.

RH: The larger the person, the larger the shadow.

PB: ... As Jung said.

RH: How do you think Jung dealt with his shadow?

PB: Not very well, I'd say, because he did not have an equal to help him. That is the danger of the big personality. He had two women. But nobody was up to Jung, really, I don't believe.

RH: Do you think he is a bad role model in that respect?

PB: He was a man of his time. For his time he was way ahead.

RH: What do you feel is the danger of being around someone with a big, glowing personality?

PB: The narcissistic demands. I don't have the energy to be around that.

Jungians and Jungian Psychology

RH: What do you think of how things have changed now, with all the discussion of ethics? Do you think we are better off today?

PB: We have had to do a lot of shadow cleaning up from the first-generation Jungians. We have worked to become aware, I believe, where they were not. But we have also become identified with this position and are a bit self-righteous, maybe. So we are unconscious in a new way. We take our ethics positions literally, believing we see things now the right way. To my mind, that's not very psychological.

RH: Janis and I have done several interviews with some of the older Jungians and they have all been so easy to talk with. It seems to me that nowadays we have some Jungians who are so heady that it is hard to know what they are talking about. Do you find that?

PB: Jungian talk is often more psychoanalytic nowadays.

RH: You seem more grounded.

PB: I so much appreciate the older Jungians, especially when I see them in films or read interviews with them, because they are such intact, authentic people. It makes me proud to be a Jungian, proud of my heritage. There may be places where I disagree with what one or another of them says, but I am enormously proud to be descended from these people.

JH: That was our feeling, too. They all started with the same fundamental body of knowledge, and it became part of them and they lived it out in their own way. They were all with this man [Jung] at one time, and they each went in a different direction, very different, but very alive.

PB: And so authentic. You can see their shadows right there on their faces. They don't hide. I have a huge appreciation for them.

RH: How do you maintain authenticity with so much regulation and with so much focus on ethics?

PB: When I trained, we developed by dealing with our analyst's shadow, peculiarities, and boundary violations. We got stronger by coping. (Or didn't—there were causalities, of course.) People nowadays might say we didn't really get analyzed because we did not have proper containment— and there is some truth to that. But also the lack of boundaries means we were not hothouse babies.

RH: How do you see all the blaming that goes on today?

PB: Our climate is quite child-centered. The metaphor for our therapy nowadays is child development.

RH: What would a Jungian say to modern collective consciousness, with all the blaming, lawsuits, etc.?

PB: There are many different kinds of Jungians. Some Jungians would talk as I am. Some would focus more on legal realities. Many would say, "You must be aware of analytic boundaries and follow this ethical code, or you will hurt your patient." We assume the looser boundaries of the early days were damaging everybody. I'm not so sure that was always the case, though nowadays the same behavior probably *is* more damaging. But by the same token, a lot of people nowadays may not be attended to.

They are not supposed to be hugged, even though they may really need a hug. I knew an analyst who took psychotic people into her home to take care of them. Nowadays, ethics committees would be all over you for that. But I'll bet it helped some people enormously.

RH: With all the work you have done on yourself and all your Jungian work, do you feel more conscious now than you have ever felt?

PB: I feel more weathered. I have a fuller sense of myself. I am more well-rounded. But I can't say I feel all that more conscious.

RH: But having spent as much time as you have, always trying to see the shadow, what has that done to you after all these years?

PB: [*Laughter*] It's undone me.

RH: Has that made life better?

PB: It has made me wiser, but also a whole lot weaker. Seeing the shadow does not help the ego. I feel richer, fuller—and my heart and soul have grown. My humanness has developed. So, in that sense it has made life better.

RH: Do you feel you can relate to people better because of your work with the shadow?

PB: I have more of an appreciation for people, since there is no question of any of us being right.

RH: I know you said you are not focusing much on death now, but rather on aging.

PB: On falling apart! [*Laughter*]

RH: Does Jungian psychology help you with the aging process?

PB: It is supposed to [*laughter*], but so far it has not helped.

PB: I never thought I would have trouble with this part of life. When I was 23, I was in some ways doing second-half-of-life stuff, since I was in Zürich studying symbols, being reflective. Then I had to come back to do the first half with profession, community, family, home, and such. I have now circled back into Stage II of the second half. Because I had done so much internal work early on, I thought that would be easy. But I really do not like falling apart and getting old. I hate having less energy, forgetting names, the sag and wrinkles — no fun.

JH: We would be worried about you if you thought it were. [*Laughter*]

AUTHENTICITY

RH: You feel as though you have maintained authenticity. You seem very real to me. How did you do that?

PB: Slam poetry helped get me real. Going off and doing crazy things helped me get real. Also, I have a motorcycle.

JH: Wow!

RH: A motorcycle?

PB: I don't ride quite as much nowadays, because it hurts when I fall off. But I have crossed the country three times.

JH: On the motorcycle?

RH: You've got to be kidding!

JH: By yourself or as part of a group?

PB: By myself twice and one time with a guy. But I like most of all to ride by myself. I had one pretty bad accident, and I'm still wrestling with whether riding is worth it or not. I love being that close to things. Riding through the deserts out West with the gorgeous vistas—these are the most wonderful experiences. You smell the smells, sense the landscape as it changes color and shape, feel it with your body because your body tilts with the road. Of course, it is tricky doing it as a woman. I wear a helmet and zip on one of these big all-weather touring suits so nobody can tell what gender I am.

JH: And you take the back roads, I suppose.

PB: As much as possible. Of course, it is crazy to start riding a motorcycle at my age. Before that, on the farm in Connecticut, I had horses—which somehow felt quite similar.

RH: Where do the inspirations come from to do these crazy things?

PB: I get seized by a passion. I do not know why my psyche works this way, but for me it is important to follow these irrational passions.

RH: Is it more important to follow them at this age than at earlier ages?

PB: Oh, I always followed them, but the things I was seized by at earlier ages made more sense—going to Zürich, becoming an analyst. These things ultimately made sense. Now, the things I am seized by are off the map. There was a question of whether I should run for an office in the International Association, since I generally love organizational stuff, but it was not where I was seized.

RH: So you try to follow the passion.

PB: Yeah. And there are the dreams. For instance, when the question of getting involved with the International came up, I did the *I Ching* and what I got was "stagnation." So that was clear. The psyche just said, "Nope, that is not what you are going to do right now."

JH: Neat!

RH: This has been fun.

PB: Thank you both for pulling all this out of me.

Postscript: Since the time of this interview, Patricia Berry has become one year older and moved to Brunswick, Maine, where she is in a new relationship and ready for the next adventure, she says.

MURRAY STEIN, PH.D.

Murray Stein is a graduate of Yale University (1965), Yale Divinity School (1969), and has his Ph.D. from the University of Chicago (1985). In 1973 he received his Diploma from the C.G. Jung Institute in Zürich. He had a private practice in Wilmette, Illinois from 1980 to 2003 and was a training analyst with the C.G. Institute of Chicago. Since 2003, he has lived in Switzerland and is a training analyst with the International School of Analytical Psychology in Zürich. Murray is an ordained minister (retired) in the United Presbyterian Church. He is a founding member of the Inter-Regional Society of Jungian Analysts and was the first President of the Chicago Society of Jungian Analysts (1980-85). He is a former President of the International Association for Analytical Psychology (2001-4). He is the author of several books, including *The Principle of Individuation, In MidLife, Transformation, Jung's Map of the Soul,* and *Jung's Treatment of Christianity,* and is the editor of *Jungian Analysis.* Murray and his wife, Jan, have two children, Sarah and Christopher, and four grandchildren. They also have a Maltese terrier named Popageno. We interviewed Murray in the winter of 2002.

• 9 •

DEEPENING THE SOUL
MURRAY STEIN AT 59

In fact, I have always thought of my work as an analyst as being in
line with a pastoral vocation.

—Murray Stein

ENCOUNTERING JUNG

ROB HENDERSON (RH): How did you get interested in Jung?

MURRAY STEIN (MS): When I was in Washington, D.C. doing an
intern year between my second and third year of Divinity School, Betty
O'Connor of the Church of the Savior [and author of *Journey Inward,
Journey Outward*] suggested I read Jung. So I visited a local bookstore and
found *Memories, Dreams, Reflections*. I couldn't put it down. It's the only
book that has actually changed my life. After that, returning to Yale
Divinity School in the fall of 1969, I ran into Russell Becker, professor of
pastoral care, who had just returned from a year in Zürich at the Jung
Institute. We hit it off immediately, and I spent the year studying with
him. He recommended me to the Institute, where I went upon graduation
from Yale Divinity School. It was a matter of one thing leading to another,
doors flying open all along the way.

RH: What was it about *Memories, Dreams, Reflections* that changed
your life?

MS: What I found in this wonderful book was a whole new way of
looking at life. The notion of the unconscious was utterly new to me—at
least in the way Jung uses this notion. My meager exposure to the idea of
the unconscious previously had been a smattering of Freudian
superficialities. When I read *Memories, Dreams, Reflections*, I immediately

began recording my own dreams and trying to decipher them, using the glossary in the back of the book (shadow = dark threatening figures of the same sex; anima = beautiful women, etc.). I was also impressed with the grasp Jung had on religion and religious images and feelings. The book bowled me over. I couldn't put it down. I still find it extraordinary and read from it regularly. Never mind that Aniela Jaffé is responsible for it. The feminine touch improved it, in my opinion.

RH: What are a couple of your favorite stories about Jung?

MS: I arrived in Zürich in 1969, eight years after Jung died. His spirit was still alive and well, however, in the Institute. Barbara Hannah was the first lecturer I encountered. She was giving her "Cat, Dog, Horse" lectures—but mostly she told stories about Jung. I don't recall many specifics, but what emerged was a rendition of "tales about the wise old man." Almost everything Jung did and said was, in her view, a teaching. It was sort of like listening to one of the Apostles talk about Jesus after the resurrection. I witnessed the making of the Gospels. It was quite inspiring. At the time, I was a complete newcomer to the Jungian world and had no critical judgment whatsoever. When von Franz lectured, it was more like listening to God speak than hearing a mere Apostle. She spoke with the voice of Jung himself, and I thought she understood it all, had the complete picture about Truth, Reality, and Life. So all of my Jung stories were filtered through these mouthpieces. One of my favorite stories about Jung, nonetheless, was told to me by Ulrich Hoerni, his grandson. It seems that while at Bollingen, Jung would fix himself porridge for breakfast every day. He cooked the porridge in an iron pot, and when he was finished with the meal, he would take the pot to the lake and put it in the shallow water. Fish would come and eat the remainder of the oatmeal from the pot. After a while, the fish learned the routine so well that they would already be there waiting for *their* breakfast when Jung came along after *his* breakfast. I find this story touching and amusing. It shows a relationship between Jung the man and his natural surroundings.

RH: What did you learn about Dr. Jung from his grandson, Ulrich Hoerni?

MS: Ulrich is extremely knowledgeable about Jung's writings and life, and being Swiss and having grown up there during the 40's and lived in the culture for his entire life, he is much more aware than most people of the context in which Jung worked. He and I have had many long discussions about the 30s and 40s, regarding the position of Switzerland during the years of Nazi domination in Germany, and Jung's attitudes toward the Germans in that period. For instance, the JAP [*Journal of Analytical Psychology*] recently published an interview that Jung gave in 1942 to a Swiss magazine, *Schweizer Illustrierte*, with a commentary by Jay Sherry. I did not realize that at that time it was the consensus in Europe that Germany could easily win the war and that the Nazis and the Germans would dominate Europe for a long time to come. This, of course, created a very particular climate of dread and anxiety in Switzerland, which was culturally and economically—if not politically—closely bound to Germany. If you read the interview with this context in mind, what comes through is quite different from the impression one gets when one reads Jung's remarks from the perspective of what we know now, namely, that Germany was in fact about to bring about its own inevitable defeat by attacking Russia and getting bogged down in an unwinnable war on the Eastern front. So I guess what I've learned from Ulrich is quite a lot about the Swiss culture and mentality, its politics and awareness of its delicate relations with the giant countries that surround it. We have to keep in mind that Jung was Swiss through and through, although intellectually and culturally he far exceeded those quite specific limitations and boundaries. It is important to distinguish between various levels in our discussions about and appraisals of Jung: the scientific, the psychological, the religious, the political, the personal (family and relationships), to name a few. Besides that, Ulrich has told me quite a few stories about his grandfather. He is the family member in charge of managing Jung's written legacy and as such has been privy to all the documents, such as the *Red Book* (which will be published in a couple of years, incidentally) and other personal materials, such as letters, diaries, and so on.

JUNGIAN ANALYSIS

RH: Given your background at the Divinity School at Yale, do you consider your professional work to be a ministry?

MS: I received ordination in the Presbyterian Church in 1973 for a special ministry as a Jungian analyst and teacher in Houston, Texas, and

I have continued to be associated with the local presbytery here in the Chicago area. In fact, I have always thought of my work as an analyst as being in line with a pastoral vocation. While I was studying at Yale Divinity School, it became evident to me that the church is a collective association and treats the "average" layperson. But of course the "average person" does not actually exist. Everyone is unique, special, and individual. So what is the church doing? I wondered about its effectiveness and relevance. If it missed the individual, the only dimension it could treat was the collective. Social action made sense because it involves collective action. But spiritual life was getting shortchanged, I felt. The church was not offering much of value in this regard—at least not the Protestant church that I grew up in and knew. And in practical terms, I couldn't see how a minister could attend to the needs of all the individuals in his or her congregation. He or she is dealing with the whole group, and the job is largely administrative and political. Sermons are aimed at the general collective level of the group's attention span and understanding. There isn't time to meet for long sessions with individual church members. I was much more interested in reaching the individual and deepening the soul work there. So when I discovered Jungian psychotherapy, it seemed to me to hold the answer to what I had been searching for all along—a way to deepen and extend the spiritual life of the individual. By this I do not in any way mean avoiding the everyday issues of internal and interpersonal conflict, defensiveness, anxiety and all the rest. But I feel that the Jungian approach in analysis takes all of this material into account in an individual's life and includes it in the overall enterprise of becoming conscious and integrating the transcendent dimension into life.

SEPTEMBER 11, 2001

RH: In terms of analytical psychology, how do you understand the nightmare of September 11?

MS: Well, nightmare is certainly a relevant term. The whole event had and has a dreamlike quality. It's surreal in a way. Many patients have expressed the same feeling. "Unbelievable," is a term that springs from the lips. Yet this is not fiction, nor dream, but physical reality. I've had many thoughts about it. One thing that seems apparent to me is that this is a product of the collision of cultures at a world historical level. I've asked a number of economists and political thinkers what they see to be the limits of globalization. Many of them have looked at me in a puzzled way. To me, it seems that this economic and political phenomenon is running into a wall wherever it meets traditional cultures and particularly those rooted in the Muslim religion. Islam and the West have become polarized, as we witnessed in Iran over twenty years ago and increasingly in many other parts of the world since then. My notion is that we must learn much more about Islam and Muslim culture, and we must make much greater efforts to dialogue with the intellectual, political, and religious leaders of the countries controlled or influenced by Islam. If the great teachers of Islam would declare that people who kill others in these terrorist acts will go directly to Hell for eternity rather than to Paradise, a lot of violent behavior would cease immediately. If children were not taught to hate America in their schools from the early years on, they might have a better perception of who and what we are. On the other side, we must become much more conscious of the shadow of Western imperialism, expansionism, and dominance that goes under the guise of globalization these days. Globalization and modernization pose a dire threat to traditional peoples, not only because they cause economic dislocation, but because they attack cultural, philosophical, and religious roots. The psyche is deeply affected by this challenge posed by Western science and values. In short, I believe what is needed is much more dialogue between the West and Islam at multiple levels, and a willingness on our part to listen to their perceptions about us. Otherwise, we are only shocked and surprised at the incredible hatred so many people around the world harbor toward us.

RH: When the ego gets hit and wounded by the shadow, it quite naturally seeks to get even, as is seen in our country now preparing to strike back at the terrorists. What would analytical psychology suggest to the ego?

MS: Well, I guess what analytical psychology always says to the ego is, pause for a moment and reflect. Reflect on your defensive reactions, reflect on your shadow motivations, and try to clarify the reality situation you find yourself in. Once that work has been done (and this includes examination of unconscious material, of course, like dreams and fantasies), then take action based on your best and most conscious judgment. In the present situation, it is extremely important to identify our outrage and defensive emotional reactions to this attack on our population. It is equally important to protect our country as far as possible from similar attacks in the future. But we must act with great consciousness because the perpetrators are elusive and hidden. It becomes easy to project onto whole groups of people (the "others out there" in the Muslim world) and lash out at all of them. Most of them are suffering terribly from their corrupt and cruel political overlords and are trapped in a horrible and helpless situation. The mature ego is patient and takes long-range decisions that do not need to show immediate results. The worst thing we could possibly do is to try to muscle our way out of this difficult situation simply on the basis of our massive military superiority. The ego must be aware that it is in great danger of creating a situation that will damage its long-term interests in a fundamental way, namely, entering into an all-out war with the Muslim nations. This would be the height of folly, from the ego's self-interested point of view.

THE UNCONSCIOUS

RH: What are some of the ways you work with the unconscious in your own life? I am thinking of dreams, active imagination, etc.

MS: In the past few years, I have found active imagination especially useful—in fact, invaluable. Also, I observe and reflect on my dreams with a friend or my wife or sometimes a close colleague. I also try to watch for synchronicity in relation to dreams and active imagination. And then there is the constant work on my unconscious in my practice as I observe and work with countertransference. I think of analytic relations in terms of mutual transference and "fields between." This is endlessly fascinating and rich terrain, and I feel enormously privileged to be in the profession I have chosen (or that has chosen me). I imagine, however, that people in any profession can do the same, if they choose to watch their projections and emotional reactions to the people they work with. Teachers, for instance, project massively onto their students. So the unconscious is all around us, whether we're waking or sleeping.

SPIRITUALITY

RH: How do you see God in Jungian analysis?

MS: I wrote a paper on "Psychoanalysis and Spirituality," which will be published soon in *Quadrant* [*Quadrant* XXXII: 2, Summer 2002]. In it, I make a distinction between positive spirituality and negative spirituality, following Isaiah Berlin's famous distinction between positive and negative liberty. Positive spirituality would try to program God into the session, so to speak, by using prayer, meditation, or other positive techniques. Negative spirituality simply lets the spiritual happen when and as it will. I recommend the latter. If God moves into a session with a dream, a synchronicity, a transference or countertransference reaction, then that should be openly acknowledged and received. These moments do happen in analysis, but I don't think you can program them without falling into denominationalism.

MARRIAGE AND FAMILY

RH: What are some of your current views on marriage and divorce?

MS: I think of marriage as a complex psychological relationship with conscious and unconscious aspects, grounded in an archetypal energy constellation. There is a sacred factor involved here, no doubt. Marriage invokes the union of time and eternity because it calls forth love. As an ongoing reality, for most people it becomes a test, ultimately, of their capacity to maintain integrity, inner and outer. I like Jung's notion of container and contained with respect to marriage, only I look on the relationship itself as the container. Sometimes it is a warm bath, sometimes a seething cauldron or an ice-cold tray. Such images come to mind. Of course, marriage has legal and economic aspects, but these are peripheral to the core reality of interpersonal fields and the dynamics that operate between the two personalities involved. Divorce may be a failure to withstand the demands of marriage, a failing grade on the test. On the other hand, it may be a turning point in a deepening individuation process. Every marriage is unique, and each divorce is different. Everything depends on the context and the people involved.

RH: What does it mean to maintain integrity within a marriage?

MS: Integrity must be understood in relation to individuation. To maintain integrity is to keep one's individuation process going. What often happens in a marriage is that one person loses him/herself in the other and then has to go through the separation process all over again, as though from attachment/dependence on parents in the family of origin. For a time at least, integrity is lost. There is a loss of soul. Because the archetypal pattern underlying marriage is one that seeks to unite the opposites, the conscious personalities can get so pressed into its service that they lose their individual connection to the Self. Then there is a huge confusion of personalities, which features projection and projective identification and results in a kind of polarization of shadow. Out of this stems the dynamic of manipulation. What the call to integrity does is call the person to an individual center, from which intimate relationship can grow without distorting the person's individuation process. The challenge of marriage is to maintain integrity, hence individuation while living in intimate relationship with another person at multiple levels within the container created by the marriage archetype. I have found two books important and informative in this regard: Adolf Guggenbühl-Craig's *Marriage Dead or Alive* and John Beebe's *Integrity in Depth*.

RH: Do you feel that remaining true to your individuation process is more important than trying to make sure the relationship is going all right?

MS: Well, there is always the need to strike a balance because in fact individuation is impossible without intimate relationship. Also, real intimacy is impossible without individuation. So these must go hand in hand. Practically speaking, there are many moments in a long-term relationship that demand a conscious decision to go one way or the other. The best advice would be that if your natural inclination is more towards relationship, you need to emphasize individuation, and vice versa. This is a lifelong process, and it is impossible to 'arrive' at an ideal point and stay there.

RH: You are a father. How has Jungian psychology affected your parenting?

MS: The children of professionals always suffer the parental deformations that arise from their parents' training, education, and passions—no less so the children of Jungian analysts. Probably psychotherapists and psychologists are generally too intrusive with their kids, understanding everything in developmental terms, keeping their eyes peeled for incipient pathology, commenting on behavior and interpreting stray and offhand comments. The result is that the child develops defenses against this and goes into hiding. I've had to cope with this problem with my own two children. They've had to cope with me, too. We joke about it. Neither of them is much interested in academic psychology, but both know about the shadow, the anima and animus, thinking and feeling types, archetypes and myths. They both love movies—the contemporary religion, with its villains and heroes. And both are hooked on music—the feeling side of popular culture. The positive value of Jungian psychology for them, I believe, has been that we have attempted in the family to honor dreams, to respect individuality, and to take typology into account. With both children, I have now what I consider to be a quite wonderful, healthy, and open relationship, but it has not been without turmoil. I think Jungian psychology has helped us to be more open with each other, even though that is sometimes almost intolerable. We are able to show affection and anger, and we tend to laugh a lot when we're together.

ANALYTICAL PSYCHOLOGY

RH: As the newly elected [in 2001] President of the International Association of Analytical Psychology (IAAP), what do you see as some of the important issues in the Jungian psychology world?

MS: Well, I guess the issues could be divided into three general groups: the tensions and polarizations within the IAAP itself; the relations (past and present) between the IAAP and other psychoanalytic and depth psychology organizations (e.g., the IPA [International Psychoanalytic Association]); and the issues that arise between the IAAP and the wider world. Each of these groups can be broken down into a number of major subtopics. In the first group, for instance, there is the perennial tension between classical Jungians and developmental Jungians, which itself contains a large number of issues (emphasis on analysis of dreams, for instance, vs. analysis of transference). In the second group of issues, there is the historical relationship between Freud and Jung and the institutional outcome of their split. In recent years, this divide has begun to come together in many interesting ways. Today we stand on the verge of being able to begin bridging that chasm. In the third group of issues, we have the whole panoply of concerns about psychotherapy and government agencies, insurance companies, and other external pressures on our profession. There is also the important matter of openings in areas of the world, such as Eastern Europe, Asia, and South America, that before the last decade were completely off limits for analytical psychology. Today that picture has changed completely, and some of our most dynamic growth areas lie in those parts of the world. There is also the whole area of applications of analytical psychology to non-clinical topics such as politics, organizations, cultural conflicts, religion, etc. As you see, it is a large and complex set of issues that confronts the IAAP, and the officers are out there on the frontlines on a daily basis.

RH: Since you began in analytical psychology, do you feel Jung is more known and understood now, and what impact do you see his ideas have made in the world?

MS: I'm astonished, frankly, by the enormous impact Jung's ideas have had in the world. Some of his influence has not been quite so obvious; it has happened by way of inspiring others to do great things. For instance, the lie detector test, the Rorschach test, the Myers-Briggs type inventory, and the Thematic Apperception Test were all to one degree or another inspired by Jung. It is the same with Alcoholics Anonymous. These have been mighty movers in the twentieth century and will continue to be in the twenty-first. Jung's influence on the arts, on theology, on literary criticism, on the study of the history of religions has also been immense. This does not even mention his influence on psychotherapy, which was perhaps his most focused and direct contribution. To my mind, psychoanalysis would never have left the Jewish circles in Vienna without Jung's influence on European psychiatry. Jung was Freud's door into the mainstream of psychiatry and psychotherapy, which is why Freud wanted Jung to be the first president of the IPA. Jung was the spearhead. Is his work well understood? That is another question. His writings are so complex and multidimensional that it is a rare student who grasps the

196

unity in the complexity. It is there. Jung has a vision, informed and bounded by strong philosophical views derived from Kant and Schopenhauer, which he displays in his formal and informal writings. To grasp this, one has to read and master a great deal of material, not the least of which are his numerous letters, the transcribed seminars, and his autobiography. Most of the biographies of him fail to capture the immensity of the man, his mission and his vision. Biographers are defeated by the sheer size and complexity of the man. Jung was a lot like Goethe, a creative phenomenon of the mind and spirit on the one hand and a somewhat banal bourgeois middle-class European man of his times on the other. As I say, his influence has been immense. Yet the intellectual grasp of him has been lacking.

THOMAS KIRSCH, M.D.

Tom Kirsch was born in London, the only child of Hilde and James Kirsch, co-founders of the C. G. Jung Institute of Los Angeles. He is a graduate of Reed College, the Yale School of Medicine, and the C. G. Jung Institute of San Francisco. He is also the past President of the International Association of Analytical Psychology. Since 1967, he has been in private practice in Palo Alto, and has served for twenty-five years on the faculty of the Department of Psychiatry at Stanford University. He is currently on the teaching faculty at the C. G. Jung Institute of San Francisco and has lectured in various psychological training programs around the world. His recent book, *The Jungians: A Comparative and Historical Perspective* (Routledge, 2000), has won wide acclaim as the first book to trace the history of the field of analytical psychology. He has also published journal articles and book reviews. Tom and his wife Jean, who is also a Jungian analyst, have a daughter, Susannah, and Tom has a son from his first marriage, David, who is married and has twins. I interviewed Tom at his office in the winter of 2004, after we shared a wonderful lunch together at a delightful Greek restaurant in downtown Palo Alto.

GROOMED TO BE A JUNGIAN

THOMAS KIRSCH AT 67

> To confront the shadow in one's self means you have to make some real changes based on those realizations.
>
> —Thomas Kirsch

ENCOUNTERING JUNG

ROB HENDERSON (RH): What are your memories of Jung when you met him as a child?

Thomas Kirsch (TK): Since both my parents had analyzed with Jung, he was part of our household and a phantom that was behind everything that went on in my childhood. He was definitely bigger than life. In 1955, as a college student, I was making the grand tour of Europe along with two other students, when I developed appendicitis. My mother, who was in Zürich at the time, had me come to a hospital there to have my appendix taken out, and it happened to be around Jung's 80th birthday. My mother dragged me into the receiving line to meet Dr. Jung, and Jung liked it very much that she had done that, as he did not like people obeying the rules all the time. He gave me a very warm handshake, and there was something very open about him towards me that made a deep impression on me. That was my first meeting. The second time was in 1956, when I was traveling with my parents to Europe. They had gone back to Germany for the first time since the war, and we went to Zürich. Emma Jung had just died the previous November. My father went out for afternoon tea with Jung and he took me along. The three of us sat out in the garden for about an hour and a half.

RH: Did you speak with him then?

TK: I had read a few things that he had written, and I mentioned to him where he had said that everything was relative and that there were no absolutes. I said to him that that statement was itself an absolute. He chuckled, and I could tell he liked the idea that I would challenge him. I do not remember what his reply was, but it was not in keeping with my personality at that time for me to have challenged him in that way, even if it was done gently. Even now, I do not challenge people that easily on intellectual matters.

RH: Did you meet him a third time?

TK: Yes, in 1958. I was in medical school, and I was not happy. I was having problems with a relationship, and I went to Zürich for analysis. My father was teaching at the Jung Institute, and he had an appointment with Jung that he could not keep, so Jung said it was all right if I came instead. I had an hour with him, and I was prepped beforehand as to what I should talk about—at the time, Jung was interested in flying saucers. My analyst, C. A. Meier, told me that I had some dreams that Jung would find interesting in relationship to flying saucers. As I walked into his office, Jung said to me "so you want to have an hour with the old man before he dies." I do not remember a single thing from the hour after that.

RH: Incredible!

TK: What I was bringing to the hour was not really what I wanted to bring. I did not know that at the time. I was being the dutiful student who was bringing to Jung what he might be interested in to further his research. Each of these three meetings with Jung in their own way made me quite a Jungian, coupled with what my parents had given me.

RH: You have learned a lot about who Jung was from your parents and other people?

TK: From my parents and all the people coming into the house, I sensed that Jung was idealized, and clearly I idealized him as well—and I probably still do, since one thing I have done all my professional life is defend Jung in a number of situations. But I did find in meeting him that there was something very powerful about being in his presence.

200

RH: What was that power?

TK: There was some kind of wisdom and knowledge that I sensed in this man—though it is possible that my being prepped for the meeting had something to do with it. I felt an aura around him. He wasn't a guru to me, nor was he trying to be full of wisdom. He was actually quite down-to-earth. He was very direct.

RH: Why do you think you do not remember anything from your hour with Jung other than that one thing he said?

TK: I think it was because I was in such an altered state being in the room with him and because I was thrown off by his directness, which I had not been prepped to deal with. Besides, what I was bringing to him was not truly where I was at the time. At the time, I was caught up in trying to decide where to go to medical school and what to do about a relationship with a woman that I was involved in. And I was not involved in flying saucers [*laughter*], which is where he was, so my problems did not mesh with his.

RH: Was it your sense that he was not interested in where you were and mostly oriented to where he was?

TK: I do not think I even gave him a chance to ask where I was. I came in to see him with my own agenda, which was what would be interesting to him, so I do not even know if I was afraid to tell him where I was.

RH: What do you remember about sitting in the garden with Jung and your father?

TK: What I remember was that Jung showed us the sculpture he had done in memory of Emma. She had died the previous November, and Jung was in mourning.

RH: What do you remember about how he and your father spoke to each other?

TK: Nothing specific—but I do remember there was an easy flow between the two of them. My father was very scholarly, and he had a tendency to put almost everyone he knew down a little bit. I saw my father behave absolutely deferentially with Jung in a way I had never seen him do with anyone else in my whole life. It was a revelation.

RH: So you met at least one man who was above your father.

TK: My father was so deferential that I could not believe it.

RH: Do you have brothers and sisters?

TK: I was the only child of my parents, but they both had been married before and had children in those marriages, so I have four half siblings. One of them has died. A lot got projected onto me. You asked about my childhood memories of Jung. My mother wanted to have another child, which turned out to be me, and Jung responded by saying that any cow could do that.

RH: What do you think he meant?

TK: You see, I was supposed to be the child of analysis, the conscious child. My parents had both been in analysis so they might have expected their children after analysis to be more conscious and less troubled.

RH: So what was Jung trying to say?

TK: I think he was trying to tell my mother that I was just another baby—not to put too much on "this child." She did anyway.

RH: Do you have a lot of letters from Jung that you inherited when your parents died?

TK: I do. I actually have the correspondence between my father and Jung. I have the letters my father received from Jung, and now I am trying to get the letters my father sent Jung. They are in Zürich. I have been told there are over 300 letters from my father to Jung. I have about 40-50 letters from Jung to my father. I would like to work that into a book, and that is where my energy is now.

RH: So that is your next book?

TK: That is my next book. I have some first editions of Jung's books that he signed for my Dad, and I have a picture over here on the wall that he signed.

RH: How do you feel that the phantom presence of Jung in your family affected you as a child?

TK: I remember my mother saying to me that I could be any kind of Jungian analyst I wanted to be. [*Laughter*]

RH: So you were groomed from Day One to be a Jungian analyst.

TK: Jo Wheelwright often said to me and anyone else that would listen that my mother stuck an archetype in my mouth when I was weaned. [*Much laughter*]

RH: I can just hear Jo saying that. [*More laughter*] I assume that when someone idealizes someone else, they are doing it out of some need they have.

TK: That is the case, in my opinion.

RH: What need did your parents and other first-generation Jungians have that led them to idealizing Jung?

TK: I would say there were two major areas. The first is the timing of World War II, which meant that many people who were in analysis with Jung were cut off abruptly from Jung for a period of at least six years. If you are in analysis with someone, ideally you would prepare to terminate the analysis and go through the process of ending. These people had no chance to make any kind of normal termination. And with the War on, they could have no contact with him whatsoever, so that left people with an over-idealization of Jung. That is one factor. The second factor is that Jung's position in the world was marginalized. He was definitely the minor personality in relation to Freud. It was a time when Freudian analysis was in the ascendancy. Jung's position was mainly that of a dissenter. Now, we see his psychology as something in its own right. The Freudians made a point of knocking everything Jung did. What I have realized in my 40 years as a professional is that psychoanalysts know terribly little about what Jung wrote about after 1913. From their point of view, whatever he wrote after 1913 was tainted with mysticism and anti-Semitism and had nothing to do with psychoanalysis, so they could just disregard it. There was something cultish about the atmosphere around Jung, because one was so much in the minority; one had to defend him in order to have an identity of one's own.

RH: Has the unresolved transference of the first-generation Jungians been passed down to succeeding generations, and are we still working on these issues?

TK: We definitely are still working on them. Some of the splits in later-generation Jungians had to do with the kind of transferences that the first generation had. For example, in Los Angeles, because my parents were uprooted, they looked to Jung and they adopted Switzerland as their home country as a place they could go back to after the War, since they could not go back to Germany. Everyone who trained in Los Angeles in the early 50s went to Zürich. That was a necessary part of their training. There were probably twenty people who came from Zürich to lecture in Los Angeles. There was a special fund to bring those people over. There is still a residue of that kind of feeling. Some Jungians have sought Freudian psychoanalysis as a reaction against the over-idealization of Jung by their teachers and analysts.

RH: So you feel your parents and their colleagues did not deal with the shadow of Jung?

TK: They recognized the shadow of Jung to some extent, but they made it sound like something positive. For example, there is a story that Jo Wheelwright liked to tell. Maybe he told you this one when you interviewed him. In 1938, he once went to see Jung, and he heard Jolande Jacobi being thrown down the stairs. [*Laughter*]

RH: I heard that one.

TK: OK. Now you laugh about it—but look at it seriously. Many people may have wanted to throw her out symbolically because she could be very provocative, and Jung did not like her managing his ideas in the world. However, to throw her literally down the stairs! Many Jungians see it as charming, but biographers have taken it as an indication that Jung detested women. I would say that's shadow stuff. My parents could not talk about Jung's shadow. One area in which my Dad did talk about it was anti-

Semitism, and he questioned Jung about it too. He said he was satisfied with Jung's explanation, but there were others who were not. That is the problem with reading Jung—you can interpret the same facts and say what a shit he was or what integrity he had in standing by his guns and not letting anyone change his ideas and not backing down when pushed. That could be seen as either good or bad.

RH: You have written in *Psychological Perspectives* what I think is a beautiful remembrance of Franz Jung [Jung's son]. I have wondered if you identify with Franz in any way.

TK: I did feel that. I do not say that my father was in any way as great as Franz's father, but both Franz and I found ourselves in the role of the son who is supposed to follow in the footsteps of the father. I think we both felt that our fathers did not really provide us with a model, and that left us as sons at a bit of a loose end. When I spoke with Franz, I had the sense that he wished his father had given him more direction, helped him more. I think his father was trying very hard to stay out of his way, so Franz would find his own way. I had trouble with my father and his authority growing up. He did not understand what it was like to be an American kid growing up in United States. He expected me to be more like a European, reading all the great philosophers, and I was interested in sports and things of that nature. He couldn't understand that. I was never the scholar my father was. At the time of his death, he owned 25,000 books— and he had read them all. I was much closer to my mother, and I felt Franz was much closer to his mother too. Here, there was a certain similarity. Another thing about Franz was that he loved to talk. He would go on and on and on. Obviously, someone hadn't been listening to him somewhere earlier along the line.

RH: That's interesting, because I had the same feeling the two times I met Franz. In fact, both times I had to excuse myself.

TK: I had to excuse myself too. That happened several times because he did not know when to stop.

RH: I also felt when I spoke with him that he was determined to make sure that we would never talk about anything negative about his father or mother.

TK: He never said anything negative about them directly to me either, but I just sensed that he wished his father would have done more for him. I liked him. He looked and sounded a lot like his Dad—and that was a little unnerving.

RH: Anything else you would like to say about Jung?

TK: Yes. Jung became a very important symbol in my analysis. He became a self symbol for me. He became an inner figure in helping me to find myself in a larger way.

RH: So if you ever dreamt of Jung, that dream generally addressed what was going on in your life. He became a very important symbol for you.

TK: Very important.

RH: Have you had a lot of dreams of Jung?

TK: Not a lot—but my initial dream in analysis when I came to Palo Alto involved Jung. He was a young-looking man in the dream and represented me and my relationship to myself and my ambition in what I was going to do in relation to his psychology.

DEPTH PSYCHOLOGY

RH: You said once that Jungian analysis and depth psychology are under attack today in our medicated society, where insurance no longer pays for long-term treatment. How do you feel this will affect depth psychology and Jungian analysis as a vocation?

TK: What I think will happen is that there will be fewer practitioners of depth psychology and Jungian analysis—and that is not necessarily a bad thing. What Jung wrote about and talked about was getting in touch with the unconscious. I am not sure that he cared too much about how we do it, but he was concerned that we get in touch with that level of our psyche. No matter what people do as far as medication goes, it will not take away people's interest in their own inner development. Look at the recent FDA ruling about the potential suicidal effects of the newer antidepressant medications. There will always be a place for people who are interested in this long-term work. I do not think that Jungian analysis is for everyone. In 35 years of practice, I have seen a lot of people who *think* they want Jungian analysis, but that is not what they want at all.

RH: What is it that they do want?

TK: They want some quick fix. And they usually pay lip service to integrating the shadow. They do not really want to look at the shadow elements in their own lives.

RH: Why do you feel that is? Why are the shadow and depth avoided?

TK: Because if you avoid it, you do not have to make any real changes. To confront the shadow in one's self means you have to make some real changes based on those realizations.

RH: Do you feel our society is becoming shallower?

TK: I feel very appreciative that I live in the Bay area because I think it is still a bastion of something of more depth and spirit than what is going on in most places I read about in the United States.

RH: That's interesting. Why do you think that is?

TK: I think it is partly the politics, but the politics is an outgrowth of a certain psychological sense, maybe it is the New Age influence, or being close to the gateway to Asia, or that there has been a mixture of East and West here for 150 years. There is a lot of ferment here. New England is another area that I love in that regard.

RH: Some people feel the United States is the West and East Coasts and there is some land in between.

TK: I agree with that. [*Laughter*]

INTERNATIONAL JUNGIAN COMMUNITY

RH: What are some of your reflections on Jungian psychology in the world after your years in leadership with the International Association?

TK: For one, I discovered that Jungian psychology is so much influenced by where it is practiced. It is just amazing. The cultural norms of the country make such a difference in the ways Jungian analysis is practiced wherever it is.

RH: You have shown some of that in your book, *The Jungians*. Any surprises you found in how it is practiced?

TK: I became President of the International Association when the Iron Curtain fell—when the Berlin Wall came down. What amazed me was the amount of interest in Jung's psychology that had gone on underneath and out of the awareness of the authorities in Eastern Europe and the Soviet Union. People did not have any possibility of analysis but they had picked things up off the Internet and out of old translations of Jung. Somehow books had gotten in. They had hidden these books and studied them secretly, and when it became possible, these people interested in Jung emerged.

RH: Did you discover a secret society of Jungians?

TK: No, it was individuals who had somehow found friends or colleagues, or books by Jung, or something on the Internet.

RH: I know some of your friends were wondering how you would feel once you left the presidency of the International Association. How has it been?

TK: Through my parents, I met a lot of international Jungians who came to Los Angeles. I have been connected to the international community from a very early age. I gave it my fullest and really put my heart and soul into the international work. Writing the book, *The Jungians*, helped with my transition. What has happened now is that I am more interested in the history. I am not interested now in writing about dreams and other aspects of clinical practice, but rather in history. I just practice as I do. I do not know if it is Jungian or whatever. I just practice as I do.

RH: Why have you become interested in the history now?

TK: Part of it is my typology—I am an extraverted intuitive feeling type. That means I am somewhat like you. I love stories. I feel it is something I have and can give, and many other people do not have and cannot do. So I have some kind of legacy of what I have experienced that I want to pass on, since after I'm gone it will be gone too, if I don't pass it on.

RH: What trends do you see going on in Jungian psychology today?

TK: I see two opposing trends. On one side, I see many people gravitating toward psychoanalysis and object relations, and I see the danger there of losing the deeper connection to the psyche. On the other side, I see many people veering towards taking Jung in a fundamentalist fashion. I do not like either of these extreme trends. There is a strong clinical tradition in Jungian analysis which has not been properly spelled out and needs to be spelled out more clearly. I feel that is one of the strengths of the professional San Francisco Jung group. There is a strong clinical value here.

RH: Are these deepening Jung's vision or, by elaborating only certain areas, skewing the overall vision?

TK: I think that the two extreme tendencies, which I just mentioned, undermine the real value that Jung offers. Jung had such broad interests that it is understandable why people have taken certain parts of his thinking and tended to make it more than it actually was meant to be. Jung's intuitions went in many directions.

RH: Can you give me an example, Tom, of when something went too far?

TK: I cannot give you a specific example, but I think about the number of people who have told me that a dream has told them to act in certain situations. I follow my dreams closely, but I am weary of people who live too much by the unconscious. This living by one's dreams can go too far. Where is the position of consciousness then?

PSYCHOLOGICAL TYPES

RH: One of the things I read that you had written, which touched me, Tom, was that it is important to you to be true to your typology. Is your interest in history an instance of that?

TK: Yes. I am not an alchemical Jungian. I appreciate alchemy, but I do not read alchemical texts. I would rather read biographical stories about people.

RH: What have you learned about the extraverted intuitive feeling type?

TK: I really knew that extraverted intuitive feeling was my primary function when I saw the kind of trouble I have had with introverted sensation. I have a lot of trouble with my back, and I have had to do exercises and physical activity all my life in order to balance out my life. What I have learned from extraverted intuition is that intuition can be 180 degrees wrong as often as it can be right. The reality that it is often right about people or things can make one begin to believe that it is always correct, and then one is in trouble. One forgets that one can be mistaken as well. What I have learned about the feeling function is that people like the good feeling that it gives, but it can also be used in a manipulative way and it can be dictatorial. Through feeling you can make people do things that they do not really want to do. One has to be careful with one's feeling function. It is not just an absolutely wonderful thing.

RH: Somewhere I read that you feel your responses now are much more introverted than they were in the past. Do you think that comes from an intention now to develop your introverted side?

TK: I am not sure that is really true. Recently, I saw a man that I had seen twenty years ago, and he said he found me less doctrinaire than I used to be. One of the ways I have changed in clinical practice is that I do not push for dreams the way I used to. When I started, bringing dreams in to every session was a kind of homework one did when in analysis. I still write down my dreams, since I find it helps me remain somewhat centered. I want people to bring in dreams, but I hope they are more spontaneous. It used to be if you did not have a dream, you had the feeling that there was nothing to talk about—you should just go home or to the movies. [*Laughter*]

RH: What do you talk about then if patients do not bring in dreams?

TK: Well, you talk about what is going on in people's lives. What I tell my patients now is: I want you to talk about whatever is emotionally significant for you right now as you are in the room with me, whether that is a reaction to something I said or a dream or wherever it takes you.

RH: Do you think that is because you are now dealing with the unconscious coming out in lots of different ways rather than just in dreams?

TK: Yes. I will tell you who really influenced me on this was John Weir Perry. His word for archetypes was "affect images." My job as an analyst is to connect the affect with the image, and if I can do that, something happens within the psyche of the individual, and some kind of positive change takes place.

RH: But that does not have to be in a dream.

TK: No.

RH: What has it been like for you to be an extravert in the largely introverted Jungian community?

TK: Because of my Jungian upbringing, for a long time I thought I was an introvert. [*Laughter*]

RH: That's interesting.

TK: It is. You know most people grow up here with the value that they are expected to be extraverted in American society. My parents thought I should be an introverted intuitive thinker.

RH: Because that's what Jungians were?

TK: Yes, and that's what Jung was. I struggled with it. I was a good student, so I could pass off as one. But I had so much trouble reading. I was a good reader. I didn't enjoy reading, partly because my father was such a voracious reader and kept putting me down for not knowing more about subjects that he knew about. I had some kind of paralysis about reading. But then I realized that my nature was more to go out and meet people and do things. That naturally worked for me much better. It was only through my analysis that I discovered that I am really an extravert. The intuition was always there, but feeling was stronger than thinking. That's why becoming involved with the International Society was quite natural for me. It put the extraverted intuitive feeling part of my nature to work.

RH: What do you feel extraversion is?

TK: I am not quite sure how to answer that. Extraversion is finding one's primary value through an outer object, be it place, person, or thing. There is less energy going towards the inner subjective object, and the extravert depends highly on that connection with the outer object.

RH: Do you ever try to develop your introverted side?

TK: I have an introvert for a wife. She is the opposite of me. So I have been forced to … [*laughter*] … kicking and screaming all the way. [*Laughter*]

RH: I have a similar situation, as my wife is introverted and I am extraverted, and that is why talking with the Wheelwrights was fun. They had the same thing in their marriage. You have a marriage of the opposites too. What have you learned about that kind of marriage? I often tell people that I think about 70% of marriages are that way.

TK: What I have learned is that there is a great deal of value in introversion. My wife has helped me a lot. I developed back problems when I was 27 or 28. She helped me to look for other forms of treatment, other than the traditional medical treatment. Her point of view has been invaluable to me. I do not think I would be sitting with you today if I had not followed her lead. I probably would have had some surgery that would not have helped me at all. I would be much more in chronic pain than I am.

RH: I am glad. You think that is one thing that came from your marriage of the opposites?

TK: It came from the marriage of the opposites. What I have given her, on the other hand, is that she was very shy, and she has come out much more in the world than she would have done otherwise.

RH: What is your advice to people in a marriage who are more opposite than similar?

TK: It is a common phenomenon that marriage contains opposite typologies. Opposites attract. We are fascinated by that which is undeveloped in ourselves, and we unconsciously see that in the other and are quite taken by it. As we get into the relationship, we realize that the other also is very problematic, and we have to find a way to negotiate with that other side. This can often bring a person into analysis, because eventually we have to bring much more of that which we have projected onto our partner back into our own psyche.

DREAMS

RH: How do you deal with your own dreams?

TK: Over the years I have been in analysis for the most part with one person, Joe Henderson. And I still am. It has been a long time. It is not analysis in the classical sense. I bring my dreams to him. I write out my dreams in my journal as I always have, and I work on them. I still see him every other week. I think I am much better at dealing with my own dreams now. Joe is over 100 now and is still very much there.

RH: Would you say your dreams are important to you?

TK: Absolutely. I still get up in the middle of the night and write a dream down. Recently we had to put a dog down, and I had some dreams that were extremely significant. So, I still keep pretty close tabs on my dreams.

RH: Have you learned any new tricks on remembering your dreams?

TK: No. As I heard you say, it is a kind of spiritual practice with me. In fact, I would say it is one of my spiritual practices—a major one.

RH: What are some of your other spiritual practices?

TK: Well, another activity that I find very spiritually uplifting is swimming for half an hour a day. It helps with my introverted sensation and it also gives me a chance to let my imagination go where it will. Often it is the time when I think about the meaning of a particular dream.

RH: What do you do with your dream journals when they are filled?

TK: I have them all lined up on my bookshelf. I have kept every one of them going back to 1962.

THE SHADOW

RH: Has the notion of the shadow helped you in relationships with your family and friends?

TK: That's not the way I would put it. I see the light and dark in myself, my friends, and family. I do not use the term shadow. I am specific about what I see in people.

RH: You find it more helpful to be specific like that?

TK: I don't like the term "shadow." I think using terms such as "shadow" can short-circuit an experience. I would rather describe the experience than put a label on it. The labeling bothers me.

RH: Do you feel the same way about diagnosis?

TK: What I look for is *evidence* of psychosis, because I think there is a great deal of difference in working with people who have a psychotic process going on and those who have either a neurosis or character disorder. The specific *DSM* [*Diagnostic and Statistical Manual of Mental Disorders*] diagnosis is not as important to me.

RH: Do you still do insurance?

TK: I will fill out my part of the insurance form so people can get reimbursed. But they have to pay me first in full. I will not go to insurance companies to get reimbursed.

RH: Why is that?

TK: Because insurance companies generally want to hold onto the money and make it as difficult as possible for you to get paid. I figure it is the person's responsibility to pay me. I will do my share in filling out my part of the insurance form. Then they can deal with getting their reimbursement.

LIFE AND PRACTICE AS A JUNGIAN ANALYST

RH: Can you talk about your calling as an analyst?

TK: My calling to be an analyst came much more through my mother than my father. It came through my father later. But I feel much more akin to my mother.

RH: How do you understand your calling to be an analyst?

TK: I had a very close relationship with my mother—perhaps too close. However, through her I saw something about life that really made sense to me. She was very connected to her own unconscious, sometimes to her own detriment, but I also saw in her a deeper sense of how it helped her to make meaning out of her life. This influenced me deeply, although it has taken me many years to put words to the experience.

RH: Is that why you talk about having a positive mother complex?

TK: Absolutely!

RH: Tell us about a positive mother complex and how it impacts sons.

TK: It can impact a son in lots of different ways. In my case, people see me as friendly, optimistic, positive about things—that's the *positive* side of the positive mother complex. There is a creativity and openness to the inner and outer world. You expect good things to happen. The *negative* side of the positive mother complex is the expectation that you should get everything you ask for and that you will always get your own way. You are less able to accept limits and to give in when things do not go your way. I generally expect things to go in what I think is a positive way.

RH: You have had to struggle when things do not go your way?

TK: Quite a bit.

RH: What have you learned from that?

TK: I have learned that to have a positive mother complex is not always that positive. [*Laughter*]. It has some down sides to it too.

RH: What's it like when you don't get your own way at this stage in your life?

TK: I can get pretty moody and depressed and down. I've had to develop a thicker skin—get tougher. There is a certain softness that comes with the positive mother complex. I hope I am a bit tougher now than I used to be.

RH: You have been a Jungian analyst now for 35 years. What is it like seeing patients now after all these years?

TK: I still very much enjoy the work. I feel more comfortable with what I am doing, less anxious about whether I am doing it right. Somehow, my experience with seeing a lot of people has enabled me to see more things. I know I am less tense in the hour. I do not see as many patients now. I do about 20 hours a week now, and I used to do about 35. I now have time to write. It is just enough for me.

RH: Have you ever thought of retiring?

TK: I like seeing people, and I like the lifestyle generally. Financially, I could afford to retire. My models for keeping going are all those who died in the saddle. I have a commitment to my work and do not want to stop. It's the kind of work I can do as long as I want, as long as my head works.

RH: And who are your main role models?

TK: Joe Henderson and my parents.

SEXUALITY

RH: What do you think was Jung's view of sexuality?

TK: I remember the first time I heard something on that topic from a psychologist in 1963 who said that Freud wrote about sex, but Jung did it. I was terribly affronted by that remark. Recently, I read a review of Deirdre Bair's new biography of Jung, and someone in the book said something similar. Sex is sex, but sex is also a drive to a spiritual connection. It is a movement of energy to something that one wants to join with, so it is both something instinctual and something spiritual. Jung talked about both of those aspects, especially in the *Psychology of the Transference.*

RH: What is the spiritual connection that sexuality leads us to?

TK: Sexuality, in its broadest sense, is teleological. At its deepest level, it leads us to wholeness, and this includes our relationship to something outside ourselves, which can be called by many different names. It is most often connected with our deepest religious values.

RH: The fact that Jung did it so often is used by some as an excuse for doing the same thing themselves. If Jung did it, then it is OK for me to do it too.

TK: But remember that Jung never set himself up as an example for us to follow. What he did was live out his own fate, but he never recommended his fate to others. Jung did have his relationship with both Emma and Toni, but it was not easy for any of them. Deirdre Bair, in her recent biography, *Jung*, which I mentioned earlier, has looked at this question from many angles, and she documents how everyone involved suffered. It was not an easy choice. Sexuality is a problem in doing analysis, since we are listening to highly intimate material. Jo Wheelwright used to say that therapy is a highly personal relationship in an impersonal setting. That balance between what is impersonal and personal is a tricky one. If we have personal needs, we can attempt to fill these needs in the therapeutic setting.

SPIRITUALITY

RH: That is well said. Are you a spiritual person?

TK: I don't to go church or to a synagogue—if that's what you mean. I am not a "practicing" anything. I keep track of my dreams—that's the kind of spirituality I practice. I love classical music, and listening to it is another way of engaging in spirituality for me. I'm a practical person.

RH: What happens to you spiritually when you listen to classical music?

TK: Obviously, it depends upon the music being played and the performers who are performing it. When the music touches me deeply, I find tears coming to my eyes without words to express the feeling. I am transported into some other space. This does not happen as frequently any more.

RH: Do you feel God is in the room when you are doing analysis?

TK: I do not consciously think of it that way. But if you put it that way, I would agree that there is some greater presence there.

RH: Do you feel that whatever it is that is greater has an impact on what happens between you and the other person?

TK: There have been synchronicities in my practice that have been hard to explain. There is often an uncanny connection between some of the experiences that people have had and my own life. These experiences have forced me to look at my own issues in a new way. I would call this my fate.

RH: You would not say it is God? Why do you hesitate to call it God, especially since Jung had that inscription above his front door, "Invoked or not, God is always present"?

TK: I could not put that above my door because Erasmus is not somebody I read. That would be more like something my father would do. I just wouldn't use a religious metaphor, but it is not because I do not value it.

RH: That touches on the issue of whether Jungian psychology is or is not a religion. Where do you stand on that issue?

TK: I think up through to the 1940s Jungians had a lot of aspects of a cult, for example, being few and intimate with each other. I do not go along with Richard Noll's contention that there is a Jung cult. I think I have a religious attitude toward my dreams. I am culturally Jewish. I feel strongly attached to that. My wife is not Jewish. My first wife was Jewish. I have not found that Jungian psychology has led to Judaism.

FAMILY LIFE

RH: Having been divorced yourself, and having had a father who was divorced, what have you learned about divorce as a Jungian?

TK: A lot! [*Laughter*] I was in analysis when I got divorced. That was one of the defining moments in my analysis. I really experienced the archetype of death and rebirth, and we can talk about that till the cows come home. I experienced first hand what it meant for me—with my positive mother complex—to fail. I failed. My marriage failed. I had to own that failure as my choice. It had to be a death. All that happened during my divorce was one of the most important parts of my growing up. Jung talks about marriage as a psychological relationship, and he says we often marry a person who is unconsciously connected to the parent of the opposite sex.

RH: Why do you feel the divorce rate is so high?

TK: If you can avoid a divorce, please do. But there are some out there who say that if it doesn't work, then move on. I would say there is a lot to be done trying to work out the predicament. Another factor in the high divorce rate is that we do not have large extended families to hold our marriages together as we used to and as some societies still do. We are a lot more isolated now.

RH: I read somewhere that you have made a conscious effort—perhaps because of your own childhood—to kept Jungian psychology and your work away from your kids. How have you dealt with Jungian psychology in raising your children?

TK: You cannot keep Jungian psychology completely out. That would be unnatural. They know I have had emergency calls, and most of our family friends are in the same field. They have met our colleagues. And inside me there is a secret wish that someday they will both go into Jungian analysis for their own personal growth. I know a lot less about their personal lives than my mother knew about mine.

RH: You have raised two children in a completely different way from the way you were raised?

TK: In many ways, I have. My first marriage ended when my son was three, and shortly after that he and his mother moved out of the area, so there was not much continuity with him. But my daughter has had two analysts for parents. One might think that her childhood would be similar to my childhood, since both my parents were analysts too, but that is not the case. In the home that I grew up in, there was a Jungian seminar at least once a week—if not more often. Patients who had just had their analysis would stay for dinner. The dining room was the waiting room. I knew all the patients my parents were seeing. Once, when I was 19 or 20, my mother said, "Stay out. This person does not want you to know she is here." Of course, I had to go sneaking around to see who it was. [*Laughter*].

RH: Curiosity got the better of you. [*Laughter*] If you grew up in that kind of atmosphere, and then you tried to raise your own kids in the opposite way, you must not have felt very good about how you were raised.

TK: I did like the way I was raised. My parents gave me lots of opportunities to develop in different ways, and I appreciated their general openness to new experiences. However, my parents talked about me to their patients, so that up until ten or fifteen years ago, whenever I gave a lecture somewhere, there would always be someone in the audience—an old gray-haired man or woman—who would come up to me afterwards and tell me that he or she remembered me from when I was very young and had interrupted his or her analytic hour when I came home from school. That was touching in one way, but in another way, it left me feeling very vulnerable, as I had no idea what my parents had said to their patients about me. It did not feel quite right. In my practice, I have not remained in close contact with ex-patients. There are some former patients of mine with whom I still have close contact, because they are now colleagues in the field, but I feel that is different.

ANTI-SEMITISM

RH: The issue of anti-Semitism and the Jews is an important one for you, isn't it?

TK: Yes. It's because there's a common myth about Jung—that he was anti-Semitic and that he was a Nazi or that he collaborated with the

220

Nazis. That has been given as a reason for discounting everything he ever wrote—we can't believe him because it's clear that the guy was a right-wing zealot. Deirdre Bair's book is one you need to read, as it deals in detail with this part of Jung's life. In her book, she discloses that Jung was Agent 488 in the OSS [Office of Strategic Services] and sent reports to Eisenhower. This certainly should raise doubts in the minds of those who think Jung was a Nazi.

RH: Wow! I have never heard that said about Jung. Is this the first time it has been talked about?

TK: Ten years ago, I read an article in a Swiss-French journal that talked about Jung's contributions to World War II. There is a letter in the *C.G. Jung Letters* in which Jung writes to my Dad about his—Jung's—supposed anti-Semitism. I am Jewish. My parents were Jewish, and they were in analysis with him when he was supposed to be a rabid anti-Semite. So maybe, some say, it was just personal. He was OK with my parents, according to them, on the individual level, but on the collective level he was terrible. This might be the case. But I've had to deal with it. Thirty or forty years ago, most psychoanalysts were Jewish. The American Psychoanalytic Society was 90% Jewish at one time. It is a big issue. If I could meet Jung in some afterlife, I would raise the issue of anti-Semitism with him. I would ask him why, when he was asked about it, he would make such circuitous remarks? He couldn't just come out and say what he meant. As Jo Wheelwright has said, Jung was not *pro*-Semitic. He may not have been anti-Semitic, but he was not pro-Semitic, either.

RH: So where does that leave you at this point?

TK: My dad said that Jung was not interested in Judaism because he could not find the numinous in it, and it was only after the war that he was able to explore the Hasidic and mystical traditions in Judaism such as the Kabalah. Then he developed a more positive feeling toward Judaism. I would like to have Jung clarify this. This is very important to me.

RH: Given what you now know, do you feel Jung was anti-Semitic?

TK: Prior to World War II, I think anti-Semitism was endemic in most of Europe. I would include Jung among those Europeans who accepted the *status quo* in regard to the Jews. He, like so many others, had no idea what the Nazis had in mind. As I have said before, I do not believe Jung was pro-Semitic. Whatever connections he may have had with the Nazis, he became disillusioned just prior to World War II when their true colors began to show. You can see that in his correspondence with numerous American and English friends and colleagues. Furthermore, Jung had a number of Jewish patients in analysis during this period, and not one of them—as far as I know—left analysis with him on account of his so-called anti-Semitism.

RH: You would include your parents in that group of Jewish patients, right?

TK: My mother came from an assimilated German Jewish family whose roots in Germany could be traced back to the 14th century. She frequently stated that Jung helped her to reconnect with her Jewish roots. My father came from an Orthodox Jewish family of Eastern European origin, and Jung helped him to find a way out of that orthodoxy and at the same time remain connected to his Judaism.

First-Generation Jungians

RH: Having met a number of first-generation Jungians, I sense something different about them. There is something very alive and authentic about them, and it is easy to connect with them and understand them. When I talk with a lot of Jungians of our generation, on the other hand, I feel as though a lot of them have intellectualized Jung. Do you feel that way?

TK: It is very interesting that you come at it in that way. When I first came into analysis, my mother told me that it was important to see somebody that had been in analysis with Jung—and nobody else would do. There is something different about those first-generation Jungians, I think, in the way they were touched. It is not intellectual. But with the next generation, the experience becomes more intellectual because direct firsthand knowledge has been replaced by what can be gleaned from books and is therefore not so close to the original source.

RH: Do you feel your analysis is different because of working with Joe?

TK: I do not think that consciously. People think I am very classical, but in reality I am not nearly as classical as people think. I am labeled a classical Jungian. In some ways, I guess, I am classical, with my emphasis on dreams—but I do not have a couch. I feel I am much more a clinical Jungian.

RH: You seem different to me, as we have talked. I am telling myself maybe that is because you are a feeling type, and a lot of Jungians are thinking types.

TK: That's interesting. I think that's true. My major influences have been Henderson, Wheelwright, Meier, and my parents. Those were my mentors—they shaped me. Jung was an important presence for all of them. I know that my wife at times wishes I would see somebody else. I think she feels it would be helpful for me to get another perspective on my psyche. If Joe had not been around all this time, maybe I would have.

RH: What do you think the major contributions of your father and your mother were to Jungian psychology?

TK: My father was an extremely scholarly man who was recognized as such in the field, and he had the ability to amplify symbols in a powerful way. My own assessment would be that his intuitions and understanding of the larger Jewish question, along with his understanding of religious experience, were of major significance. If he had not understood what was going on in Germany in the 1930s, I would not be here today. My mother had a deep sense of being able to touch people at their core. She influenced a great many people in their Jungian path, and although she wrote little, her influence is widely felt through these people who were in analytic training with her.

RH: You wouldn't refer yourself to a Jungian other than Joe?

TK: Not at this point. Maybe I am too first-generation. There is nobody above me any more, age-wise or experience-wise. I would have to do something else.

ENDINGS

RH: How do you wish to be remembered by the Jungian community?

TK: As a responsible analyst who practiced with integrity. Hopefully, my book about the history of the Jungians will have lasting value. Also, I hope that time will prove that the decisions I made as President of the IAAP were the right ones.

RH: Do you hope your book will be seen by the larger Jungian community as one of your major contributions to Jungian psychology?

TK: I hope so.

RH: The book is very important to you.

TK: It is. It was very important for me to do it.

RH: Having met Jung when you were younger, if he were to reappear today, what would you want to ask him or say to him?

TK: One of the things I would ask him would be why he did not come forward and say something publicly about his views on the Jews and anti-Semitism. For 40 years I have been defending Jung on that subject. I know my parents feel their lives were saved because of their contact with Jung, not because of what Jung did, but because he helped them get in touch with their own psyche and that helped them to realize what was going on.

RH: How do you find your life now, Tom?

TK: My parents wanted me to be a spokesperson, as it were, for Jung and analytical psychology, and I have defended him on many occasions. But as I get older, I like not being so much in the limelight any more. It is nice to be quieter. I do not mean introversion. I am not giving a lot of public lectures. I see others doing very public things and part of me thinks that would be fun, but I've said no to places so many times now that they will not invite me any more. When there is a specific issue that interests me, I still want to reach out and speak out, but otherwise I prefer to remain in the background.

RH: Tom, it has been a lot of fun sharing these moments with you. How do *you* feel about it?

TK: I feel very good about what we just did together.

As a child I felt myself to be alone, and I am still, because I know things and must hint at things which others apparently know nothing off, and for the most part do not want to know. Loneliness does not come from having no people about one, but from being unable to communicate the things that seem important to oneself, or from holding certain views which others find inadmissible. [*Memories, Dreams, Reflections*, p. 356.]

—C. G. Jung

FRED GUSTAFSON, D. MIN.

Fred Gustafson was born in Rockford, Illinois. He is a graduate of Augustana College in Rock Island, Illinois and the Lutheran School of Theology in Chicago. He received his doctorate degree from Andover Newton Theological School near Boston and a Diploma in Analytical Psychology from the Jung Institute in Zürich. He is a Training Analyst with the Jung Institute of Chicago and past president of the Chicago Society of Jungian Analysts. He is in private practice as a Jungian analyst and pastoral psychotherapist in Watertown and Milwaukee, Wisconsin. He is also an ordained minister of the Evangelical Lutheran Church of America. He is the author of *The Black Madonna* (Sigo, 1990) and *Dancing Between Two Worlds: Jung and the Native American Soul* (Paulist Press, 1997), and the editor of *The Moonlit Path: Reflections on the Dark Feminine*, (Nicolas-Hays, 2003). He and his wife, Karen, have two children, Andrea and Aaron. We interviewed Fred in the winter of 2003.

• 11 •

GROUNDED IN THE EARTH
Fred Gustafson at 63

I also like sitting in the dark, in the night, when things are quiet, perhaps by a fire, or just by myself and listening to the sounds in the world around me and in me. They come from another place than the ego.

—Fred Gustafson

Encountering Jung

Rob Henderson (RH): How did you get interested in Jung?

Fred Gustafson (FG): I had just finished seminary and decided to go on for graduate work at Andover Newton Theological School [ANTS] in the Boston area. I was planning to get an advanced degree in psychology and pastoral counseling. At that time, the psychology department of ANTS was headed by a man who had been closely associated with Jung, Dr. John Billinsky. As a result of that association, the entire department was influenced by Jung's work. It was there that I began reading Jung and talking to those involved in the department about his work. I became fascinated. Here was a man who spoke to my inner world. I had been in academia for eight years by that point, but never had there been such an unpacking of the psyche as I now experienced. I did some initial psychotherapy at the time—mostly shadow work—with the late Dr. Henry Brooks, a wonderful man who drew me into myself in a way that opened all kinds of doors to self-discovery. I know now that that period of my life laid the groundwork for moving deeper into analytical psychology. After graduate school, I accepted a parish in Upper Michigan—a mission that required a lot of collective involvement. It drew my extraverted side out. Up to this point, I had been a flaming introvert. I needed that time to figure myself out, but only two years into my four-year stay there, I knew I had to move on. It was then that I applied to the Jung

Institute in Zürich and, amazingly, I was accepted. When I think back now, I realize how naïve I was at that time about what I was going to face with such a move and a career change, and being married with two small children, and not having much money. I am grateful I was naïve, and for the most part, I believe we need to be when we are young if we want to get seriously into life at all.

RH: What are your favorite stories about Jung?

FG: I thought about this—and decided on this one, which I believe I got from my analyst, Dr. Adolf Ammann. I don't know how much truth there is in it or whether it is just part of the lore that developed around Jung—but I like it, so in my imagination it is true! It goes like this: Since Jung had a weak feeling side, in spite of all the wonderful work he did, it was not until his later years that he decided to do anything practical about it. In the past, when Christmas came, he left the buying, wrapping, and delivery of all the many gifts he had to give out to someone else, probably Emma. Now, in the later years of his life and wanting to work on his feeling side, he decided he should go out and buy all the individual gifts himself—and he did. He selected them carefully to match the people he was giving to, took them home, wrapped each one himself, and then had himself driven around to deliver them personally. In this way, he hoped, he would exercise his feeling function, making it much more concrete in personal action rather than just an idea in his mind. Many times in my practice I have shared this story with people who have had trouble expressing their feeling side or even getting to know that they had one—as a way of demonstrating to them that it is necessary to get in touch with our feelings when we perform a feeling act. Anyway, whether the story is authentic or not, it seems to fit the person I imagine Jung to have been, namely, a person who never stopped requiring himself to individuate.

RH: It sounds as though you have found Jung to be a tremendous inspiration. How has he inspired you?

FG: This question can be answered in many different ways, and that probably is an indication of how many diverse regions of the psyche Jung touches in all of us. But, strangely, the word that came to me was "mysticism." It is a word that has been distorted in our times and, in that distorted form, applied unfairly to Jung's work. However, in its purer meaning, it describes why Jung's work has remained as a template in my own work and my personal life. So much of what we have around us is trivia and bounces around on the surface of life. We know how this can happen to the field of psychotherapy and the world of religion. So much has failed here. For me, the mystical life is what Jung calls us back to when he plunges us below the surface to see what the ordinary eye of our assumptions and prejudices does not. In this word "mysticism," I hear depth as well as height. Did not Jung say that as the universe is so very deep and infinite, so is the human psyche? But that is not all there is to it. The mystical refers to the mysteries of life and death, meaning and madness, knowing and not knowing, loving and hating, struggling and yielding to the struggle. This is the stuff toward which Jung points us. Our call as human beings is to be intimately in life and all it has in store for us, with all of its conscious and unconscious drama. Jung's work reminds us of the vital place of the spiritual journey we all take. That's what I mean by mystical—not something that detaches us from life, but throws us headlong into it. So far, Jung's work has addressed this the best.

Mysticism

RH: What are some of the ways you have found to access and develop the mystical side of yourself?

FG: Good question. I find that nature is a good place to start because it is simply that, natural. It is basic to our being, and it can—if we take the trouble to look into it just a little bit—show us our place in the grander scheme of things. I also like sitting in the dark, in the night, when things are quiet, perhaps by a fire, just by myself, listening to the sounds in the world around me and in me. They come from another place than the ego. A true mystic is grounded deeply in the earth. Teilhard de Chardin, as a Christian and a scientist, could see Christ in the molecules of a leaf. Mystics of other religions have done something similar. It requires imagination and a willingness to apply all the incarnational theology that Christianity talks about to the real living world around us. When we do that, we align ourselves with the cutting edge of post-Newtonian physics and the latest explorations in the regions of chaos and string theory. Such an understanding, whether it comes from the world of depth psychology, or religion, or physics, challenges us to think of ourselves as part of a grand cosmic order. Jung said we are all an experiment of nature.

RH: Can you share an experience you have had in nature that might have touched your mystical and sacred side?

FG: My wife and I and another couple recently took a week off to vacation in Central America, in Belize. We spent the first three days in a jungle lodge and planned to follow that with a canoe-caving expedition. On our second morning, we made the arrangements for the trip and met our Mayan guide, Philip. Philip was a botanist and bird expert, a gentle man quite prepared to lead four tourists through an interesting experience. To get out of the jungle, we had a three-mile ride over a bumpy road until we reached the main highway that would eventually lead us to the waterway that would take us deep inside the cave. On the way out, Philip suddenly stopped and pointed to a tree where a large white hawk was perched. Quite spontaneously, I said, "Good sign." He said he hardly ever spotted them, even as an experienced birder. We saw a total of four by day's end! When we reached the highway, he pointed out the largest mansion I think I have ever seen with armed guards protecting the estate. Philip explained that the owner had built this fabulous residence on top of a Mayan ruin. All four of us moaned. I said, "It would make me nervous to live there thinking of all the spirits in that place." Philip responded with, "You could have some really bad dreams there."

By this time, without expressing it aloud, we were beginning to realize that maybe we all had something in common. We had several miles to travel, and it was during this part of the trip that Philip began talking about his people. Long ago, they had been pushed out of the Yucatan Peninsula further into Mexico. Then pushed further south to the site of their present village, which he said he would drive us through on our return trip. On the way, he pointed out the sacred tree of the Mayans, the Seiba tree, and explained how the sun was the principal god they honored. At this point, I couldn't keep my mouth shut. I told him that all four of us had been ceremonially and culturally connected with the Lakota Sioux people in North America, and that they, also, had a sacred tree, the cottonwood, around which they danced for four days when performing the Sun Dance, recognizing the sun as the great life-giver. Now all five of us knew without saying it that we could be safe talking about such matters. We had stepped past the idea of us four as tourists and him as tourist guide.

When we reached the cave and launched the canoes, he suggested we wait until everyone else got out so we could be alone in the cave. On entering the cave, he said he had to tell us something. He declared that we now would be entering the domain of the underworld gods. This was the Mayan underworld, a place where, long ago, they had buried their dead and offered food to the spirits of that place. We would be beneath the cosmic tree. It was sacred. Archeologists had long since removed the bones and most of the pottery, except for a few remaining pieces, which were now protected. Our two spotlights illuminated this dark space, revealing multicolored rock formations and stalactites hanging as silent witnesses to past events. About a mile in, Philip suggested we go no further. At that point, we asked if we could offer two Lakota Sun Dance songs as a way of honoring this place. He agreed. We sang the first song in total darkness in this Mayan underworld. When we finished, to our surprise, we heard further into the cave singing of a different kind. It turned out to be a Mennonite group. It must have been a choir on tour, because they were near perfect in their singing. There was nothing sentimental about what they sang—it was some hymn. Their singing caused us to stop and listen as they got closer and eventually passed us in silence. I should tell you that the waterway was only 15-20 feet wide. When they were some way off, Philip said he wanted us to sing the second song and that he would offer a prayer in his Mayan language when we finished. We did and then he started to pray. As he did, we heard the Mennonite choir sing again far away in the distance. I was deeply struck by this moment: it was a living metaphor of how it should be for all of us. Here was a Mayan holy man praying in the total darkness of this underworld, in his language, with a Christian hymn being sung far off in the distance, like a backdrop of support. Here there was no overpowering of the deep instinctual world that lies within us all. That's the way it should be.

When Philip finished, he told us he had made an apology to the gods for not bringing an offering, but that he had prayed for our welfare. I told him that the Sioux would offer tobacco, and wondered if that would be all right. He said it would, and I asked for a cigarette from one of our smokers and carefully took off the paper—and then, to my horror, I dropped the filter in the darkened water. A little fish quickly rushed up, grabbed it, and took it down. Then, to my relief, it floated to the surface again. Once more the fish grabbed it, and then it came to the surface again. Then it got lodged under the canoe. I was able to retrieve it in the end, but the incident was a reminder that when we are in a sacred place, we need to do things with great care.

On our return trip, we went through Philip's village and were invited to attend a small once-a-year carnival that was being held that very evening. We did. As we circled the small carnival grounds with all the villagers out, we tried to locate Philip. This was no easy task, as the evening was dark and the lights of the carnival were dim. Indicating a man standing off at a distance among a group of people, I asked my friend if he thought that was Philip. My friend said he wasn't sure. As we continued to look, we saw the man smile and wave at us. We went over and were introduced to Philip's wife, his children, their spouses and all the grandchildren, and we got to shake hands with everyone. Philip told us later that the day had not turned out at all the way he expected. How true that was for us as well! I was left with a deepened awareness that people of like spiritual minds and hearts find each other regardless of religion, race, or country of origin. It is an experience I will never forget.

NATIVE AMERICAN SPIRITUALITY

RH: I know you are very drawn to Native Americans. What has inspired and guided you in this love?

FG: It is difficult to answer just where my connection to Native American spirituality comes from or began. Why are any of us drawn in certain directions? Yet, my interest in Native Americans has been with me all my life. There have been several events along the way that have played a part, all acting like stepping stones in the process that brought me to where I am today. The first of these happened when I was a young boy. My mother told me my great-great-grandmother was Cherokee. This in itself is not a great piece of information to inspire a journey. Many people have such a background, and some claim it even when it is not true. Anyway, it caught my attention and faded in and out of my consciousness as the years passed. I later did find out this Cherokee great-great-grandmother's name and some of the history surrounding her. What really drew me into a more conscious involvement with Native American life was a conference I attended in 1983 on Native American spirituality, conducted by Indians for non-Indians. I mentioned to a good friend I was with that I really wanted to do a vision quest sometime. He knew individuals who could help and promptly put me in touch with Native peoples and through a series of interesting and even synchronistic happenings, I found myself on the Rosebud Sioux Reservation on June 25, 1983, starting the first day of a vision quest. Incidentally, June 25 was the day Custer was defeated. After it was over, and as we were leaving the reservation, I said to my wife that I probably would not be back, that I had done my thing, so to speak. Well, when a person is on the right path and the spirits behind it have a say in it, things don't always work out as we think. In fact, I went on to do three more such vision quests and started sun dancing in 1987—and have been doing this every summer since then.

Just what is behind this we can define only in terms like Jung's Self or what native peoples call the spirits. It does not matter to me. All I know is that it has gone deep inside me, changed my life, and brought me closer to what I think the deep essential human is for all of us. We all have an indigenous history—a history that for the most part has been forgotten and buried beneath centuries of forces that have separated us from the body of the earth and the earth that makes up our body. To return to it cannot but bring healing to the soul and deepen one's connectedness to all things and to a more vibrant spiritual life. This will be true regardless of our religious or non-religious backgrounds.

RH: How do you think Jung would react to your interest in Native Americans?

FG: I think Jung would be fascinated by this interest simply because he believed that a deep study and experience of primitive peoples was essential to understanding the basic behavior of the psyche. I must say here that the word "primitive"—like the word "aboriginal"—has been misused and abused in our modern era. Both words really mean "of the first order," or "from the origins or the beginning." When you think of it that way, they become more than words; they reflect a need to look back in an attempt to understand the long evolutionary history that has brought us all to where we are in the 21st century. I am referring here to our original ancestors, the base upon which we stand and which still cries out for recognition today. Personally, I prefer the word "indigenous" because it means "to be born within," which I take to mean being born within the context of the whole human race. Jung was interested in the North American Indians. He even visited the Taos Pueblo in the 1920s. So I think he would look favorably on any of us North Americans who took Native Indian spirituality seriously simply because we are indigenous to this continent in the same way that it is. Despite the tragic fact that Indian people have suffered and still suffer much at the hands of our dominant culture and are today the most neglected minority group in our country, we are affected by our involvement with these original inhabitants of this land. Jung said that the conqueror takes on the attributes of the conquered. Look at our country—at how many cities have been given Indian names, at how much our constitution was affected by the Iroquois Confederacy. Look at the Native influence in the jewelry we wear and the recent fascination with Native people and their history. Above all, look at how often Native imagery appears in the dreams of non-Native Americans.

As for my participation in Indian ceremonial practices, I am not sure what he would think about that. I am inclined to think he would have no objection to it inasmuch as it has been part of my ongoing individuation process. Jung was not against religion nor religious practices so long as they carried living symbols that reflected the deepest layers of the Self. I have experienced living ritual in these practices that have brought me closer to not only myself, but to other people and to the world in general. Indian ceremonial practices are embracive, that is, they speak of "all my relatives" when they are celebrated. All the ceremonies are performed for the sake of the entire creation. How could Jung be against something like that? Yes, I think he and I could have had a fine conversation about these matters.

TYPOLOGY

RH: What have you learned about introversion and intuition?

FG: The issue of typology has been an on-again-off-again interest of mine throughout the years since I first read about Jung's research. At this point in my life, I am ever more impressed by this great contribution to the understanding of human behavior, interpersonal relationships, and myself. For a long time in my analysis, I thought I was an introverted intuitive. I functioned so well that way. It made so much sense given my understanding

234

of myself and how I saw myself relate to the world and my family and friends. Only later, when I took the MMPI [Minnesota Multiphasic Personality Inventory], did I discover that I am an introverted feeling type with a secondary intuitive function. If I thought things made sense before, they made even more sense now. What so many of us Jungians tend to forget is the liberating role of the secondary function in our lives. It frees us from the tyranny of the primary attitude (in my case, introversion) and the primary function (for me, feeling). It keeps us from being lopsided. The second function makes possible a reversal in attitude. In other words, it shows us how narrow our viewpoint is if we think of ourselves as only introverted or only extraverted, or as operating in the realm of only one function. As an introvert, I have become quite good at extraversion. I speak in public without much difficulty, I love to mingle with people, I have taught courses and have led groups and organizations over the years. But, when it's all over and done with, I want to be magically picked up out of these situations and put in a cave somewhere to recover. These experiences often carry a touch of the magical for me, though from time to time I have to come up for air in some private introverted space.

Living with other Jungians over the years, I have found that many of us can get defensive about our type, fearing that others will see us primarily from that one single perspective, with all the prejudices that can go with it. I have been guilty of this myself. Earlier on, I had a thing about extraverts. I was inclined to see them as superficial, self-serving socialites who had difficulty being in the inner life, as if introverts have such an easy time of it! Of course, thinking types were too cold, not in touch with their feelings, and couldn't care less about relationships. Sensation types had no imagination, and so forth. Then, too, I thought that being an introvert, I was seen by others as socially withdrawn, too much in myself. Besides, with the feeling side being dominant in me, what intelligent contribution could I possibly make to the group? To the extent that we go no further with ourselves than our typology dictates, these categories become self-fulfilling prophecies. These were of course prejudices, but as prejudices tend to go, they were really projections one onto another, as well as introjections into ourselves. The only goal they served was to put distance between all of us. So, as I said at the beginning, I have really come to appreciate typology simply because as my own projections have calmed down and become understood, I have learned to appreciate much more deeply the valuable place that all psychological types have in bringing about wholeness in the collective or the personal. We need each other's perspectives. None of us can do it alone. At the same time, I now value much more intensely my own typology as an introverted feeling intuitive type. For example, I have to take responsibility not to assume that just because I have a feeling understanding within myself that the world will know this. I have to extravert it, get it out, and trust that it will have a role to play in the world at large. My secondary extraverted intuitive side also needs to give some substance to itself by connecting with some sensate data and logic wherever possible. This is work, but it is profitable. The end result for me is to value the diversity of people's insights. I have many good extraverted friends, for example, and I am amazed at how introspective and deep they are, since I once thought this was the prerogative of the introvert! I am now also quite amazed that I can keep up with the thinking types and that they do have a wonderful feeling life, even if it comes around the track behind everyone else. Jung really gave us a useful and practical contribution in this area of typology.

RH: How has your understanding of typology affected your relationships with your wife, your children, and your friends?

FG: Understanding typology in my head and practicing it in my heart are two different matters. How blind we can be on these matters of psychology, whether it be typology or other psychological insights, when it comes to people who are close to us! Usually deep understanding comes, if it comes at all, after verbally defended positions have worn a person down. Whether one is psychologically aware enough at the beginning of a relationship, or while the relationship is evolving, or near ruin, the deep remembering and practice of typological discrimination is invaluable. It can result in a deep "ah-hah" or "that makes sense now" reaction that can release one from one's own lopsided opinions as well as from that of the other. In my own case, it has helped me in coming to a better understanding of my wife and two children. For example, my wife has a strong sensation/feeling side, which can drive me nuts at times, especially when I am focusing on something intuitively and she gets into the sense details. I leap directly from A to Z while she takes into account every letter in between. The other side is that after several years of this kind of interaction, I am beginning to take responsibility more consciously for the details of my life. I now actually make lists—at times—of things that need to be done—something that is quite routine for sensates. I have come to appreciate the fact that if I had not worked on developing my sensation function, all the things that I would have left undone would have been assigned to my wife to carry out for me. That is just one very small example, but when things like this are compounded many times over, they can lead to great tension in any marriage or relationship. As for my children, my daughter is an introvert, my son an extravert. I do relate to them differently at times on account of this, but because of my Jungian background I can do it in a more discriminating matter. In other words, I am more aware of which issues to engage when I am relating to them, and which ones to not fret over. I have learned to be open to a deeper appreciation of the different gifts they bring. As an introvert myself, I have come to appreciate my extraverted friends and not only appreciate them, but actually enjoy being their company. This, too, is because I have worked on developing and strengthening the weaker, extraverted side of my personality. The difference is that I am a sprinter, and they are long distance runners when it comes to living out extraversion. In all these various relationships, I am grateful for Jung's contribution in the area of typology, for it has helped to break down the many unnecessary barriers that arise between individuals and their family and friends.

SEXUALITY

RH: That's a wonderful way to put it. Are you familiar with that line in one of Fellini's films, "When I see a beautiful, sexy woman, I feel more religious"? As a Jungian and a minister, what do you understand that statement to mean?

FG: First of all, this idea of a beautiful, sexy woman is highly subjective. I have seen women who by all typical American standards might be considered beautiful, but who nevertheless do nothing for me. By contrast, I have encountered many women who do not meet such culturally determined standards of beauty and yet radiate a strong animating presence. So, something else is going on here other than external beauty. "Animating" is the keyword here, because it calls to mind the anima. If looking at a beautiful woman is akin to a religious experience, as Fellini suggests, then the beauty must be judged by something other than the socially sanctioned norms of external beauty. The experience touches something deep inside me.

In the presence of such a woman, I feel moved in my body, my mind, and my soul. It is a total response of the entire being. Can it get more religious than that? The vast majority of images in our collective culture are designed to appeal to us merely at the level of the instincts. But that is not what I am talking about. It certainly includes that, but is much more. I remember hearing that the actor Matt Damon once confessed that when he was introduced to Sophia Loren, he was unable to speak. He lost his voice. We could say he was paralyzed. I would say he was transported to the realm of gods and goddesses, and this, by the way, is what a religious experience really is. I feel the same way sometimes when looking at a painting or sculpture of a beautiful woman. Such great works of art can transport us to realms beyond the everyday world of externality. I think in some ways this experience is true for women as well, inasmuch as it can touch something deep within them and invite out into their own field of consciousness a deeper understanding of their own beauty as women. So when you ask me how I would understand this as a minister and a Jungian analyst, I am somewhat at a loss, not because I cannot speak of this theologically or psychologically, but simply because this kind of language always falls short of describing such moments. It is best at such times to let ourselves, like Mr. Damon, be overcome by a failure of words and simply allow ourselves to be transported to wherever it is She wants to take us.

What is the great Dream? It consists of the many small dreams and the many acts of humility and submission to their hints. It is the future and the picture of the new world, which we do not understand yet. [Letter to Herbert Read, September 2, 1960, *C. G. Jung Letters, Vol. 2: 1951-1961*, Princeton University Press, 1976, p. 591.]

— C. G. Jung

In the deepest sense we all dream not our of ourselves but out of what lies between us and the other. [Letter to James Kirsch, September 29, 1934, *C. G. Jung Letters, Vol. 1: 1906-1950*, Princeton University Press, 1973, p. 172.]

— C. G. Jung

What the dream, which is not manufactured by us, says is *just* so. [Letter to Herbert Read, September 2, 1960, *C. G. Jung Letters, Vol. 2: 1951-1961*, Princeton University Press, 1976, p. 591.]

— C. G. Jung

GILDA G. FRANTZ, M.A.

Gilda G. Frantz is co-editor-in-chief of *Psychological Perspectives*. She received her certification as a Jungian analyst in 1977 from the C. G. Jung Institute in Los Angeles, and has served as president of that institute as well as on its various committees. She is currently on the board of the Philemon Foundation, a nonprofit organization dedicated to publishing the complete works of C.G. Jung. A respected teacher, her research on "Tears, Loneliness, Creativity, and Individuation" led to a series of lectures that she delivered in Zürich, Davos, Tokyo, and Kyoto, and at many Jungian centers throughout the United States. Throughout the 1990s, she volunteered at a local hospital as a facilitator for groups dealing with caring for loved ones who suffer from AIDS-related illnesses. She is the widow of the late Kieffer Evans Frantz, M.D., and is a devoted mother, mother-in-law, and grandmother. She maintains a full analytical practice in Santa Monica, California, where she lives with her pug, Mr. Fu. We interviewed Gilda in the winter of 2004.

• 12 •

SOFTENING THE HEART

Gilda G. Frantz at 78

I think suffering can soften the heart.
—Gilda G. Frantz

Encountering Jung

Rob Henderson (RH): How did you become acquainted with Jung?

Gilda Frantz (GF): I fell in love with a handsome psychiatrist, Kieffer Evans Frantz, M.D., who was soon to become a Jungian analyst. At the time, he was working analytically with James Kirsch and felt ready to settle down and get married. He mentioned this to a friend of his, who coincidentally was also a friend of my family, and she introduced him to me. Most—if not all—of my friends were already married, so I guess it seemed right that I should be thinking seriously about marriage too. We met and fell in love—almost at first sight. I was 23; he was 39, although I didn't find out about the age difference until he proposed. It was through meeting him that I discovered Jung and the Jungian community in Los Angeles and eventually in the world. I had been very interested in psychology as a young person, but had never heard of Jung—although I had read Freud. This wasn't unusual in the 40s, since Jung's books did not have a wide readership back then. At the time we married in 1950, there were probably less than 100 analysts in the entire world, and many of Jung's works had not been translated into or published in English. Kieffer and I married after a short courtship, and suddenly I found myself in the midst of a group of analysts who had fled Germany on account of the Holocaust and who were many, many years my senior! Being so young in the midst of people 13 to 25 years older did present problems. I think they saw me from the outside in as opposed to the other way around—and I expected them to see me as I really was instead of seeing only my persona. Eventually, I went into analysis with Max Zeller, who helped me with the problems of growing up. He was very kind, but my real analysis began years later with Hilde Kirsch and, still later, with James Kirsch.

RH: What are some of your favorite stories about Jung?

GF: Your question is a very interesting one, because it sounds as if what you are asking about is the mythology surrounding Jung. There were several stories that I heard, mostly in the form of anecdotes during lectures, that have remained with me. For example, I recall Hilde Kirsch saying that Jung once commented to her that blind suffering is the worst. I will say more about this later on.

There were people in Los Angeles who had had a deep relationship with Jung. People like James Kirsch, with whom Jung carried on a correspondence for 40 years or more. One of my favorite stories is Hilde's account of going back to see Jung after being away during the war: he remembered everything about her last visit, including the last dream she had told him. I have tried to follow that model in my own work—that is, focusing on being so present that I am able to recall everything about a person with whom I work, especially his or her inner world. Recently, I had a call from a woman whom I had seen only once 20 years ago, and I remembered everything about her and her issues. She felt very seen, and that made her feel good—and it made me feel good, too.

RH: Are there any stories about Jung that have had meaning for you personally as a woman?

GF: Jung's legacy to me as a woman includes very much the encouragement he gave to the women around him to seek their own development. The stories—not the gossip—about the women around Jung have been very inspiring. I often think of Barbara Hannah, a minister's daughter and an artist, who became, under Jung's influence, an analyst and a colleague of Jung's as well as an author. Von Franz met him when she was still in her teens. Through his understanding of her genius, she blossomed, became her own person (which I think is incredible, considering how powerful Jung must have been), wrote many great books, lectured, and had a distinctive voice of her own, for which she became well known. Rivkah

Scharf Kluger and Aniela Jaffé are some others that come to mind, as does Liliane Frey. Each one of these women in those early days, influenced as they were by Jung's personality and psychology, was still able to maintain her own individuality and live her own truth. If you take a look at the film "Matter of Heart," you will be amazed at how awesome and how beautiful those women were. Of course, they are all gone now.

RH: How has Jung affected your life generally, apart from his influence on you as a woman?

GF: Through his writings, Jung has taught me how to live my life authentically and not give too much of a damn about what people think. He also taught me about suffering and how to find a way to live life meaningfully while enduring suffering. I wrote a little poem a long time ago, which was published in the book *C. G. Jung, Emma Jung, Toni Wolff: A Collection of Remembrances*—it goes like this:

> I loved the old man
> who touched my life
> with outstretched hand
> and left his mark
> upon my soul.

[Published by the Analytical Psychology Club of San Francisco, 1982]

There is one little story that just came to mind about a female client who always wore a hat. One day, for whatever reason, Jung remarked that he didn't like the hat she was wearing that day. The next time she came, she brought several boxes of new hats and challenged him to pick one out for her. Apparently, he did! I always like hearing stories about how analysands confront their analyst with a challenge to get real. I never met Jung, but I do feel very grateful for his lived life and his many books.

SUFFERING

RH: You have struggled in your life, as you mentioned to me, with profound loss. How has Jungian psychology helped you understand and deal with your suffering?

GF: I have written and thought a great deal about suffering. In my analytical career, I have treated an unusual number of individuals who have experienced physical suffering as well as emotional suffering. An unusually high percentage of women have come to me on account of the pain they have suffered having children who are handicapped or ill or who have suffered a birth injury or have a genetic problem. When women suffer a miscarriage, they often suffer deeply. In Japan, miscarriage is often ritualized, with a special service being performed for the aborted births. In my own understanding of grief in such instances, I encourage women to create a ritual when they are depressed as the result of having undergone a miscarriage or an abortion.

RH: Why is ritual so important? How does it help?

GF: Ritual is very important because it adds a spiritual dimension to the experience, something that is often missing in such cases. It is this element of spirituality that Jung offers to anyone who is going through any type of ordeal. I remember Hilde Kirsch giving a lecture about her work with Jung in which she quotes Jung as saying that even in the darkest of times, he was, by the grace of God, given a tiny speck of light, which gave him hope. That comment has meant the world to me, because I myself have looked for that tiny sliver of light slicing through the pain and darkness that I have experienced personally. Ritual can provide that speck of light, that glimmer of hope.

RH: You see a connection between loneliness, loss, and suffering, don't you?

GF: Yes—and I have experienced all three. Within nine months of my husband's passing, I was asked to give a lecture at a conference here in Los Angeles on the theme "From Chaos to Eros." I agreed to do it, even though I had never given a paper before, and I chose to speak on the subject of loneliness. My paper was titled "On the Meaning of Loneliness." The insights I gained from writing that paper have helped me—as they have helped many others—to understand loneliness, which can be experienced as profound suffering after the loss of a loved one. In writing the paper, I came to realize that if the ego is in an alienated state, separated from the Self, it suffers greatly, but if there is a relationship to the Self, then meaning is found in the loneliness, and one can go on to the next stage of development, a relationship between ego and Self.

RH: Did Jung have anything to say about this—about loss and loneliness?

GF: A great deal. I've always valued Jung's work in alchemy, especially what he has written about *mortificatio,* that place of pain and suffering on the journey toward individuation. In Jung's *Letters,* there are many about suffering written by people to Jung about their loss. Another of Jung's contributions that relates well to dealing with loss and suffering is active imagination. Personally, I have found that when suffering strikes, it is very helpful to use active imagination to work the experience through. You may be familiar with Albert Kreinheder's book, *Body and Soul,* which provides many examples of how active imagination can be used to dialogue with pain. It's a beautiful little book that addresses the suffering in physical illness, written by an analyst who wrote elegantly and without footnotes. The process of active imagination has helped me tremendously. When I lecture on active imagination, I always used Dr. Kreinheder's book as a reliable and creative source of information about this process.

RH: You mention active imagination. That is something you do by yourself—on your own. What role, then, does analysis play—if any—in all of this?

GF: Some people think of analysis as an antidote to suffering. However, it is very important to remember that being in analysis does not protect us from suffering. I think when we are young we secretly believe that if we work on our "problems," we will somehow develop an immunity to suffering. Of course, this is not the case. What analysis *can* do is help us not to suffer *blindly.* That's doing a lot, I think. Bitterness can be a major part of suffering, but if it is all one is left with, then you might say that the suffering has failed in its task of softening the heart. In one active imagination episode, I saw my heart split open and some plant or tree had taken root there. This was shortly after my husband's death, and it was only later that I understood the transformative meaning behind the image. Jung found a way, not to remove human suffering, but to make it meaningful. I think it is one of his very special contributions to human understanding.

LONELINESS

RH: We've talked a bit about loneliness in general and the paper you wrote on it, Gilda. But what has loneliness been like in your life personally? And, as a Jungian, what are some of the ways you have found helpful in dealing with it?

GF: My initial response to the question was a definite feeling that I didn't want to talk about that subject, but I've changed my mind. I *will* tell you about my personal struggles with loneliness. I was a lonely child—introspective. I spent a lot of time trying to figure things out for myself. I was separated from my parents at around age 4 or 5 and lived with a beloved aunt and uncle and cousin in a city far from my parents. I missed my mother terribly, but she had to work—it was the Great Depression—and sending me to live with her brother was the only solution she could think of. My uncle and his wife were wealthy, even in those economically depressed times. They lived in a spacious and beautiful home. I had my own room and beautiful clothes. There was a woman who did the ironing, another who did the cleaning, and a housekeeper who cooked and looked after me and my cousin. The furnishings of the home were beautiful. Each day at around dusk, I would go into my aunt and uncle's library. I loved that room with its dark red leather-upholstered furniture, studded with shiny brass tacks that gleamed, and built-in walnut bookshelves lined with fine books. I would read nursery rhymes for a while—I learned to read when I was around 4 years old. Then I would look out of the window as night approached, watching the sun go down and thinking about how much I missed my mother. I would cry silently and alone, sniffing and snuffling with tears and deep sadness. That was the loneliest I had been in my entire life, until my husband died very suddenly when I was 48 years old.

RH: Was that a different kind of loneliness?

GF: Yes. The loneliness I felt as a widow was very different from what I had experienced as a child. It was an enveloping kind of loneliness. On the weekends, the house felt as though it was sealing me

246

in and I was alone with my grief. It was a wrenching and oppressive sense of being utterly alone in the world. To help myself I would meditate, do breathing exercises, and write in my journal. And I read, not books, but my late husband's journal, and I found that sustaining. As I read his inner thoughts and the work he did with his dreams, I felt a sense of renewal and closeness to him. I had never seen his journal before his death.

RH: And what came out of that experience?

GF: About 9 months later—I had been in training to become an analyst for 2 or 3 years by then—I was asked by Russ Lockhart to present a lecture at that conference I mentioned before. I had never given a lecture before, but I boldly agreed to do it on the condition that I could speak about where I was at that time. I called the paper "On the Meaning of Loneliness," and the tape and paper are still in use at the library at the Institute in L.A. I've heard it has helped many people. There were three other excellent speakers beside myself: Russ Lockhart, Betty Meador, and Mel Kettner. I took two weeks off from work, stayed at home almost the entire time, and wrote the paper. Our library at home was so extensive I never had to leave the house to do the research, and during those two weeks I never felt lonely for even a moment.

RH: And what did you discover from your research?

GF: What I found out was that divorce, separation from a loved one, bereavement are all circumstances in which a separation between ego and Self can spontaneously occur. There is a complex set of circumstances that brings the separation about, and an equally complex set of circumstances that heals it. I used Saul Bellow's *Henderson the Rain King* as a way of showing the transformation from chaos to Eros. In the story, the hero, Henderson, goes to Africa in order to find a way to quiet an inner voice that says, "I want, I want, I want," over and over in his head. In his attempt to understand this voice, Henderson discovers in Africa that which enables him to feel whole for the first time in his life. Jung's writing, and the writing of those who followed, helped me understand the psychological meaning of loneliness. This was in 1976. Now that I am in my seventies, I feel at home with myself, more content, and happy to be alone. I have experienced other deep losses since then, which have taken me back to being lonely. That happens with profound loss, but I have, by the grace of God, been fortunate to find my way back to life. That is the experience of being human.

HOMOSEXUALITY

RH: As a Jungian, what is your understanding of homosexuality?

GF: I truly believe that homosexuality is not a choice or a lifestyle. It is there from birth. I haven't done the depth of research necessary to prove this, but I have interviewed a number of gay men and I am convinced that each of them felt he was gay going as far back as his earliest childhood memories, well before the age of five.

RH: What sparked your interest in talking to gay men?

GF: I began to do these interviews when my son died of AIDS. After years of silence from Ronald Reagan, who was President at the time, I felt I had to do something proactive to compensate for Reagan's lack of interest in helping or even expressing compassion for the gay men who were suffering and dying from this plague. I thought Reagan would speak up when his fellow actor, Rock Hudson, died or after Magic Johnson acknowledged that he had contracted HIV from—as he called it—partying. I thought Reagan would say something after Ryan White died—he was the hemophiliac teenager who became infected with the virus through a blood transfusion with tainted blood. When Arthur Ashe died, surely Reagan would honor this great African-American tennis star—but still there was silence. And finally, when babies began to die, having been infected at birth by their infected mothers, and Reagan didn't say one word about AIDS, I gave up hope.

RH: You sound angry.

GF: I am! Angry that gay men and women are made to feel like pariahs in our society and are ignored even in illness and death. Many gay men and women have felt the sting of society's rejection from early childhood. I read a scholarly book on homosexuality titled *The Homosexual*, published in the early 70s, in which the authors stated that in interviewing hundreds of homosexuals they came to the conclusion that most of the psychological difficulties found among homosexuals stem from their rejection by society.

The most powerful punishment any group can inflict upon a member is banishment from the "tribe." Our homosexual children grow up in a society that banishes and scorns them from childhood and this continues throughout their lives. Our American culture rejects anyone who is different. What a reversal for a nation whose European settlers were seeking religious freedom! We attempted to destroy the native people we found here, and one way or another, we destroy anyone who does not fit the American ideal of "normal."

RH: You said your son died of AIDS. Was he gay?

GF: Our son was almost 3 when he began exhibiting certain feminine characteristics—or at least that's when they became more visible. By the time he was 4 and the trend had not reversed, we started to feel concerned. My analyst, unfortunately, knew nothing about homosexuality, and with great authority informed me that what was producing this feminine behavior was an unconscious relationship between me, the mother, and him, the son. My analyst husband didn't support this diagnosis, but I readily accepted total responsibility for my son's condition. This is not uncommon among women. Most women feel responsible for whatever befalls their babies.

RH: And has Jungian analysis changed since then in its understanding of homosexuality—has it changed with the times?

GF: That's very much an individual matter. The question each analyst today needs to ask himself or herself is: Am I, as an analyst or therapist, as blind today as some analysts were 50 years ago? Not necessarily about homosexuality, but about all aspects of contemporary life. Our profession has very powerful tools which can be very helpful, but when we make an error, our assumptions can do great harm. One of Jung's warnings to humankind was to beware of collective infection and collective thinking. We analysts need to ask ourselves constantly if we are thinking collectively and, if so, how to find a way to extricate ourselves from being carried along on the wave.

RH: And your son—what happened to him after that diagnosis?

GF: He grew up to be an ethical, idealistic, studious, artistic man, very cultured, with enormous integrity and intelligence. As an adult, he became a skier and a hiking enthusiast, and was physically strong as well as

249

handsome. He never felt AIDS itself was evil, but did feel that the way people *reacted* to AIDS was *evil*. He was speaking in particular about Ronald Reagan, as well as about people who felt—and feel—that homosexuals "deserved" this disease. Our son somehow found a way to accept his fate, knowing that he was a victim of a plague that struck down people indiscriminately. He was conscious and careful from the moment he knew he carried this awful virus. He never complained during his entire ordeal, but he cried on the day he learned of children suffering from AIDS. Carl [Gilda's son] never asked himself, "Why, me?" He always said it was useless to ask that question because the answer could very well be, "Why not you?" Thousands died, and he was one who died too. He was forty years old. He died just as doctors were beginning to prescribing the "cocktail" that would help to boost the immune system—the T-cell count—and hold the disease at bay. Had it come even six months earlier, he might be alive today, enjoying life—and contributing to society. It could have come earlier if those in power had done something about it, but they are still dragging their feet. After all, it's mostly homosexuals in this country that have the disease, so what's the hurry? That's what they think!

THE INDIVIDUAL AND THE COLLECTIVE

RH: Your son's story is deeply moving, and it leads directly into my next question. You already mentioned the danger of being carried along on the wave of the collective. One of the struggles in life for the individual is how to hold onto to yourself and at the same time hold on to your membership in the collective, whether that be marriage, family, community, culture, or society. How do you see the struggle?

GF: This is a very tough question, because when you are being "carried along by the collective," you don't even know that it is happening—not until much later. As Jung wrote, the Unconscious is unconscious, and that makes it even more difficult to know how to extricate oneself. Take the stock market as an example. Many people, including myself, were caught up in the euphoria over the rise in the market a few years ago, and either began investing or raised the level of their investment. Then one day the market did an adjustment, and everything that was up came crashing down. Many people lost half—maybe more—of what they had invested in the market and ended up kicking themselves for not selling sooner, but the reason they didn't had more to do with being in the grip of the collective than with their innate intelligence. I lost money too, and knew deep down before it happened that I should get out, but I didn't. In retrospect, it all looks so obvious, but the infection of greed began to spread, and that part of our shadow manifested itself, albeit unconsciously.

RH: Can analysis help in any way?

GF: It is very important in analysis that we convey the knowledge of collective infection to our analysands, because if we don't, then they will not benefit from the understanding of how easy it is to be gripped by a political movement, a cult, or something similar. How do cult leaders—like Jim Jones, who convinced hundreds of people to drink poison and commit suicide—how do they do it? What possessed Jim Jones's followers to the extent that they went against their natural instinct to survive? Von Franz lectured in L.A. about the Nazis and gave an example of someone who worked in a bank and needed the job badly. The employees were told to join the Nazi party and although they didn't really want to, their need for security and money influenced them, and they did things they normally wouldn't have done. So the shadow relating to money influenced them, as much as anything else, and they became one of Hitler's supporters—almost against their will, one might say.

RH: How do you keep from getting carried along by the collective in your own personal life?

GF: Well, one way to avoid getting trapped in identification with mass thinking or mass action is to assert one's individuality constantly—go one's own way, no matter what. When I wake up in the morning, for instance, I never turn on the TV, nor do I listen to the evening news. I am interested in what is happening in the world both locally and internationally, and I read the newspaper, but I don't feed on those "sound bytes" of information—or misinformation—all day. In other words, I don't saturate my psyche with collective thinking if I can help it. My life isn't like other people's lives, because I do very little of what other people do. I try to follow my inner promptings rather than the outer promptings, but being human, I am just as vulnerable to collective forces as anyone else. As much as is humanly possible, one

251

needs to question oneself constantly and check in regularly to make sure one is staying connected to the soul and not being led by the outer world. However, as Jung wrote, we do not individuate alone on an island. We need to relate to people if we are to gain a true understanding of ourselves. My favorite example of a man who resisted collective thinking was Thoreau. If you read his journals, you will realize how much he struggled against the wastefulness of his generation, and how he forced himself to listen to his inner voice against the insistence of the outer collective. Jung, too, went his own way. Unfortunately, as Emerson once wrote, society doesn't reward us for being our own person; on the contrary, it usually punishes the person who goes his or her own way. But that should not stop us. It is through suffering that punishment willingly that we individuate.

RH: How do you know if your inner promptings are the voices of your individuality or something from the collective that you have internalized?

GF: Von Franz once urged us to get to know the voices who speak to us all the time, to be able to tell the "good" ones from the "bad." The way she put it was that if you hear a knock at your door, you don't simply fling the door open. First, you ask who is there and if you know the person, you open it; if the person doesn't sound right, you don't. Not every prompting we get from within is a desirable one. The inner voice that prompts us to go through the light at an intersection is not a helpful inner voice, especially if we end up in a collision. We need to get to know the characters who are our daily companions and learn to discern who is friend and who is foe. It takes work and time to get to know whether the inner voice is actually internalized collective thinking or the promptings of the soul. When we become familiar with the inner world, we learn who each of the characters is and whether to follow his or her dictates or not. Does this make sense?

RH: Yes, at some deep intuitive level it does.

GF: We all do the best we can, but the Unconscious is indeed unconscious, and Jung said he guarded his consciousness lest it be stolen from him. That means we can lose all we have attained by allowing it to drop back into the unconscious again. So I guess the way to guard what we have found is to stay conscious, stay alert and live always in the realization that we can lose what we have worked so hard to attain if we allow ourselves to go to sleep.

RH: What do you see for the future of analytical psychology?

GF: There is a short answer to your question: I rarely think about the future of analytical psychology! I think more about the future of the planet and what my grandchildren will have to face. Now that I am on the Board of the Philemon Foundation, however, I am excited about their plan to publish all of Jung's works that have not yet been published. They plan to put out what is to be called *The Complete Works*. This project does make me think positively about the future of Jung's work. Our planet is in such a precarious position that it feels a little indulgent to worry about what will analytical pychology be like in the future. But I can add a few random thoughts. I think that Jung's work will be around for a long, long time— longer than any of us can imagine. It may go through the spasms of trying to integrate other modalities and theories, but in the end it will stay true to Jung's ideas. There are many people who have never become analysts, but who are deeply committed to Jung's concepts and have found that they have helped them live a fuller life. If the analysts don't keep Jung's work alive, then the people who have benefited from the work will. I think the people in the Analytical Psychology Clubs and lay societies around the world will keep analytical psychology alive. Dilution may weaken a tincture, but if one allows it to cook down a bit, it can regain its potency. So it might be with Jungian psychology. C. A. Meier, one of Jung's colleagues, told me that in his opinion the most important thing analysts can do is research. That might be the answer.

MORE SPRING JOURNAL BOOKS

Collected English Papers, Wolfgang Giegerich
    Vol. 1: *The Neurosis of Psychology: Primary Papers Towards a Critical Psychology*, ISBN 1-882670-42-6, 284 pp., $20.00
    Vol. 2: *Technology and the Soul*, ISBN 1-882670-43-4
    Vol. 3: *Soul-Violence*, ISBN 1-882670-44-2
    Vol. 4: *The Soul Always Thinks*, ISBN 1-882670-45-0

Dialectics & Analytical Psychology: The El Capitan Canyon Seminar, Wolfgang Giegerich, David L. Miller, and Greg Mogenson, ISBN 1-882670-92-2, 136 pp., $20.00

Northern Gnosis: Thor, Baldr, and the Volsungs in the Thought of Freud and Jung, Greg Mogenson, ISBN 1-882670-90-6, 140 pp., $20.00

Raids on the Unthinkable: Freudian and Jungian Psychoanalyses, Paul Kugler, ISBN 1-882670-91-4, 160 pp., $20.00

The Wounded Researcher: A Depth Psychological Approach to Research, Robert Romanyshyn, ISBN 1-882670-47-7

The Sunken Quest, the Wasted Fisher, the Pregnant Fish: Postmodern Reflections on Depth Psychology, Ronald Schenk, ISBN: 1-882670-48-5, $20.00

Fire in the Stone: The Alchemy of Desire, Stanton Marlan, ed., ISBN 1-882670-49-3, 206 pp., $22.95

Disturbances in the Field: Essays in Honor of David L. Miller, Christine Downing, ed., ISBN 1-882670-37-X, 318 pp., $23.95

Three Faces of God: Traces of the Trinity in Literature and Life, David L. Miller, ISBN 1-882670-94-9, 197 pp., $20.00

Christs: Meditations on Archetypal Images in Christian Theology, David L. Miller, ISBN 1-882670-93-0, 249 pp., $20.00

Hells and Holy Ghosts: A Theopoetics of Christian Belief, David L. Miller, ISBN 1-882670-99-3, 238 pp., $20.00

Electra: Tracing a Feminine Myth through the Western Imagination, Nancy Cater, ISBN 1-882670-98-1, 137 pp., $20.00

Fathers' Daughters: Breaking the Ties That Bind, Maureen Murdock, ISBN 1-882670-31-0, 258 pp., $20.00

Daughters of Saturn: From Father's Daughter to Creative Woman, Patricia Reis, ISBN 1-882670-32-9, 361 pp., $23.95

Women's Mysteries: Twoard a Poetics of Gender, Christine Downing, ISBN 1-882670-99-XX, 237 pp., $20.00

Gods in Our Midst: Mythological Images of the Masculine—A Woman's View, Christine Downing, ISBN 1-882670-28-0, 152 pp., $20.00

MORE SPRING JOURNAL BOOKS

Journey through Menopause: A Personal Rite of Passage, Christine Downing, ISBN 1-882670-33-7, 172 pp., $20.00

Portrait of the Blue Lady: The Character of Melancholy, Lyn Cowan, ISBN 1-882670-96-5, 314 pp., $23.95

Field, Form, and Fate: Patterns in Mind, Nature, and Psyche, Michael Conforti, ISBN 1-882670-40-X, 181 pp., $20.00

Dark Voices: The Genesis of Roy Hart Theatre, Noah Pikes, ISBN 1-882670-19-1, 155 pp., $20.00

The World Turned Inside Out: Henry Corbin and Islamic Mysticism, Tom Cheetham, ISBN 1-882670-24-8, 210 pp., $20.00

Teachers of Myth: Interviews on Educational and Psychological Uses of Myth with Adolescents, Maren Tonder Hansen, ISBN 1-882670-89-2, 73 pp., $15.95

Following the Reindeer Woman: Path of Peace and Harmony, Linda Schierse Leonard, ISBN 1-882670-95-7, 229 pp., $20.00

An Oedipus—The Untold Story: A Ghostly Mythodrama in One Act, Armando Nascimento Rosa, ISBN 1-882670-38-8, 103 pp., $20.00

Psyche and the Sacred: Spirituality Beyond Religion, Lionel Corbett, ISBN 1-882670-34-5

The Dreaming Way: Dreamwork and Art for Remembering and Recovery, Patricia Reis and Susan Snow, ISBN 1-882670-46-9, $24.95

HOW TO ORDER:

To order online: Go to the online store at our website:
www.springjournalandbooks.com

To order by telephone: Call (504) 524-5117

Spring Journal Books, 627 Ursulines Street # 7,
New Orleans, Louisiana 70116, USA